Small Miracles

A 2-in-1 Edition of Heartwarming
Gifts of Extraordinary Coincidences

Small Miracles

A 2-in-1 Edition of Heartwarming Gifts of Extraordinary Coincidences

Yitta Halberstam
&
Judith Leventhal

ADAMS MEDIA CORPORATION
Holbrook, Massachusetts

To my sons Yossi and Eli—my own "small miracles." — YHM

To Jules and Arielle, my miracles of miracles. — JFL

Published by
Adams Media Corporation
260 Center Street, Holbrook, MA 02343

ISBN: 0-7394-0213-7

Printed in the United States of America.

Cover art by Barry David Marcus.

Contents

Small Miracles, Volume I

Preface

by Dr. Bernie Siegel

I'm writing a new book and it's coming to a close, and I want to conclude it with the words "The End." But suddenly, to my own surprise, an inner voice tells me, instead of writing "The End," to write "The Beginning." Hmm, I say to myself . . . well, that makes sense! Because if the people who are reading the book have read it well and absorbed its message, then hopefully, it will be the *beginning* of a new life for them!

But then I start to wonder . . . where did that impulse to write "The Beginning" come from? It wasn't in my plan; I know that. Something, or someone made me write it. Perhaps it was God.

Often, I don't know what I'm going to write until I see it down on paper. I used to find myself asking aloud: from God knows where did this come? Now, I know.

Once, when I was about four years old, I almost choked to death on a small toy that I had taken apart. I was alone in my room and no adult was nearby. So there I was choking, and suddenly, for no apparent reason, I vomited. The tiny parts of the toy came flying out and I could breathe. But later, I asked myself in amazement, "Now who did that? Who made me vomit? Was it God or an angel or spirit who entered the scene and made me vomit?"

But this book isn't about me, or about strange occurrences, or acts of fate or guilt or fault if no angel intercedes. It is about coincidences, the seemingly random acts that turn out not to be so random at all. How they happen, to whom, and why? Is God behind the orchestration of these "coincidences?"

I believe that *nothing* is a "coincidence." It's all part of creation and God's plan and our response. We just have to be open to seeing it. We have to want to see it and participate in creation. For example, when I was born, the man printing the birth certificate asked my parents my name. The name spoken was "Benzion—son of Shabsi," but the man transcribing it onto the birth certificate didn't understand the Hebrew name and created his own rendition of my name. Thus, my name, as it appears on the birth certificate, is "Shepherd." God had already determined my calling; to be a shepherd in the community as a spiritual, and intellectual, leader.

A common coincidence that I experience all the time is that I find pennies wherever I go. When I enter a hotel room for the first time and it's been freshly cleaned, vacuumed, spotless, I can often count on finding a penny on the threshold. In the airport, in a restaurant, even sitting atop my luggage, I'll suddenly spy one solitary penny. Now, what does that mean? What does it say on a penny? "In God We Trust." It's not the value of the money that's important, but its message, its wholeness—a reminder that God is directing my energies, God is here and I am on my path.

Here's another example: My wife and I own a cat named Miracle, and we decided to get her some company. A neighbor's cat had a litter of kittens and we were invited to choose one of our liking. I brought an adorable-looking kitten back home, but he and my wife didn't hit it off. The match didn't work out, and I had to bring him back to the original owner. My wife was sorry but the owner assured us there was no problem, all the other kittens had already been adopted—all, that is, except one. Somehow, no one seemed to like this last one, because she had grown up in a barn, was dark-brown, and very fearful of people.

"Oh, what's her name?" I asked and the owner answered casually, "Penny." I hadn't been planning to try the experiment a second time, but the minute I heard the name, I knew it was right. So we adopted Penny and she and Miracle get along just fine. She was named Penny by a child who saw her being born and said, "She looks like a Penny."

So why do coincidences happen to some people and not to others? I believe that I look for coincidences in my life and have faith and so I find them. If you stay rooted in the intellect only, and disregard the spiritual aspects of life, you won't have them. If you learn to become more fully conscious, more aware of what's going on in your body and stop and listen to the universe, to keep journals, to write poetry, then coincidences will happen. Behave as if you have coincidences in your life, expect them, when you are ready to receive them, they'll come. You develop the intuitive in yourself.

This uses the exact same principle as "Behave as if you're the person you want to become," and that is whom you become! Once, I demonstrated this to a student of mine who was skeptical about our own ability to create coincidences. I was lecturing at a school an hour away from my home and when the lecture was over, I said to my student who rode back with me, "Watch this. I'm going to drive back home using an entirely different route than I ordinarily use, to show you something." Sure enough, about half a mile away from my home, I passed my wife driving her car, and she started waving and signaling. I rolled down my window and she said, "Oh, honey, I'm so glad to see you! I wanted to get in touch with you! I wanted to change the time of our tennis match and I didn't know how to reach you." My friend was shocked. Because I had faith and knew that a coincidence would occur, it did.

So go with the flow. Allow things to happen. Maintain a certain rhythm and harmony with the universe. Don't try to rush things. Get on the universe's schedule. And practice! When the phone rings, before you pick it up, say out loud who you think it is. After a while, you'll find you're always right!

Our daughter Carolyn is even better. She knows when the phone is going to ring and is great in gambling casinos.

Once, a patient of mine had an appointment with another doctor and was sitting in his office, waiting for his appointment. The doctor was running late, and the waiting room was crowded with irate people. After an hour had passed, several of them rose from their seats and left. My patient was tempted to do the same but something stopped him. All through the next hour, he kept glancing at his watch, wondering if it wouldn't be wiser, after all, for him to get up and leave. Finally, after two full hours had passed, the nurse came into the room and called out "Kirimedjian!"*

He jumped to his feet, but saw to his surprise that across the room, another man had also risen at the summons. Both men stared at each other in shock, because the name is extremely odd and unusual, and what was the likelihood of two men bearing the same uncommon name being in the same doctor's waiting room at the same time? Curious about the man's identity, my patient approached him and discovered . . . his father, whom he hadn't seen in twenty-two years! His mother had gotten divorced when he was a young child. At that time his father had been an alcoholic and abusive parent, and as a result hadn't been given any visitation rights at all. Kirimedjian grew up never knowing his father at all, to the extent that he didn't even know what he looked like, until that moment in the doctor's waiting room! Now, here's the rub: If my patient had given in to his impulse to leave, he never would have met his father! But because he allowed himself to "go with the flow" and waited, a reconciliation with his father was able to take place.

A couple of years ago, I was teaching at a college, and I wanted the students to confront the issue of their own mortality. I created an exercise where I asked them to write out their own death certificates.

---

*Note: Names followed by asterisk are pseudonyms.

I instructed them to write on the certificates both their age and the cause of their deaths. I joined them in this exercise, and wrote on my certificate that I was going to die at the age of ninety-eight by falling off a ladder while working on the roof, despite my family saying I shouldn't be up there at my age doing that.

Several years later I climbed up on the roof with a pole saw to cut branches and clean gutters before we went on vacation. As I stepped off the roof, the top rung of the ladder broke off. I fell straight down and landed on my feet and fell backwards, hitting my head, but received no significant injury.

Again, I ask, how did that happen? Why didn't I get tangled in the ladder? Who or what guided or protected me and placed me safely on the ground? An overworked spirit or angel, good luck, intuition, reflex, coincidence, or God knows?

I'll leave it to you to answer. I have my experience and know the answer.

Introduction

There are moments in life when we catch our breath and glimpse God's presence. Sometimes it is when we see the radiant face of a sleeping child, sometimes it is when we hear a fragment of melody that stirs awake an unfamiliar yearning. These moments—which flicker for a tantalizing instant and then vanish in a flash—convey to us a sense of the Divine.

Every leaf, every blade of grass bears God's imprint. But these days most of us are urban dwellers leading hectic lives, and have lost the connection to the earth that enriched our forefathers and helped them see God. Obscured by skyscrapers and the haze of polluted skies, we can barely see the stars, let alone sense a Divine Presence.

Living as so many of us do lives of alienation and despair, how can we help ourselves reconnect: to God, to one another, to our very selves?

Beyond nature, there are teachers—other experiences that can help us along our journey. These guides, beacons of light and signposts in the labyrinthine wilderness in which we wander, offer us gentle instruction and compassionate encouragement as they firmly propel us back to the path from which we may have strayed.

These epiphanic experiences, common to us all, can help lead us to our unfulfilled destiny. They occur within the great universal flow of energy, and require nothing more than our sheer awareness of their presence. When consciousness is cultivated and perception is heightened, these experiences can serve as vital tokens of growth and transformation. To encounter these moments in their fullness and richness, to be aware of their message and hear their music, is truly to know God. And predominant among these experiences is the phenomenon we call *coincidences*.

Coincidences have been variously defined as "luck," "chance," "a fluke," "something out of the ordinary," or a "random conjoining of inexplicable events that defies our sense of the reasonable." We firmly believe that coincidences are much more than simple accidents or quirks of fate. To us, coincidences are blessings, the spiritual manna that hosts of angels send down to illuminate our Path. They are vivid, striking, awe-inspiring examples of Divine Providence. They are acts of God.

It has often been recounted that when the poet William Blake watched the sunrise, he would greet its arrival with an exuberant shout: "Holy! Holy! Holy!" This is how we feel when coincidences unfold in our own lives.

Thousands of years ago, God spoke to man through the sublime miracles he performed on massive and grandiose scales. In modern times we are bereft of that privilege. Today we wrestle with a hidden God, a concealed God, a God who no longer parts seas, stops the sun, or turns people into pillars of salt. Instead we have coincidences—smaller, more personal, everyday miracles. For when a coincidence does take place, it is nothing more and nothing less than God tapping us on the shoulder, whispering, or at times even shouting: "I'm here! I'm with you!"

"Coincidences," the writer Doris Lessing once said, "are God's way of remaining anonymous." *Small Miracles* attempts to strip away that facade of anonymity, and demonstrate that these seemingly random moments are instead the full and vital expressions of God's handiwork. In our own personal lives, we have been touched many times by God's radiance. In this book it is our goal to share the abundant blessings of this celestial light.

Coincidences can also be seen as opportunities for change, vital keys towards expanding our consciousness. If we can learn to become more aware of and attuned to coincidences, more cognizant of their significance, then we will evolve to a higher state of being. When we integrate both the experience and the meaning of coincidences into our lives, we open ourselves to the enriching possibilities, the blessings, and the sense of harmony with the universe that they offer.

We have written this book out of a deep sense of appreciation for God's guiding hand. Both of our fathers were Holocaust survivors whose lives were saved by inexplicable sets of uncanny coincidences. When we were children, both men independently recounted the tales of the miracles that permeated their sagas. Our respective fathers' survival was not the consequence of chance, but rather the result of divine providence. While each of these great men died over ten years ago, the message and the spiritual legacy they have imparted to us endures.

Today, both Judith and I continue to filter the inordinate number of coincidences occurring in our lives through a spiritual prism. Separately, we each embark upon a path of pursuing their deeper meaning from a spiritual perspective rather than a psychological or paranormal one. The more aware we are, we find that coincidences are constantly unfolding in our lives, sometimes at a dizzying, but certainly always exhilarating rate.

The coincidences contained in this book come from personal interviews, as well as various other sources, including newspapers, television, books, and magazines. Some are heartwarming, some awe-inspiring. Some are a nudge in a particular life-changing direction. Others demonstrate how the universe answers a question. Still others offer signs to the protagonist, a confirmation that he or she is on the right track or has done the right thing. But as much as the stories poignantly convey God's presence, they also equally impart profound teachings and precious moral lessons that can enrich our spirit and empower us to live our lives more fully. To help you along your journey, we have interpreted many of the stories, adding a few lines of commentary to reflect on their meaning and inherent value.

We hope that after reading these stories you will be able to absorb the small miracles that come into your life with an expanded mind and a different eye. As you will see, coincidences can nourish in times of hunger, enlighten in times of confusion, and comfort in times of need.

A story is told of a holy man who radiated an unusual aura of inner peace and joy. An unearthly, almost celestial glow shone from his body, and attracted vast crowds who pursued him everywhere. "Blessed one," they cried out to him, "are you a God?" "No," he answered. "Are you an angel?" "No." "Are you a prophet?" "No, I am simply awake."

We hope that *Small Miracles* will awaken you to the rich promise of a bounteous universe and the splendor lying dormant within your soul. Coincidences are everywhere and can happen any time. When your soul is ready, they will come. All that is required is that you open your heart.

I don't know if it's the hard-nosed reporter in me or the incurable romantic, but for some strange reason that I cannot fully explain, I constantly find myself poring over the "personals" in various newspapers week after week. I have been married for nineteen years and am certainly not looking for another spouse, yet I'm utterly riveted by these ads. The drama of everyday life is reflected by them, and they pay eloquent testimony to the hopes, dreams, and endurance of the human spirit.

Once in a while, I find an ad that I actually think is appropriate for a single friend of mine or for my widowed mother, and I refer them to the box number, urging that they respond. But most of the time, I just read these ads out of idle curiosity and an insatiable desire to know what lurks in romantic hearts.

One day I was scanning the personals column of a local newspaper, when I was stopped short by one particular ad. "Wow, that's unusual!" I thought. "Could this be for real?" The ad that caught my attention read: "Henrietta—do you remember we met and courted at Camp Tamiment in 1938? I've never forgotten you. Please call me. Irving . . ." and a phone number was listed, rather than the more common box I.D. "Is this some kind of joke?" I wondered aloud.

But all night long, I couldn't get the ad out of my mind. "Those personal ads cost a lot of money," I thought. "Why would someone waste so much money on a joke . . . and what's the joke here, anyway?" Finally, in the morning I couldn't take it anymore, and decided I just *had* to know the truth. Gathering my courage, I dialed the number in the ad.

As soon as the mature voice answered, I knew this was no joke, but the real thing. At that moment, I almost regretted my decision to make the call, hoping that it would not raise the elderly man's expectations, even momentarily. "Uhh . . . this is *not* Henrietta," I said quickly, "and I hope you don't mind . . . but I was so intrigued by your ad, I just had to call and find out . . . what's the story?"

Gracious and courtly in a manner that is unfortunately out of style these days, Irving amiably accommodated my inquisitiveness, and recounted the following story:

"In 1938, Henrietta and I were both counselors at Camp Tamiment, an overnight camp in Pennsylvania, and we fell in love. We were sure we were right for each other, that we'd found 'the one.' However, Henrietta's parents didn't agree. She was seventeen at the time, and they felt she was much too young to get involved in a serious relationship. So in the fall, to get her away from me, they sent her to stay with an aunt in Europe, and she lived there for several years. There she met another man, whom she married. Heartbroken, I eventually married someone else. I never loved my wife in quite the same passionate way I loved Henrietta, but we did have a good marriage. She died three years ago, and I've been very lonely ever since. Lately, I've started to think about Henrietta a lot, and I've begun wondering if she's still alive. And if she's alive, whether she's still married. And if she's single now, could we reignite our old love? Well, you get the picture. Maybe I'm just a foolish man, but I was just hoping against hope that somehow Henrietta would see the ad. Or at least someone who knows her. I realize my chances are very slim, but I sort of thought at least I should give it a try."

I was very moved by Irving's recital, and found myself marveling at the essence of hope that resides in the human spirit, the trust and resilience that animate the soul. Irving's faith in the possibilities of the future, at the age of seventy-one, was indeed touching. I asked Irving if he would mind if I wrote a story about his search for Henrietta, and he instantly agreed, but unfortunately the editor of my magazine didn't like the idea at all. However, since I was fascinated to learn the outcome of Irving's quest and had also formed an affection for him over the phone, I kept his number and called him from time to time to see how the story played out. Sadly, he never got the phone call he was waiting for.

In 1993, two years after I first made contact with Irving, I was riding the IRT line of the New York subway system and was again engrossed in reading the personals columns of a local paper, when I heard a soft chuckle beside me. "Looking for a new husband, my dear?" the woman sitting next to me inquired with a laugh, looking pointedly at my wedding band and then at the personals page spread clearly on my lap.

"Oh," I blushed, a trifle embarrassed. "I just read them for fun. You know . . . out of curiosity. Don't you ever have the yen?" I asked her.

"Not me," she said, shaking her head adamantly, "Too much pathos in those pages. They would break my heart, those ads." She turned to me with a warm smile, "But isn't it always fascinating, the different perspectives different people have on the same things?"

My interest in her quickened. "What an intelligent woman!" I thought delightedly. "In a way, you're right," I agreed, "there *is* a lot of pathos in these pages." And I began to tell her the story of Irving's tender quest for Henrietta. She seemed mesmerized by the tale, and listened to my recital with rapt attention. "Well," I concluded at the end of my account, "I wish I could give the story a happy ending and tell you Irving found Henrietta, but unfortunately that wasn't the case. Either Henrietta's already dead, or she lives in another city, or she just doesn't read the personals."

"It's the third choice, my dear," the woman said, patting my arm gently. "Trust me, I know."

Startled, I looked at the lined face that held vestiges of a regal beauty that had long since lost its bloom. "Do you still have his number?" she asked.

Comment

Hope is something that brings sunshine into the shadows of our lives. It is our link to a better tomorrow. When hope is gone, so too is our life force. And when hope is kept alive, so too is our determination to go on.

I was walking down a dimly lit street late one evening when I heard muffled screams coming from behind a clump of bushes. Alarmed, I slowed down to listen, and panicked when I realized that what I was hearing were the unmistakable sounds of a struggle: heavy grunting, frantic scuffling, the tearing of fabric. Only yards from where I stood, a woman was being attacked.

Should I get involved? I was frightened for my own safety, and cursed myself for having suddenly decided to take a new route home that night. What if I became another statistic? Shouldn't I just run to the nearest phone and call the police?

Although it seemed like an eternity, the deliberations in my head had taken only seconds, but already the girl's cries were growing weaker. I knew I had to act fast. How could I walk away from this? No, I finally resolved, I could not turn my back on the fate of this unknown woman, even if it meant risking my own life.

I am not a brave man, nor am I athletic. I don't know where I found the moral courage and physical strength—but once I had finally resolved to help the girl, I became strangely transformed. I ran behind the bushes and pulled the assailant off the woman. Grappling, we fell to the ground, where we wrestled for a few minutes until the attacker jumped up and escaped. Panting hard, I scrambled upright and approached the girl, who was crouched behind a tree, sobbing. In the darkness, I could barely see her outline, but I could certainly sense her trembling shock.

Not wanting to frighten her further, I at first spoke to her from a distance. "It's OK," I said soothingly. "The man ran away. You're safe now."

There was a long pause and then I heard her words, uttered in wonder, in amazement.

"Dad, is that you?"

And then, from behind the tree, stepped my youngest daughter, Katherine.

— *Greg O'Leary**

Comment

Many people fear that their good actions will go unrewarded. How often do we hear the cynical aphorism "No good deed goes unpunished"? Yet here is a vivid example of the fact that precisely the opposite often holds true. By resolving to risk his life for an unknown woman, the father ended up saving his own daughter's life. And in his determination to help another, the father discovered the amazing force and power of the will. Under ordinary circumstances, he would have been unable to summon up the physical strength to fight off the rapist. Yet his will was so great that he drew strength from an unknown and untapped source. We have capacities of which we are not even aware. In setting out to do a good deed for another, this man did a wonderful deed for himself!

*W*hen my son Joey turned eleven, he was suddenly stricken with panic disorder, which evolved into agoraphobia. His anxiety attacks were so severe that he spent close to a year confined to his room, while my husband and I searched frantically for a cure. Finally, after eleven months of sheer hell, we found a psychiatrist who prescribed Prozac, a drug that achieved wonders. My husband and I were tremendously grateful that God had returned our son to us from the nightmare world into which he had been plunged.

During this time, we had visited a series of practitioners to determine the cause of our son's problem, and had discovered along the way that he was learning-disabled. All the years that he had been in school no one had picked up on this fact, which we were told had contributed to or even totally created the anxiety problem. Now that he was cured of panic disorder, we had to find a school that specialized in learning disabilities. This was not so easy, we soon learned to our dismay. Given his recent medical record, nobody wanted him.

All the schools that specialized in learning disabilities claimed that their students had an educational problem, not an emotional one. Our son would not fit in, they maintained; they were not equipped to handle someone like him. All the psychologists I spoke with insisted that all LD (learning-disabled) children possess emotional components as a result of their disability, but when I repeated their words to school officials my protests fell on deaf ears. He was rejected by every school we applied to.

There was one particular LD school that I really wanted to get Joey into, because it had an excellent reputation and was close to home as well. I had campaigned hard to get him into this school, but they kept turning me down. "Please give my son a chance!" I begged. But nobody wanted to, and I was growing more desperate by the minute.

One evening, I happened to attend a charity event, where I found myself seated next to an older woman named Barbara with whom I was vaguely acquainted. I knew her to be a prominent society figure, very wealthy, very influential. Suddenly, before I could think or stop myself, I found myself—to my own shock and horror—pouring out my heart to her about my continuing travails with Joey. Even as I unburdened myself to her, I felt the inappropriateness of what I was doing. "Why are you telling this woman your troubles?" I scolded myself even as I continued to describe my litany of woes. But to my own mystification and chagrin, I found I just couldn't stop. I didn't stop, in fact, until I had completely exhausted every single last detail of my struggle to get Joey into the LD school of my choice.

When I was finally finished, I was appalled at myself. What had I gone and done? But to my surprise, Barbara neither distanced herself from me nor looked at me with disdain. Instead, to my complete surprise, her eyes filled with tears, and she patted my hand consolingly, reassuringly. "Honey," she said warmly, "you've told your story to the right person! It just so happens that I live next door to the founder and director of the school, and it also just so happens that I am one of their major league contributors. In fact, I have thrown many parlor parties for this particular school and raised tremendous amounts of money. You can consider your son a new student of this school. I give you my word— you can depend on it!"

I couldn't believe my incredible luck, my great fortune! What a godsend, to have been seated next to Barbara! Sure enough, true to her word, she used her powers of persuasion and influence, and my son was accepted by the school for the coming year, where he excelled and—for the first time in his life—was placed on the honor roll.

My sense of indebtedness to Barbara was infinite, and so I kept up with her, sending gifts and cards. I called her before each holiday to wish her well, and a bond was forged between us. During this time, I learned from other people that she had experienced many problems with her own two children. The older one, a son, was a drug addict who had recently disappeared, and the younger one, a daughter, was mildly retarded and problematic in many different ways. My heart ached for Barbara, especially when she inquired, frequently, about my son's progress, and seemed genuinely delighted to learn that he was doing well.

Our relationship continued to develop for about a year—and then Barbara's husband died suddenly. I traveled to the suburbs for the funeral, where I would meet her family for the first time. As I stood on the line that slowly filed past the mourning family to offer condolences, I was suddenly struck by a familiar figure sitting beside my friend. "Who's that young woman sitting next to Barbara?" I asked the woman behind me. "Why, that's her only daughter, Nancy," she answered, "you know . . . the retarded one." I gasped, as I felt goosebumps erupt on my arms. Now everything was suddenly clear. Now I knew for certain why Barbara had been fated to be the agent of redemption for my son.

Twenty-five years before, when I had been a high school student in a private school, a mildly retarded girl whose name I had forgotten had joined our class in senior year. Although our school was not equipped for special ed cases, her wealthy parents had prevailed upon the school administration to give the girl a chance and allow her an education within a mainstream context. Their wealth and influence had overcome all objections and the girl had been admitted, albeit with great hesitation.

Life in this school, however, was not easy for this young woman. She was viewed as both an outcast and a pariah. She was cruelly shunned by virtually everyone—everyone that is, except me. I had always championed the underdog. I had great sympathy for those on the fringe, and had always made an effort to reach out to them—as I reached out to this girl.

On our high school graduation trip to Washington, D.C., no one wanted to room with her in the hotel. I volunteered, and although the experience wasn't an easy one, I was glad that I had done so. After graduation, the class dispersed and separated, striking out in different directions. Some I hadn't ever seen again, some I had forgotten about. Like . . . Nancy.

For it was Nancy who was the young woman sitting next to Barbara. It was Nancy, long-lost, long-forgotten Nancy, who was in fact Barbara's daughter. During our senior year together, I had never met nor spoken with Nancy's mother, and we had never had occasion to be introduced. Yet our lives had apparently become inextricably connected, our destinies fated to intersect. As the line slowly worked its way towards the mourners, and I drew closer to Barbara and Nancy to pay my respects, my eyes filled with tears.

Twenty-five years ago, I had helped Barbara's daughter. Twenty-five years later, Barbara had repaid the favor and helped me with my son.

Perhaps our own memories are sadly too short, but happily God's is blessedly long.

— Blanche Purcell*

Comment

When we perform a charitable deed or benevolent action, it doesn't disappear into a vacuum or a spiritual black hole; ultimately we can expect to be repaid. Sometimes, we are repaid within a matter of moments or hours after executing the kindness, and can immediately see the connection between our deed and our reward. However, there are deeds that take decades to be repaid, but when they finally are, we often gasp at their fitting symmetry! Of course, virtue is its own reward and the desire for compensation is rarely the reason we perform acts of kindness. Nonetheless, it is heartening to receive a nod of acknowledgment from God every now and then, an affirmation that we did the right thing and that our deeds are duly registered with a universe that remembers.

For fifty-two years, Robert Adkins thought his best friend, Roy Stump, was dead. After all, hadn't he cradled his dying friend's head in his lap and then watched a medic remove his dog tags?

"Everyone in the platoon was sure Roy was dead," Robert recalled one day in April 1996 as he chatted with a stranger in a waiting room at Lorain Community/St. Joseph Regional Health Center in Lorain, Ohio. Robert was waiting for his wife, Juanita, to return from cataract surgery. The stranger was waiting for his brother-in-law, also in surgery. Somehow, the conversation turned to World War II.

"We were stationed in Holland and were watching a buddy defuse an anti-tank mine when it blew up," Adkins said. The man working on the mine was killed, and shrapnel struck Stump in the head, chest, and other parts of his body. The worst injury was the gaping head wound that Adkins tried to tend by applying pressure with his handkerchief, unmindful of a smaller wound in his own forehead.

As they continued to talk, Robert, now seventy-two years old, was astonished to learn that the stranger, like him, had served in the 787th Anti-Aircraft Battalion in 1944. Skeptical about the coincidence, they began grilling each other, as if in a test.

"Who was the platoon sergeant?" Robert asked the stranger.

The man answered correctly. "Was anyone killed in that battalion?" he shot back.

"I just told you, my best buddy, Roy D. Stump," Robert replied.

The man smiled and said, "I hate to disappoint you, but I am very much alive."

Robert sat stunned. "I thought he was going to have a heart attack," Stump remembered. "I hadn't recognized him at first, but I knew who he was as soon as he said his nickname was 'Sloop.' Mine was 'Little Red.' I had bright red hair then," said Stump, stroking his gray crewcut.

To prove his identity, the seventy-one-year-old Stump produced a faded copy of his discharge papers and a driver's license with his name on it. Then the two men hugged and "everybody in the waiting room thought we were crazy," Robert said.

Stump had been critically injured, but he hadn't died as the other platoon members had believed. An emergency operation in a field tent had saved his life, and he had been transferred to a hospital in Belgium, where he remained for eighteen months, recovering from forty-two wounds, including one that left him with a metal plate in his head.

By the time he got out of the hospital, the war was over and he had no idea where the rest of the platoon members were living. He often wondered what had happened to his buddy, Sloop.

He always credited his friend—along with an Army-issue combination Bible, almanac, and dictionary and a leather wallet he carried in his breast pocket—with saving his life. Shrapnel had torn through the wallet and Bible into his chest but had missed his heart.

In an odd twist of fate, both men moved to Lorain, Ohio, after the war and raised families there. For more than forty years, they lived only a few miles apart and never knew it. "I probably drove by his house three or four times a week and didn't even know he lived there," Roy Stump said.

The men have had no difficulty in picking up their friendship where it left off. The night after their chance meeting, they had dinner with their wives, and later that week they went to the speedway together. And, like the kids they were forty-two years ago, they exchanged pocket knives.

arol Anderson was a young widow whose husband had died of cancer at thirty-five. Bob Edwards was a young widower whose wife had been killed in a car accident at twenty-nine. Both marriages had been extremely happy, and both Carol and Bob were sure they would never love or marry again. After many lonely years of pain and suffering, they met at a church dinner and started courting. When they got engaged and then married, they told everyone "it was miraculous that they had found each other." Their relationship was strong and loving. The only trouble spot in the marriage was that they had diametrically different opinions on what to do about the past.

Carol longed to bury it; Bob needed to explore it. Carol never wanted to talk about either of their previous marriages. Bob, on the other hand, was eager to know the most minute details of Carol's life before they had met, and was hurt that Carol showed such a complete lack of interest in his. "Why raise ghosts?" Carol would ask when Bob would persist with his gentle probings and soft inquiries. "Memory should be preserved, not obliterated," he would reply. This went on for years, with Carol's perspective ultimately prevailing. As a result, they never shared stories, pictures, or mementos from their first marriages.

Ten years later, Carol felt that their marriage was secure enough to withstand any assaults from the past. "Okay," she told Bob one day, "I'm ready to talk." She began telling Bob about her first marriage and pulled out several snapshot albums she had hidden from him all these years. "These are from our honeymoon," she said, starting to leaf through the pages of one album. "We went to France. Oh . . . here we are at Lourdes."

"You went to Lourdes?" Bob said with mild interest. "So did we."

"Well, I guess half the world goes to Lourdes," Carol laughed, "no big deal. Everyone's looking for blessings and miracles in their lives."

"Wait a second, Carol, turn back a page," said Bob suddenly. "Let me see that snapshot again of you and Ralph at Lourdes." Carol obligingly turned back the page.

"Carol," her husband asked tensely, "Who's that couple in the background?"

"I have no idea," she said. "Just as the photographer snapped the picture, a couple walked by and got caught by the shutter. I can see why you asked, though, thinking they were with us. In the picture, it does look as though they're standing behind us, almost as if they're posing, but it's just an illusion.

"You're wrong, Carol," Bob said slowly, "it wasn't a mistake, it was destiny. You see . . . that couple in the background . . . is me and my first wife."

⮞⮞⮜⮜

Comment

Millions of people travel to Lourdes each year. What were the chances of Carol and Bob not only being at the same place at the same time but also "coincidentally" appearing together in a photo at the holy shrine? When the picture was taken, they lived in different parts of the United States, and were not members of the same association, organization, or tour group. They were not connected to each other in any way—except in God's plan. The people who make pilgrimages to Lourdes are more often than not the ill, the infirm, and the elderly, rather than young people like Carol and Bob. Life had just begun for each couple, and seemingly neither Bob nor Carol needed a miracle. But they did . . . only they hadn't known it at the time.

*A*s a young bride in the summer of 1972, Faith Peterson* came to the Adirondack cottage of her in-laws for a visit. Her doting husband, Kevin, took her rowing in an idyllic lake framed by pastoral woods. In the boat, sighing contentedly, Faith languidly swished her fingers through the cool water, enjoying the bracing feel of the wet cold against her warm hand.

Curling up in a corner of the boat and half-dozing, Faith continued running her hand through the water until she suddenly became aware that her diamond engagement ring had slipped off her finger. "Oh my God!" she shrieked to her husband as she sat bolt upright in the boat. "My ring's gone! It must have fallen into the water!"

"That's impossible," Kevin said with skepticism. "You probably left it in a drawer at the cottage."

"No," she insisted, "I never take it off, never. And besides . . . just as we were about to climb into the boat, a woman at the dock complimented me on it. So I know I had it on."

"But how could it have fallen off your finger, Faith?"

"My hand was in the water, Kevin, and the ring was a little loose to begin with. It must have just slipped off . . ."

"Okay, don't worry, I'll find it," Kevin reassured her, and dove into the shallow lake to begin searching the bottom.

All day long, he dove again and again into the crystalline waters of the placid lake, confident he would successfully ferret out the missing ring. After all, there was no powerful current coursing through the lake that could have carried the ring away, and there was little debris below the surface that could have trapped it. But each time that his head bobbed to the surface, the story was the same. "Not yet!" he would yell bravely to Faith as she sat forlornly in the boat, peering anxiously at him. "I'll find it this time for sure!" he would smile valiantly, descending into the water for yet another foray.

Finally, at nightfall, Kevin called it quits. "I'm so sorry, honey," he said to his disconsolate spouse, putting an arm around her shoulder. "I tried my best."

"I know you did, Kevin."

"And it's not as if the ring isn't insured. We'll get you another one."

"Kevin, you're sweet and I know you mean well, but another ring just won't be the same. This is the diamond you gave me when you proposed, when we pledged our eternal love. I treasured it as a symbol, for its meaning and sentimental value. Any other diamond will just be an expensive rock. No, it's the original ring I want," Faith said stubbornly. "If I can't have the one I lost, then I don't want another. Let's use the insurance money for something practical, like furniture."

"Okay, honey," Kevin shrugged, too drained from the day's rigors to argue. So Faith never got a substitute—not even when they were wealthy and could easily afford one.

In 1992, when Faith and Kevin were a middle-aged couple with teenage children of their own, they took their family to the same Adirondack cottage where they had vacationed as newlyweds. Kevin had inherited it from his parents when they had died, but had since that first visit never returned to the cottage, preferring to rent it out instead. For years, they had sent their children to overnight camp, but this summer the kids had rebelled. "C'mon, Dad," they argued, "we're too old for camp. Let's go to the Adirondacks for the summer and use Gramps's cottage."

When they arrived at the cottage, Kevin was excited. "Let me take you out to the lake," he said to his kids as his wife was unpacking. "You don't mind, do you, hon?"

"No, go ahead, enjoy yourselves! It's actually much easier for me to finish when you're all out of the way," Faith said, laughing.

"Hey, Dad, can I take my fishing rod along?" asked the youngest.

"Sure, I hear the fish are really biting today."

When they returned home a few hours later, Kevin and the kids proudly held aloft their prize catch of the day: a huge trout that weighed in at seven pounds. "Guess what's for dinner?" Kevin winked at Faith, as she directed the requisite "oohs" and "aahs" at her youngest, who was glowing with unmasked pride. "I never caught such a big one before," he said.

"It sure is a great catch," Faith agreed, as she placed the trout on a cutting board and slit it open with a knife.

"It sure *is* a great catch," she repeated, staring in shock at the entrails of the fish. With a sweeping motion of her hand, she beckoned her husband to her side.

Inside the belly of the trout was Faith's diamond ring.

Comment

When you cherish the emotional value of a gift, it can never really be lost, for what you carry in your heart is yours to keep, forever.

Every Sunday morning, at exactly 9 A.M., the twenty members of a church choir would assemble in the chapel of their small Southern Baptist congregation for a one-hour rehearsal before services. The choir consisted of long-time members who were dedicated, enthusiastic, and extremely punctual.

One Sunday morning, the tranquil air of the sleepy Southern town was suddenly pierced by a loud blast. Residents rushed outdoors to see what was happening, and then watched in anguish as flames spurted out the windows of the small church. They checked the time, glancing at their watches, the clocks on their kitchen walls, the alarms on the night tables in their bedrooms. It was ten minutes past nine.

Gasps, wails, and shrieks filled the air as the townspeople raced towards the church. The volunteer firemen who had preceded them by a few minutes shook their heads mournfully as they arrived. In just seconds, the church had been totally consumed by flames. "It probably was a gas explosion," one of the firemen said. "It happened too fast. None of the choir members could have gotten out in time. I'm sorry. It doesn't look like there are any survivors at all."

Everyone reacted differently. Some people bowed their heads and turned away in silence, griefstricken. A few women crumpled onto the charred grass. Others collapsed into one another's arms and emitted heartrending sobs. Paralyzed by shock, people didn't seem to notice the sudden convergence of twenty automobiles pulling into the church's parking lot at the same time. No one seemed to observe the twenty red-frocked figures running towards the church.

"Hey, what happened?" they heard a familiar-sounding alto voice inquire, shattering the silence that had fallen over the mourners.

"Yeah, what's going on?" chimed in another well-known voice, a mellifluous soprano. "My God, the church is in ruins!" shouted an unforgettable baritone. In wonder, astonishment, and dazed disbelief, the townspeople gazed at the miraculous sight of all twenty choir members—vital and alive—streaming in their direction.

For the first time in twelve years of ongoing choir practice, every single one of them—for separate, different, and unconnected reasons—had come late.

he dinette set was in a sorry state of disrepair. Pressed into service as props for such childhood games as musical chairs and Fort Apache, it was badly battered—a mere shadow of the gleaming chrome set that had once graced our kitchen. Stuffing was spilling out of the seat cushions. It had become a real eyesore, and I felt embarrassed each time a visitor entered my home.

In February 1996, I came into a little money and decided to splurge on a new dinette set. I scouted the neighborhood stores that had been recommended by savvy friends, and finally found a set that made my heart sing. I fell in love with its smooth, sleek, contemporary look, the clean, sharp angles of its matching chairs, and its black and white Formica finish. For me, buying a dinette set was a virtual event, and I felt thrilled that I had encountered one that I liked so much. I was, however, less than thrilled to learn its price tag: $680, more than the budget I had allotted in my head. "You have great taste!" the storeowner congratulated me. "You've chosen one of the most popular models we sell." I sighed. Story of my life: champagne taste on a beer budget! I really didn't want to spend that much money, but this set really tempted me. I stood undecided in the store, until finally the practical side of me took charge, and I regretfully told the storeowner, "Sorry, but I just can't spend that much. Thanks again." As I departed the store, I threw one final, yearning look at the dinette set of my dreams.

The next week, I called a friend renowned for extraordinary bargain-hunting abilities, and she gave me a list of dinette outlets in the neighborhood that sold cheaper models. Armed with the list, I left my home to make the rounds once again.

The day dawned gray and overcast—the kind of day that invariably makes your spirits sag and diminishes your enthusiasm, even for bargain hunting. Nonetheless, I was determined to follow my agenda, so I drove to the first outlet store on my list. Somehow, my friend had made a mistake: all the sets there were priced well over a thousand dollars, and mumbling embarrassed thanks to the storeowner, I beat a hasty retreat. By this time it was raining hard, and I ran to my car, parked a block away.

It was then that I saw her. An elderly woman, shuffling slowly in the torrential downpour, clad only in a thin cotton dress and sneakers, with no umbrella, raincoat, or rain hat to protect her from the slashing rain. She looked pale, wan, and vulnerable. She also looked vaguely familiar, and I broke off my wild dash to the car to approach her. As I advanced closer, I made the connection: She was an impoverished woman whom a charitable organization sent every year to the dress shop I owned for donations of clothing. I had an agreement with this organization whereby I gave, through their referral, free clothing to the neighborhood's poor. She came regularly, once a year, to be outfitted, but I had never seen her outside the store before.

"Linda," I asked in concern, "why are you out on a morning like this?" She began to sob. "Let me drive you to your destination," I said, propelling her to my car.

"What's the matter?" I asked inside the car, as she began to wail in an almost unearthly manner. She poured out her tale of woe and I felt stricken by her story. She had a daughter who was retarded and married to a retarded man. Unexpectedly, they had been able to carve out a happy life for themselves and had two normal children. Unfortunately, however, due to their disabilities, they were unable to make a living to sustain their modest lifestyle. Here and there they got odd jobs occasionally and some minimal government assistance, but not enough to live on. The husband's parents were dead, and Linda herself was on welfare. Unable to pay the rent, her daughter had received an eviction notice, and her daughter's landlord had warned her that if he didn't receive the overdue amount by today, she and her family would be ejected from the premises with nowhere to go.

I had three hundred dollars in my wallet. As Linda cried pitifully in my car, I pulled out a hundred-dollar bill and handed it to her. She stared at the bill in astonishment, kissed me, thanked me effusively, but continued to cry. I paused for a moment, then pulled out a second hundred-dollar bill and handed it to her. She acknowledged her fervent gratitude a second time, but her tears still flowed unabated. I hesitated the third time, but thought, "Aw, what the heck? What's a dinette set compared to the eviction of a family?" and handed her the final hundred-dollar bill. Then I drove her to the office of the charitable organization from which she hoped to solicit further help, and kissed her goodbye.

As I drove away, I was in a positive frame of mind, confident that I had done the right thing. I was proud that I had made the sacrifice. But as I neared my destination—the second dinette outlet store on my list—I began to waver, assaulted by conflicting emotions. Maybe I was a fool, a patsy, an easy touch. Maybe I should have just given her a hundred? Maybe the charitable organization—funded by individuals certainly wealthier than I—could have undertaken the full cost of the rent, and my sacrifice had been needless. By the time I reached the dinette store, I was no longer sure that my three-hundred-dollar donation had been necessary or even justified.

But as soon as I entered the dinette store, my anxiety about the money dissipated, as my attention was drawn to the dinette set of my dreams—the exact same set I had fallen in love with the week before—standing in the center of the showroom. "Excuse me," I excitedly asked the salesman who approached me, "how much is that set over there—the white one with the black formica trim?"

"Oh, that one!" he said. "You sure have great taste—it's beautiful, isn't it?"

"So how much is it?" I asked with mounting excitement. "Well," he said slowly, "it really *is* an expensive set, but you know . . . it's going to be discontinued soon so I don't mind giving you the floor sample. It's ordinarily much more money, but I'll give it to you for . . . three hundred eighty dollars!" Exactly three hundred dollars less than the original set I had seen the week before.

For a fraction of a second, I closed my eyes to thank God for his blessing on my charity and also . . . for the dinette set!

— Yitta Halberstam Mandelbaum

❦

Comment

To the extent that we give to others, the universe responds in kind.

That year, winter in New York City lingered lazily into late April. Living alone and legally blind, I had tended to remain indoors much of the time.

Finally, one day, the chill was gone and spring stepped forth, filling the air with a penetrating and exhilarating fragrance. Outside my back-yard window, a merry little bird kept chirping persistently, beckoning me, it seemed, outdoors.

Aware of the capriciousness of April, I clung to my winter coat, but, as a concession to the change in temperature, discarded my woolen scarf, hat, and gloves. Taking my three-pronged cane, I stepped out cheerfully onto my open porch leading directly to the sidewalk. Lifting my face to the sun, I gave it a welcoming smile in acknowledgment of its warmth and promise.

As I walked down my quiet dead-end street, my next door neighbor called out a musical "Hello" and asked if I wanted a lift to where I was going. "No, thank you," I called back in return. "These legs of mine have been resting all winter, and my joints are badly in need of an out-ing, so I think I'll walk."

Reaching the corner, I waited, as was my habit, for someone to come along who would let me walk across with them when the light turned green. It seemed to take somewhat longer than usual for the sound of traffic to cease, yet I had no offers. As I stood there patiently, I began to hum a tune that returned to me from somewhere in the back of my head. It was a "welcome to spring" song I had learned in school as a child.

Suddenly, a strong, well-modulated masculine voice spoke up. "You sound like a very cheerful human being," it said. "May I have the plea-sure of your company across the street?" Flattered by such chivalry, I nodded, smiling, whispering a barely audible "Yes."

Gently, he tucked his hand around my upper arm and together we stepped off the curb. As we slowly made our way across, we talked of the most obvious topic—the weather—and about how good it was to be alive on such a day. As we kept in step together, it was difficult to deter-mine who was the guide and who was the one being led.

We had barely reached the other side of the crossing, when horns im-patiently began blasting forth again at what was assuredly a change in the light. We walked on a few more paces to get away from the curb. Turning to him, I opened my mouth to thank him for his assistance and company. Before a single word had left my lips, he spoke up. "I don't know if you realize," he said, "how gratifying it is to find someone as cheerful as you to accompany a blind person like me across the street."

That spring day has stayed with me forever.

— *Charlotte Wechsler*

Comment

Sometimes, when we feel most alone in the universe, God sends us a "twin"—a mirror image—to buffer and assuage our sense of differentness and isolation.

He was born to a life of privilege and—as the times mandated—rebelled fiercely when he was nineteen. Donning the faded, torn denim uniform of his generation, Joey Riklis* dropped out of college, quit his part-time job, and announced to his widowed father that he was taking off for India in search of "enlightenment." Sensitive and psychologically astute, his father, Adam Riklis, withstood this blow with equanimity and grace, heeding the advice of friends who counseled patience, tolerance, and love. Joey was acting "normal for his age," they explained confidently, and the storm would soon blow over, they were sure. So Adam told his son that he understood that he was testing his wings and carving out his own unique identity, and he assured him that he accepted the convulsions erupting in his life with sympathy and understanding. But when Joey revealed one day that he had broken with his religion, his father snapped.

Adam Riklis was a Holocaust survivor. His entire family had been murdered by the Nazis, and he alone had withstood the barbaric hardships of three concentration camps. Upon learning that he was the sole survivor of his family, he had silently pledged that the religion his relatives had died for would not die with him. Although many survivors had come away with the opposite attitude, abandoning the religion of their youth in anger and pain, Adam's perspective had been quite different. To divorce himself from the religion of his murdered relatives would be no less than a betrayal of their lives . . . and deaths.

In Cleveland, Adam had clung tightly to his Jewish traditions and religious rituals, carefully incorporating them into his family's day-to-day existence. He sent his children to Hebrew day school, took them to synagogue regularly, and saw to it that they adhered strictly to religious law. He was proud that he had raised religious children who would carry on the family's heritage. But now his own son was announcing that he was scorning this very legacy, making a mockery of his family's losses. Adam could countenance anything but this.

"Get out of here!" he screamed at Joey. "Get out of my home and never come back! You are not my son. I disown you from my heart, from my soul, from my life. I never want to see you again!"

"Well, that's just fine with me," Joey shouted back, "because I never want to see you again either!"

In India, Joey traveled from guru to guru, seeking wisdom, spirituality—concrete answers to life's elusive mysteries. During his travels, he hooked up with Sarah, his female counterpart in many ways. She too had dropped out of a religious Jewish home and was looking for another spiritual path. They were certain they were "soul mates." They had been together for six years when Joey accidentally encountered an old classmate from Cleveland on a street corner in Bombay.

Joey and Sammy embraced happily. "This is unbelievable!" they told each other. They were avidly trading the stories of their respective adventures when Sammy's eyes clouded and he said somberly, "Hey, Joey, I was really sorry to hear about your dad."

"My dad?" Joey repeated dumbly. "What do you mean?"

"Oh my God, I'm so sorry. Then you don't know, obviously."

"Know what?" Joey asked, now rigid with dread.

"Oh, Joey, your father died a couple of months ago. No one wrote you?"

"No one knew where I was," Joey replied slowly, dumbstruck by the news. "What did he die of?"

"A heart attack."

"Not a heart attack," Joey said, his eyes welling with tears. "More like a broken heart, I'm sure. And I'm the cause. I killed him. I killed my own father."

"Joey, don't be ridiculous," Sarah murmured, touching his shoulder in compassion. "You had nothing to do with your father's death!"

"Sarah, you're wrong," Joey answered. "I had *everything* to do with my father's death!"

For several days afterward, Joey lived in a stupor, dazed with grief and remorse. He could not shake his overwhelming certainty that the pain he had inflicted on his father had taken his life. In the back of his mind, he had always hoped for a reconciliation. Somehow he had been sure that a loving reunion would one day take place. Now he would never be able to ask his father's forgiveness, or return to the warm embrace of his love. And he would never have the closure, the resolution, that he so desperately needed.

"Sarah," he shook his head mournfully a few days after learning of his father's death. "I can't go on like this anymore. India tastes like ashes to me now. I know you'll think I'm strange but I have to go . . . to Israel."

"Israel!" Sarah said in surprise, wrinkling her nose in distaste as only an entrenched religious rebel could. "Why do you want to go to Israel?"

"I just feel a pull, Sarah. I can't explain it, but I have to go."

"Okay, okay, so we'll go," she agreed unhappily.

When the plane landed, Joey turned to Sarah and said, "I want to go pray."

"Are you turning weird on me, Joey?" she asked in mock concern.

"Sarah, please!"

"Okay, okay," she relented, "so you want to pray, fine. You want to go to a synagogue?"

"No, Sarah, I want to go to theWall. It's the only remnant left of the First and Second Temples—considered the holiest site in Jerusalem. People believe that God's presence is stronger there than in any other place in Israel. It's where people from all over the world go to pray, to petition God, to ask for miracles. What I want to do is pray for my father's forgiveness."

"Okay," Sarah said, "let's go. But I have to tell you I don't like the direction you seem to be taking."

"Sarah!" Joey cried out in anguish. "Why don't you understand?"

"I understand only too well, Joey. I understand that you're not the same Joey I knew all these years. You used to laugh at all this crap together with me. And now you want to go pray at a wall."

"Look, Sarah, I'm in pain. I loved my father. He's dead. I feel I killed him. Why are you making this so hard for me?"

They quarreled for an hour, and finally decided to split up. "Sarah, I don't know why this is happening," Joey said sadly. "I thought you were my soul mate."

"I am," she said softly, planting a tender and regretful kiss on his cheek. "But our souls simply aren't in alignment anymore. Goodbye, Joey."

Approaching the Wall on foot, Joey looked from a distance at the clusters of people thronging the plaza. Ethiopians in African headdress, Yemenites in white traditional robes, Americans in T-shirts and little yarmulkes. All coming to press their lips against the cool stones, cry warm tears, and fervently beseech God with their personal petitions.

Joey approached a security guard, one of dozens tensely scanning the crowds. "Excuse me," he said. "Can I get a prayer book anywhere around here?"

Silently, the guard pointed in the direction of a bearded rabbi, who was dispensing religious paraphernalia—yarmulkes, prayer books, women's scarves—to the uninitiated.

Donning a borrowed yarmulke and clutching a prayer book, Joey made his way to a section of the Wall. Watching the others and simulating their movements, he rested his head against the smooth stone of the Wall, tried to encircle it with his arm to create an aura of privacy, and began to silently pray. He thought the words would seem foreign after all these years and that he would chant them haltingly, but instead they flowed forth from him in a familiar, comforting stream. He closed his eyes and recalled his father's intonation of these same words, as he was transported back in memory to different realms, the world of his youth. "Oh, Dad," he sobbed. "How I wish I could ask your forgiveness! How I wish I could tell you how much I loved you! How much I regret all the pain I caused you! I didn't mean to hurt you, Dad. I was just trying to find my own way. You meant everything to me, Dad. I wish I could tell you that."

When Joey finished praying, he turned around, at a loss at what to do next. Then he observed people around him scribbling notes and inserting them into the crevices of the Wall. Curious as to what this behavior meant, he approached a young man, and asked, "Excuse me, why are so many people putting little pieces of paper into the cracks of the Wall?"

"Oh, these are their petitions," the youth answered, "their prayers. It is believed that the stones are so holy that requests placed inside of them will be especially blessed."

"Can I do that, too?" Joey asked, intrigued.

"Sure. But be warned, it isn't easy to find an empty crevice any-more!" the young man laughed. "Jews have been coming here for centuries to ply God with their prayers!"

Joey wrote: "Dear Father, I beg you to forgive me for the pain I caused you. I loved you very much and I will never forget you. And please know that nothing that you taught me was in vain. I will not betray your family's deaths. I promise."

When he had finished writing the note, Joey searched for an empty crevice. The young man had not exaggerated. All of the Wall's cracks were filled, crammed, overflowing with petitioners' notes, and it took him close to an hour to find an empty space. But it turned out not to be empty, after all. When he slid his own small note into the crack, he accidentally dislodged another that had already been resting there, and it fell to the ground. "Oh, no, I've pushed out someone's note," Joey thought, a little panic-stricken, wondering what he should do with it. He stooped down to retrieve it, and holding the rolled-up paper in his palm, began searching for another space in which to insert it. But suddenly overcome by a tremendous curiosity to read the words of the unknown petitioner, Joey did something uncharacteristically unscrupulous: He rolled open the note to examine its contents. And this is what he read:

"My Dear Son Joey, If you should ever happen to come to Israel and somehow miraculously find this note, this is what I want you to know: I always loved you, even when you hurt me, and I will never stop loving you. You are, and always will be, my beloved son. And Joey, please know that I forgive you for everything, and only hope that you in turn will forgive a foolish old man." The note was signed "Adam Riklis, Cleveland, Ohio."

"Sir, are you all right, Sir . . . Sir . . . ?" The disembodied voice came from a distance, shattering Joey's reverie. He didn't know how long he had been standing there, numb, paralyzed with shock, clutching his father's note in his trembling hand, tears flowing in rivulets down his face. Stunned, he turned to face the young man who had instructed him on the writing of the petition minutes ago. "Listen," said the young man warmly, draping a sympathetic arm around Joey's shoulder, "you don't have to tell me. It will be Sabbath soon, it's almost sundown. Would you like to come spend it with me?"

Three years later, Joey had returned to his religion and was a full-time rabbinical student. "I think it's time for you to marry," the head rabbi said to him one day. "My wife likes to play matchmaker and she says she has the perfect girl for you. I've told her about you, and she says she's positive she has found your soul mate. It's someone like yourself—a returnee to Judaism—who studies at my wife's women's school. Would you like to meet her? Come to my house tonight for dinner, and she'll be there."

That evening, Joey entered the rabbi's house and was escorted to the living room. There, sitting on the couch, was none other than his old love, Sarah. They stared across the room at each other in shock and awe, and Sarah blinked back tears. "How . . . how did this happen, Sarah?" Joey asked in stunned surprise.

"Well, after we split up," Sarah said, "I began to wander around Israel. 'I'm here already, I might as well see the country before I head back to India,' I told myself. So I started trekking around, and despite myself began to fall in love with the country, the people, and . . . the religion. One day, someone told me about a great women's school, so here I am!"

"Sarah, I thought about you so often all these years . . ."

"Well, I guess our souls are in alignment now," she said softly, as she turned to him with a welcoming smile.

*S*moke poured out from under the front hood of the black stretch limousine as it sped down the highway. Louis, the limousine's chauffeur, pulled over to the side of the road to flag down assistance. Concern and worry were written on his face. He stood in the cold rain and frantically waved a flashlight in the air, hoping to draw people to his plight. It was futile. Most drivers slowed down to catch a glimpse of the stalled limousine, but then blithely continued on their way.

Robert Wise* was the exception. He noted the chauffeur's predicament and felt compelled to come to his aid. He drove up to the shoulder of the road, peered out his window, and asked how he could help. "Would you please call my boss and tell him my situation?" asked the chauffeur. "And then could you please let me know what he says?"

"No problem," came the cheerful reply. Louis then provided Robert with the name of his boss, Mr. Cavendish,* and a phone number. Robert got back on the highway, drove to the nearest service station, and made the call.

A short time later, Robert returned. He relayed a message from Mr. Cavendish and then turned on his engine, ready to continue on his way home. "Wait!" Louis called out to him. "How can I thank you?"

"Oh, please, it was nothing," replied Robert.

"No, you must tell me how I can thank you," the chauffeur insisted.

"It was really nothing," came the reply, "but if you care to, you can send a dozen roses to my wife for her birthday, which is next week." Robert gave Louis his address, and the two men departed.

The following day, the chauffeur told his boss what had happened on the road. He described how difficult it had been to get assistance and how glad he had been when a kind stranger finally stopped to help. "And all the man asked for were flowers for his wife," concluded the chauffeur. Mr. Cavendish listened and was touched by Robert's modest request. He took the address and said, "Leave the rest to me."

Within the next few weeks, Mr. Cavendish arranged for flowers to be sent to the Wise home. But that was not all. For years, the couple had been struggling financially and were threatened with foreclosure. They were now blessed with a generosity of spirit. In addition to the dozen red roses, Mr. Cavendish graciously paid off the mortgage on their house.

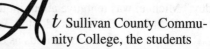

*A*t Sullivan County Community College, the students began filing in for the summer program. "Hey, look who's there," one girl said, pointing to a tall young man with curly dark hair. "It's Eddy."

"That's odd," her friend responded. "I thought Eddy had transferred to Nassau Community College on Long Island. Guess I was wrong." The two young women waved at the person they thought was Eddy. It was actually someone named Robert Shafran and this was his first day at a new college.

Moments later, a fellow running to class spotted Robert from the corner of his eye. "Hey buddy," he called out to Robert, "glad to see you. Catch you later," and he rushed by. Robert was taken aback. He knew he had never seen this person before and yet he had been greeted as if the two were on intimate terms. Just as Robert was mulling this over in his mind, an attractive young woman gave him a kiss that obviously meant more than hello.

Robert was perplexed. He had never been the recipient of such an outpouring of warmth. He was bewildered and he hoped he wasn't dreaming. Robert walked into his first class, took a seat, and settled in. No sooner had he taken a notebook out of his briefcase when a total stranger walked up to him demanding an apology. "But for what?" asked Robert, dumbfounded. "I don't even know you."

"What do you mean, you don't know me?" said the stranger. "What a sense of humor!" he chuckled.

Robert was startled and said, "Hey, I'm not who you think I am." The stranger threw Robert a quizzical look, then muttered something under his breath and walked off.

These encounters continued to happen throughout the day as Robert walked around on campus. Meanwhile a student named Michael Dominitz had heard that his best friend's lookalike had been seen on campus. Michael searched all over and then gasped when he finally spotted Robert in the distance. Indeed, there was an uncanny resemblance to Eddy Galland, his close buddy. Michael walked up to Robert and exclaimed, "Why, you're a carbon copy of my best friend!" Then he pulled out a photo from his wallet. "Here, look at this," he said pointing to a picture of Eddy, "tell me what you think." Now it was Robert's turn to stand in awe as he looked at what appeared to be a picture of himself. He was astounded, just as everyone else who had made the mistake that day. "When is your birthday?" inquired Michael.

"July 12, 1961," replied Robert.

"Oh, my God," said Michael, "That's the same day as Eddy's birthday." Michael was tentative about inquiring further, but he did so despite himself. "I know Eddy was adopted. Were you adopted?"

"Yes," said Robert, incredulous as the moment unfolded.

A few days later, Michael called Eddy at his home in New Hyde Park, Long Island, and put him in touch with his lookalike. Over the phone they exchanged vital statistics and without any hesitation agreed to meet in person. "I'll drive you out there," offered Michael, who knew the way to Eddy's house and was eager to see the outcome of this exchange.

The following day, the two met, and were stunned to discover that they were virtual "doubles." Fascinated and mystified by the striking resemblance, they had an excited conversation and discovered a number of amazing similarities. They talked alike and had identical birthmarks. They both smoked too many Marlboros, and even held their cigarettes the same way. They had the same I.Q. of 148. They favored Italian food and had the same taste in music and sports. Both had a preference for dating older women.

"Isn't this bizarre?" said Robert.

"Yes, you're my clone!" said Eddy.

Both Robert and Eddy had known that they had been adopted but had been unaware that they had any siblings. Calls were made to their respective parents and the records of Long Island Jewish Hospital were checked. That which they had sensed from the moment they had made contact was now confirmed. Eddy and Robert were twins, separated at birth.

The story hit the news and the picture of the reunited brothers appeared on the front page of newspapers everywhere. The story made for good conversation—another interesting bit of news, quickly absorbed, rapidly forgotten.

Forgotten by everyone, that is, except for one young man named David Kellman, a freshman at New York's Queens College. He called the Galland household and without skirting the issue, got right to the point. "You're not going to believe this," he said to Eddy, "but my name is David Kellman and I'm looking in the mirror and at the picture in the paper. I believe I'm the third brother." Eddy's jaw dropped open and he sat for ten minutes in total awe. "I can't believe it," were the only words that he was able to articulate.

When David arrived at the Galland residence in Long Island, Eddy opened the door and looked at him, then closed the door and then opened it again and looked and then closed it again. When he finally let David in the door, they both exclaimed "Holy cow," in unison, and stared at each other in stunned amazement. "I always knew I was adopted but I had no idea that I had any siblings," said David.

"Neither did I," said Eddy, "neither did I." They talked, they laughed, and they cried.

The records at Manhattan's Louise Wise adoption agency made it all credible. Robert, David, and Eddy were triplets, born in that order, within twenty-seven minutes of each other.

The families got together in celebration. Reporters were there to cover the story. "Looking around at the sea of new faces, what can you tell us about your new family?" asked an interviewer.

Eddy spoke up. "It's like I've known them all my life," he said, "I think the whole thing is beautiful."

Pictures were taken as David, Eddy, and Robert slung their arms around one another, each flashing a broad grin. The triplets, separated at birth, were reunited.

They went on to establish the well-known Triplets Romanian Steak-house, located in Manhattan, which still exists today.

Comment

Bloodlines may run so deep as to pierce through all barriers that threaten to stand in their way.

he ad in the paper caught my attention immediately. "Director of Programming sought for women's organization to create and coordinate conferences, symposiums, book and author luncheons, etc.," it read. "Knowledge of current affairs and contemporary literature necessary. Experience required." My heart began to thump with excitement. "Yes!" I thought with growing elation. "This is it! This is the job I've been seeking for so long. I can feel it beckoning to me. This is it . . . I just know it!" There was only one minor hitch: I didn't have the experience.

For years, I had worked in the public relations field as a writer, and I was feeling burnt out. In 1991, I was ready for a change, but was beginning to learn that it's not so easy to switch careers, especially without retraining. I had been casting about for something to do that would tap into my skills and expertise when I saw the ad. This job sounded perfect. I was an inveterate lecture-attender and a voracious reader. Putting together lectures and seminars didn't sound difficult; it sounded like fun! But how was I going to circumvent the "experience required" part? First things first: I called the number in the ad and talked my way into an interview.

My interviewers were impressed with my credentials but concerned about my lack of programming experience. I assured them that I could handle the demands of the position, and they were swayed by my confidence. I got the job.

But my confidence foundered almost as soon as I arrived at the office on the first day. "Oh, so you're *Helene Isaac's* successor," one elderly employee said with concern. "What big shoes to fill. She was a phenomenon!" Another said tactlessly, "Well, I do feel sorry for you. There's nobody in this world like Helene Isaacs!" Then a third remarked, "Well, a hearty welcome to our organization, which, you'll find, is a great place to work." Then she shook her head mournfully. "But it sure hasn't been the same since Helene Isaacs left!"

I was ready to pick up my purse and flee. How was I ever going to compete with the phantom Helene?

Then I was ushered into my predecessor's office and didn't know whether to laugh or cry. A veritable paper mountain of letters, memos, brochures, and newspaper clippings—three feet high at least—covered Helene's desk. "Uh . . . why don't you spend the day cleaning off Helene's desk," suggested the personnel director, embarrassed, hastily backing out of the room. "She was very brilliant and creative but a trifle . . . disorganized," she said in explanation as she retreated.

I put down my handbag and stared in dismay at the daunting paper mountain. What a way to begin! How was I expected to know which papers should be saved and which could be discarded? Couldn't this venerable icon at least have had the decency to clean off her desk before she left? I sighed. Just then, another staff member stuck her head into my room and said, "Oh, you're Helene's replacement; I want to welcome you. Helene was here eighteen years, you know. Do you think you could stay that long?"

I didn't think I could stay for another hour. I picked up the phone and called my friend Rose. "This was a terrible mistake!" I wailed. "How could I have had the nerve to even think for a minute that I could undertake a job for which I have no real experience! I never coordinated an all-day conference before . . . I must have been out of my mind to think I could do it. I better get out of here fast before they discover what a hoax, what a charlatan, what a fraud I really am. In fact, I think I'm actually going to pick up my handbag and go home right now!"

"Whoa! Wait a minute!" cautioned my friend. "Where's the fearless 'can do' spirit that's always infused your life? Where's your desire to stretch, to expand? Where's the woman I know and love who welcomes a challenge and a chance to grow? You *can* do it! All beginnings are hard."

"Yeah, you're right," I conceded sheepishly. "I shouldn't give up so fast. But what about this pile of papers I have to contend with?" I moaned. "What am I going to do with those?"

"Hey," Rose said, "why don't you look at it as a learning experience? Work your way through the stack very slowly, read each paper carefully, and by the time you're finished, I bet you'll know much more about the job than you did when you started."

I was inspired and heartened by her attitude. "You're right!" I exclaimed. "I'm going to see this as a challenge and a learning experience. I *won't* throw in the towel!" Blinking back my tears, I concentrated on going through the pile of papers stacked high on the desk.

When I finally got to the very last one, I blinked again. But this time it was in wonder and awe.

I picked up the old, yellowing, tattered piece of paper, dated, incredibly, 1956, and, shaking my head in amazement, knocked on a colleague's door. "Can I help you?" she asked cheerfully.

"Can you tell me who this woman was?" I asked pointing to the paper. "In the first paragraph, she's identified as Judith Mandelbaum, but in the third paragraph she's referred to as Mrs. Mordechai Mandelbaum."

"Oh, Judith Mandelbaum—she was director of programming, too. She was Helene's predecessor, and she was excellent! She retired in 1962, when Helene took over. She was an icon of the organization and she was here for ages!"

I returned to my office, smiling and relieved. And I knew: everything would work out fine, everything would be all right. I would meet the challenge of my new position and I would succeed. I would be here for a while, I was sure.

You see, *my* own English first name is Judith; my *husband's* is Mordechai. And our family name is . . . Mandelbaum!

It's five years now, and I'm still at the job.

— *Yitta Halberstam Mandelbaum*

Comment

Was this "coincidence" a reassuring tap on the shoulder? Here, engulfed by waves of self-doubt, the new employee questions the wisdom of moving into a new field. Every reference to the legendary Helene Isaacs is another assault on her self-confidence and weakens her resolve to stay on the job. But when she uncovers a link to a predecessor, she finds the reassurance she has been seeking. And, as a result of undertaking the job, which puts her into constant contact with celebrity authors, she becomes inspired and emboldened to write a book of her own—the very one you're reading now!

*T*om Stonehill* had been driving for several hours when he was overcome with the urge to go to the bathroom. It was late at night and all the gas stations he passed were closed. As time wore on, he became increasingly desperate. Finally, Tom exited the highway and drove into the first town along the road. There, he searched for a place that had facilities open to the public.

As he drove, his physical need took on heightened urgency and he started to pick up speed. Just as he began to accelerate, he heard someone on a loudspeaker instructing him to pull over to the side. It was the town sheriff. The sheriff got out of his car and approached Tom. "How fast do you think you can drive around here?" he asked in a formidable tone.

"Sir," apologized Tom, "I never drive this fast, but you see, right now I am in dire need of a bathroom."

The sheriff noted the sincerity in Tom's voice and took pity on him. "I believe there may be something open if you continue on down this road," he said, pointing straight ahead. "But you gotta watch the speed limit!" he added.

"I will," replied Tom, relieved and glad to be moving on.

Moments later, Tom spotted a light in the distance. He was sure he was approaching a twenty-four hour grocery store. But the closer he came to his destination, the more it became clear that he was headed toward a funeral parlor. Tom felt hesitant about using their facilities, but his urge was too strong to ignore. He drove up to the entrance, parked his car, and walked in.

Once inside, he was greeted warmly. "Welcome. Would you please sign in?" said Mr. Gifford,* the funeral director.

"Uh . . . I'm just here to use the bathroom," Tom said apologetically. "May I?"

"Of course you may," responded the director, "but please sign in first." Tom couldn't figure out why it was necessary to write his name down, but he did as he was told and hoped that would end the matter. Tom was about to ask the whereabouts of the men's room when Mr. Gifford said, "Please write in your full address as well."

"But why do you need my address?" asked Tom, perplexed, "I'm just here to use the bathroom for a minute."

"Please, sir, fill in the information," came the reply.

"What the heck?" Tom muttered to himself as he wrote. Then he followed as Mr. Gifford led him to the men's room.

Before leaving the funeral parlor, Tom stopped for just a moment to pay his respects to the deceased. On his way out of the building, Tom saw the sheriff. "Thank you," he nodded to Mr. Gifford and the sheriff, and with that, Tom was off and on his way back home.

Three weeks later, Tom received a phone call from a man unknown to him, who identified himself as an attorney. "I represent the funeral home where you stopped to use the washroom a few weeks ago," the man said. "You need to be in my office this Thursday at 2:00 P.M."

Tom was shaken. Alarmed, he asked, "Please tell me, did I do something wrong? Will I need a lawyer?"

"No, that won't be necessary," the attorney assured him. "Just be prompt," he said. The attorney gave Tom his address and then hung up the phone.

For the next few days, Tom was on edge. "What could I possibly have done? Why would they call me in?" he wondered aloud. That Thursday, he drove to the attorney's office with apprehension.

Tom found the office building as instructed. With bated breath and a pounding heart, he knocked on the front door. "Come in," said the secretary. The attorney stepped out, formal introductions were made, and then Tom was directed to the office. Once inside, Tom was surprised to see both the sheriff and Mr. Gifford present.

"Please be seated," began the attorney. "I have been authorized by the court to read the last will and testament of Mr. Stanley Murrow*." The attorney picked up the guest book that Tom had signed. He turned to the funeral director, pointed at Tom and asked, "Is this the man who signed the book?"

"Yes," said the funeral director. Then the attorney looked at Tom and began, "I guess you didn't know Mr. Murrow. He was a very wealthy man. He owned most of this town. However, he did not have any family and was universally disliked, practically shunned by the townspeople. Mr. Murrow has authorized me to be his executor." The attorney picked up a document and continued. "This is the shortest will I have ever drawn up. It reads simply: 'Everyone hated my guts, and no one ever got any money from me when I was alive. So any person who comes to my funeral is obviously someone who had some compassion for an old coot like me. I hereby bequeath my entire estate with all my holdings to be divided equally among those who actually attended my funeral.'"

The attorney then looked straight at Tom. "Yours was the only signature that appeared in the register book," he said. "Therefore. . . ."

Comment

There are misers who hoard their wealth, ensuring that no one will have pleasure from it but themselves. Financially, they may be well off, but spiritually they are bankrupt. Conversely, there are those who are in need, yet give of themselves generously and are blessed with an abundance of spirit. Who then is really the rich one? And who is really poor?

$\mathcal{I}t$ was Pam Altschul's first day as a freshman at the University of Michigan, far from her parents' home on Long Island. It was also Rosh Hashonah, the first day of the Jewish New Year. While her roommates were unpacking and just beginning to get acquainted, Pam was preparing to leave for the synagogue. She would have liked to stay and take part in the introductions but she felt compelled to attend services instead. It was a custom that she had observed since childhood.

Pam exited the dorm from the far right side of the building feeling somewhat lonely and isolated. As she looked around at her new surroundings, she noticed a young woman leaving from the far left side of the same building at the same time. Both were obviously dressed to attend a religious service. They crossed the lawn diagonally and met one another at midpoint. There was an awkward silence between the two women as they walked along side by side. Finally, Pam spoke first. "Hello," she began, "my name is Pam."

"Pam?" came the startled response. "Why, my name is Pam too!"

"Are you by any chance going to the synagogue?" asked the first Pam.

"Yes, I am," came the reply from the second.

A lively conversation ensued. The two Pams quickly discovered that they had much in common. They shared a common middle initial as well as first names. They had both grown up in the same unique type of ranch house in neighboring towns. Both of their mothers were teachers. Both of their respective best friends from high school were now best friends in college. And both had only sisters.

By the time they reached the synagogue doors, one more commonality was revealed. At the start of that day, both women had felt overwhelmed by the sea of new faces and both had wished that they would make at least one new friend. Indeed, that walk was the beginning of a friendship that deepened and became stronger as the years wore on.

Today, one Pam lives in Connecticut and the other in New York. Despite the distance, they continue to be the best of friends, and every Rosh Hashonah, they share the most heartfelt wishes for the New Year.

Comment

Just when you think you are alone, take one more step, walk one more block, hold on to hope just a bit longer, for just around the next corner, there may be a new friendship waiting to begin.

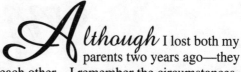

Although I lost both my parents two years ago—they died within a few months of each other—I remember the circumstances surrounding my mother's death more vividly, because they were unusual and striking.

I am a great fan of the Christian evangelical singer Curtis Stiegers. His music has always had the power to uplift and comfort me in the worst of times. When my mother was rushed to the hospital one evening, before entering the ambulance I paused to grab my black tote bag, which hangs in the corner in the front hall. It contains my Walkman and several of Stiegers's tapes. I had the feeling that I would be needing to listen to his music that night.

All night long, as doctors worked over my mother, who had had a stroke, I listened to my Curtis Stiegers tapes in the hospital waiting room. Kind nurses brought me coffee from time to time and offered me their company, but the solace I sought was from Stiegers's music. Early in the morning, the battery in the Walkman must have run out, because the music suddenly came to an abrupt halt. Startled out of my anesthetized state, I automatically glanced down at my watch and was surprised to note that it was 4:41. The night had passed more swiftly than I had ever imagined possible, and I got up to check on my mother's condition. As I walked towards the nurse's station, I saw a body draped with a sheet being wheeled out of a room. It was my mother.

When I received the death certificate, I saw to my shock that the time of death had been 4:41. Exactly the time that my Walkman battery had run out and Curtis had stopped singing!

— *Ellen Palmer**

❧

Comment

"There is a time to sing and a time to weep," Ecclesiastes said. There are moments in our lives when we *must* embrace the hard times and the pain. Since it was no longer appropriate for the joyous music to play, it stopped. The time to confront the tragedy and to mourn had arrived.

*M*y husband is the ultimate Good Samaritan. Wherever he goes, wherever he happens to be, he's always performing random acts of kindness, often for people he doesn't know, and sometimes for people he doesn't *even see*. Most of the time I am proud and gratified to be married to such a man, but once in a while I get annoyed when I think he's being excessive. When this spirit moves me—on rare occasions I must admit—I start to sulk, fume, and—if what he's done really strikes me as extravagant—boil over with rage. "Hmpph," I'll sputter indignantly, "this is all very nice, but when was the last time somebody did something like this for you or for me? Are you the only Good Samaritan left in town?"

But last week these doubts were given short shrift by a universe far wiser than I.

My husband and I were idly window-shopping one day in a local business district, where cars were parked along the curb next to meters. Suddenly, we noticed a grim-faced meter maid stomping determinedly down the street, studying each meter intently, pen poised, prepared to write tickets. My husband immediately pulled out all the change in his pockets and began running down the street, frantically inserting quarters into all the expired meters, pre-empting the meter maid. When she finally advanced upon him it was with raised eyebrows and a scowling face; he in turn flashed her a triumphant grin and a roguish wink. From a distance, I watched my husband tenderly. It struck me that he was engaging in the highest form of charity: none of the people whose cars he had saved from being ticketed would ever know their benefactor; they probably wouldn't even know they had one! I was proud of him, to be sure. Still, when he returned from his labors, that little, cynical voice that I contend with all the time had the final word: "That was beautiful, honey . . . but when was the last time somebody did that for you or for me?"

The next day, I was shopping again, this time in a different business district, and parked my car next to a meter. In a dress shop filled with luscious creations I lost all sense of time and, when I glanced down at my watch, I realized with a start that my time on the meter must have expired. I hurried out of the store and ran towards my car, parked a block away. With a sinking heart, I saw a meter maid advancing towards the car.

Now, my husband, a perfectly reasonable man in all other respects, gets totally enraged when I get a parking ticket. He considers it the height of irresponsibility and a horrible waste of money besides. A parking ticket means at least three hours of serious fighting, followed by a full day of shameful recriminations and mournful head-shaking. I have learned (painfully) to avoid getting parking tickets, at all costs.

But when I saw the meter maid just a few feet away from my car, I knew all hope was lost. There was no way I could get to the meter before she did. I almost wept in consternation.

Suddenly, I saw an unfamiliar-looking man sprint across the street, dash over to my meter, and insert a quarter. At that point the meter maid approached, and he smiled broadly at her. Then he turned and strode quickly down the street. I rushed after him to thank him, wondering, "Who could it be? Is it someone who knows me . . . maybe a neighbor, a relative . . . someone who recognized the car and wanted to help me out?" But when I caught up with him and called to him to stop, it was a complete stranger who turned around.

"You just rescued me from the meter maid!" I bubbled. "Thank you so much—I can't believe you did that! Do you know my husband by any chance, and did you recognize our car? What made you do it?"

"Oh, I don't know your husband and I don't know your car," he said. "But I happened to see the meter maid coming, and I thought, what a shame—she's going to ticket that car. All it cost me was twenty-five cents to save you from a twenty-five-dollar ticket."

I was overwhelmed, and I couldn't thank the man enough. "Oh, it's OK really," he said. "I do this all the time!"

— *Yitta Halberstam Mandelbaum*

$\mathcal{S}$*everal* years ago, the writer
Deborah Wilde* found herself
walking the streets of a small backwater village in England, a place
that was obscure and unknown to tourists. Thousands of miles away
from her home in New York, Deborah was visiting her in-laws, who
lived in the hamlet. The visit had turned into a nightmare—her strife-
filled marriage was unraveling, and that day she had quarreled with
both her husband and his parents. To escape a volatile situation, she
had announced her intention of taking a walk (even though it was
raining hard) and had stepped out into the downpour.

"What am I doing in this godforsaken place, anyway?" she thought,
dispirited. "Just what is the *point* of my being here?"

Meanwhile, a man by the name of Richard Wilson* was walking the
streets of the same village, in an equally gloomy frame of mind. He too
was from New York, and had come to meet his biological parents, who
had given him up for adoption at birth. Many years before, he had embarked on an exhaustive search to find them, and he had finally traced
them to this town. He had been in an excited, even exhilarated state
when he rang the doorbell of their home, visions of a warm, loving reunion filling his imagination. The reception accorded him, however, had
turned out to be quite different. His biological parents had been cold,
even hostile, rebuffing all overtures. After fruitlessly trying to break
down their reserve, he had finally left with an aching heart. His trip
across the Atlantic had been for nought; the dreams that had stretched
across years had turned to dust. "God, I feel so terribly alone," he said to
himself in despair. "I feel like killing myself! They were so mean—my
own parents, my own flesh and blood. What I wouldn't give right now
for one friendly face, one warm smile! Isn't there anyone in the world
who would be happy to see me?"

Just then, Deborah and Richard passed each other in the swirling
mist. Their eyes locked. They froze. Then Deborah ran toward Richard,
enfolding him in a fervent embrace. "Richard!" she shrieked happily.
"Oh God, Deborah!" he wept in relief.

The two were cousins, and close friends. Deborah's question had
been answered. So had Richard's. Simultaneously.

The true purpose of Deborah's presence in this town had finally been
revealed. She was there to give Richard solace at a time when he needed
it most.

Comment

Both Richard and Deborah were undergoing variations of the exact same experience: the painful unraveling of lifelong dreams and hopes, the loss of a certain identity, the need for a final, excruciating confrontation with the past. When they "stumbled" upon each other, they were able to give each other the comfort both so desperately needed.

A well-known editor at a major publishing house was constantly besieged by writer friends who bombarded him with book proposals and unsolicited manuscripts. One acquaintance was especially persistent, and petitioned the editor tenaciously to consider his novel. Finally, he reluctantly agreed to take a look at it. "Everyone thinks he's a writer!" grumbled the editor as he grudgingly removed the manuscript from the slush pile.

Pleasantly surprised to discover that the book had merit, the editor decided to take it home for further study. The 400-page manuscript had been enclosed in a gift box, and the editor placed the box on the front seat of his car. Before heading home, however, he made a stop at a local restaurant for a quick bite. He parked on a dimly lit street and rushed into the eatery, forgetting to lock the car doors.

When he returned to the car half an hour later, he discovered that it had been broken into and his radio removed. Worse—far worse—the gift box containing the manuscript was gone. The radio could easily be replaced, but the writer had told him repeatedly that he had failed to make a duplicate of the manuscript, and that the copy the editor had in his possession was the *only* copy.

And now it had been stolen!

The editor's heart sank. How was he going to tell his friend that the book he had worked on for three years—his magnum opus, his masterpiece—was gone? No, it wasn't right to do it now, from a pay phone on the street, with traffic in the background. He would wait until he got home, and call him from the relative calm of his study. He knew he was procrastinating, but he couldn't help it; that call would be one of the hardest things he had ever had to do in his life.

The moment he arrived home, the phone rang. It was the writer, his voice indignant. "Oh," said the editor, taken aback, "I was just going to call you . . ."

"Yeah, and I know about what," interrupted the writer angrily, "and I think it's just disgusting!"

The editor was puzzled; how could the writer have known about the stolen manuscript? He hadn't told anyone yet. "What do you mean?" he asked.

"What do I mean? You know very well what I mean!" the writer exploded. "So you didn't like my book, fine . . . you have a right to your opinion. But did you have to show your contempt by throwing it into my backyard . . . into the mud?"

Having been chased by a pair of eagle-eyed cops, the thieves who had broken into the editor's car had tossed the weighty manuscript over a fence into the nearest backyard . . . The *writer's* backyard.

Subsequently, the novel was published.

Julia Dixon* had just accidentally locked herself out of her house when the mailman came up the drive. "Mrs. Dixon!" he exclaimed in concern. "You look upset. What's the matter?"

"Oh, I don't know what I'm going to do," she wailed, wringing her hands nervously. "The door locked behind me, and my neighbor, who keeps a duplicate for me, is out of town. My husband has a key, but he's at an all-day conference at a hotel downtown, and I doubt I can reach him. How am I going to get back in?"

The mailman tried to calm the woman, and advised her to call a locksmith. "I guess that's my only recourse," she agreed, "but to tell you the truth, they charge an arm and a leg and I really can't afford an extra expense right now. Things have been tight."

The mailman commiserated with her, but pointed out that she had no choice. "Look, I better be on my way," he said, "but here's your mail. Who knows? Maybe there'll be some good news inside one of the letters to cheer you up!"

Julia looked through the envelopes. There was one from her brother Jonathan. He had visited the family the previous week and had stayed for a few days. "I wonder why he's writing so soon?" she murmured. As she tore open the letter, a key fell into her palm.

"Dear Julia," the letter read. "Last week, when I was staying at your house and you were out shopping, I accidentally locked myself out. I asked your neighbor for your duplicate, but forgot to return it. So I'm enclosing it now."

Comment

When you face a closed door and you're feeling hopeless, know that all doors can be opened, making way for you to step right in.

As a major dress manufacturer in Canada, I sold some goods to a small retail operation in Montreal, which was owned by a man who was a member of my synagogue. I had heard that he was an upright, respectable man who ran an ethical business, so I gave him credit. According to the terms we had initially agreed to, he was supposed to pay his bill of $8,724 sixty days after receiving my shipment. I was very disheartened when my bookkeeper told me that he was delinquent on his payment.

We sent out three notices, which he ignored. Finally, I picked up the phone and called him. "What's going on?" I inquired. "Look," he sighed, "I'm really sorry but I can't pay my bill. Business is terrible, and I may have to close. I don't have a penny to my name."

I didn't know what to do, so I consulted my rabbi. "Should I take him to court?" I asked. "After all, $8,724 is not a negligible amount; I really need that money! On the other hand, I feel bad for him; he's down on his luck—what can he really do?" The rabbi didn't give me much concrete advice. "Follow your heart!" he counseled.

I wrestled with myself for a long time, and finally concluded that I didn't have the heart to sue the man. I heard later that he closed his business. He moved away to a different section of the town, joined another synagogue, and I lost track of him. Several years passed, and my business prospered.

One day, I received a call from a woman whose name I didn't recognize, who asked if she could come up to my office to see me. She was deliberately vague about her intentions, but my curiosity was piqued, so I agreed to see her. When she arrived, she revealed her identity: she was the daughter of the man who still owed me the $8,724.

"All these years, my father has felt terribly guilty about the debt he owes you," she said. "He went bankrupt and was never able to stage a comeback. He still doesn't have any money, but he asked me to give you this instead." She then pulled a piece of jewelry out of her pocketbook and handed it to me.

It was a gold bracelet studded with diamonds. "It's a family heirloom," she told me, "and practically the only thing of value my father has left. He asked me to give it to you with his sincerest apologies and greatest hope that it's worth something. He doesn't know how valuable it is, but he's hoping it will bring you at least part of what he owes you." At this point, I didn't want to take it, but she insisted.

I don't know much about jewelry, but I doubted that the piece was really valuable. I tossed it into a drawer and forgot about it. A few days later, I remembered it and showed it to my father, who was also quite skeptical about its possibilities. However, he suggested that it wouldn't hurt to go to an expert he knew for an appraisal.

The appraiser examined the bracelet carefully and at length. Finally, after much time had elapsed, he turned to us and said excitedly, "This is a really valuable piece! It's worth much more than you imagined. As a matter of fact, I would like to buy it from you. I'm prepared to give you $8,724."

The exact amount, to the dollar, that the man had owed me!

— *Patrick Simone**

Comment

In our dog-eat-dog world, someone who acts generously can be made to feel like a patsy. For doing the right thing, the manufacturer has clearly won accolades and applause from a higher power.

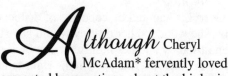

*A*lthough Cheryl McAdam* fervently loved her adopted family, she was tormented by questions about the biological one she had never known. She had been raised lovingly by doting adoptive parents who had spoiled her incessantly; she had received warmth and devotion in abundance; and she lacked for nothing. Still, despite all the blessings in her life, she could not help but obsess about her past.

Who were her natural parents? Why had they given her up? How could they have given up their own child? What were they like? And—most important—what would her life had been like had she grown up with them instead of with her adopted family? These questions plagued her continually as she fantasized about the life that might have been.

Finally, when she was twenty-one, married, and had given birth to a daughter, Kayla, she resolved to uncover the truth. She approached her adoptive parents and asked for their permission to launch a search. She loved them very much, she insisted, but her daughter's birth had reawakened her need to know her heritage. Compassionate, her adopted parents agreed to help her travel back to her roots.

Hers was a successful search—more successful than in her wildest dreams. More than anything else, it brought her a certain validation for which she had always hungered—a validation that finally laid to rest all her doubts, questions, conflicts, and fears.

This is what she discovered:

Her natural mother's first name—Anne—was almost the same as her adopted mother's, Anna. Her natural father, who had married her natural mother a year after they had given her up, was named John—the same as her adoptive father, Johnnie. Her two natural siblings bore the same first names as her adopted siblings—Carol and Wayne. And finally, when her natural sister, who had gotten married the previous year (about the same time she had) had given birth—to twins—she had named them *Kyle* and *Kaylee*, not one but two variations of her own daughter's name—Kayla.

Cheryl returned home happy, assured that her placement in her adopted family had not only been right . . . it had been destined!

Comment

Cheryl is haunted by concerns of dislocation and displacement. Perhaps, she wonders, her destiny would have been quite different had she been raised by another family . . . her biological one. However, the coincidences convey "You were in the right family all along!" The parallels here are so strong and obvious, there's no possibility of misinterpreting them. As a result of these "coincidences," the young woman acquired newfound serenity and peace of mind, and her anxiety about having grown up in the wrong family was forever dispelled.

I n the 1930s, Rabbi Samuel Shapira, the distinguished chief rabbi of the Polish village of Prochnik, was in the habit of taking long, invigorating walks into the countryside. The rabbi, who was known for his warm, loving, and compassionate ways, always made a point of greeting everyone whose path he crossed—Jew and non-Jew alike—and, adhering to a Talmudic dictum, always tried to greet them first.

One of the people he regularly greeted on his daily walks was a peasant by the name of Herr Mueller, whose farm lay on the outskirts of the town. Every morning, Rabbi Shapira would pass the farmer as he diligently worked in his fields. The rabbi would nod his head and expansively boom in a hearty voice, "Good morning, Herr Mueller!"

When the rabbi had first embarked on his morning constitutional and had begun greeting Herr Mueller, the farmer had turned away in stony silence. Relations between Jews and gentiles in this village were not particularly good, and friendships were rare. But Rabbi Shapira was not deterred or discouraged. Day after day, he would greet the silent Herr Mueller with a hearty hello, until, finally convinced of the rabbi's sincerity, the farmer began returning the greeting with a tip of his hat and a hint of a smile.

This routine went on for many years. Every morning, Rabbi Shapira would call out, "Good morning, Herr Mueller!" And every morning Herr Mueller would tip his hat and yell back, "Good morning, Herr Rabiner!" This scenario stopped when the Nazis came.

Rabbi Shapira and his family, together with all the other Jewish residents of the village, were shipped to a concentration camp. Rabbi Shapira was transferred from one concentration camp to the next until he reached his final destination point: Auschwitz.

As he disembarked from the train, he was ordered to join the line where selection was taking place. Standing in the back of the line, he saw from a distance the camp commandant's baton swing left, swing right. He knew that left signified certain death, but right bought time and possible survival.

His heart palpitating, he drew closer to the commandant as the line surged forward. Soon it would be his turn. What would be the decree? Left or right?

He was one person away from the man in charge of the selection, the man whose arbitrary decision could send him into the flames. What kind of man was this commandant, a man who could so easily send thousands of people a day to their deaths?

Despite his own fear, he looked curiously, almost boldly into the face of the commandant as his turn was called. At that moment, the man turned to glance at him, and their eyes locked.

Rabbi Shapira approached the commandant and said quietly, "Good morning, Herr Mueller!" Herr Mueller's eyes, cold and unfathomable, twitched for a fraction of a second. "Good morning, Herr Rabiner!" he answered, also very quietly.

And then he swung his baton forward. "Recht!" he shouted with a barely perceptible nod. "Right!" To . . . life!

Comment

Who would have thought a simple "Hello" could save a life? Yet sometimes the smallest of actions (or at least actions that we perceive to be small) can result in the greatest—and gravest—of consequences. The rabbi sowed the seeds of his redemption for years by engaging in polite pleasantries with a person whom others might have deemed an inconsequential peasant. Could he ever have envisioned that one day this man would quite literally hold his fate in his hands?

$\mathcal{T}$ *om* MacEnvoy* hated his daughter Trisha's cat. She had picked up the stray in the school's courtyard, promptly fallen in love with it, and brought it home, pleading, "I know you swore no more pets after the hamster disaster, Dad, but please let me keep him! I love him so much!"

"But Trisha," her father objected, "he's just a plain old alley cat. If you want a cat, let me at least get you a Persian."

"No, this is the one I want! When I saw him in the yard, he came right up to me, rubbing against me, meowing and purring. We're right for each other, Dad . . . we connect!" Tom MacEnvoy succumbed to his daughter's soft entreaties, but whenever he saw the cat, he scowled and turned away in distaste.

One morning, Tom found debris from the litter box scattered all over the floor of the dining room. Seizing on this as an excuse, he said to his daughter, "That does it! The cat goes tomorrow!"

"Please, Dad, this is the first time he's done anything like this. Something seems to be the matter with him today, he's acting so peculiar. Please give him a chance."

"No chance," Tom bellowed. "Try finding him a home today. Tomorrow he's out!"

Late that night, Trisha was startled out of her sleep by a loud thump and a flying body that hurtled into her bed. "Hey, what's going on?" she muttered as she looked in disbelief at her cat's arched body and raised fur. The cat always slept curled up on an afghan in the corner of her room. What was it doing in her bed? And it was acting so strangely, too, making angry, hissing sounds, circling wildly on her quilt. "Hey, get out of here!" she said sleepily, gently shoving the cat off her bed, pulling the covers up over her head. In a second, he was back, hissing louder than before. "What's the matter with you?" she shouted, pushing him off again, trying to get back to sleep. When he returned a third time, she threw up her hands, yelled, "OK, I give up" and climbed into her sister's bed on the other side of the room.

Just then, the floor began to vibrate and shake in an all-too-familiar manner. Books slipped from shelves, lamps crashed to the floor, objects tumbled, and furniture slid over the room. A huge chest of drawers, jarred from its usual position against the wall, toppled across the bed where only seconds before Trisha had been sleeping.

It was the Northridge, California earthquake of 1994, and the "plain old alley cat" had saved Trisha's life. Needless to say, the cat has since become a permanent member of the MacEnvoy household.

❦

Comment

Life is very mysterious and awesome, and you never know from where your salvation will come. Sometimes, it comes from the most unlikely of sources. Let us learn to regard all living things as divine and gifts from God . . . and treat them accordingly!

The tale has the elements of a classic mystery: a grieving widow; a misidentified body; a key, which, despite lottery-like odds, fits the wrong door; and a happy ending, as the husband and wife, having each learned the other is not dead, vow never to take each other for granted.

No, it is not a movie (not yet, anyway); it really happened to a Houston couple, Jose and Herlinda Estrada.

At about 5 P.M. on Feb. 11, Jose Estrada, 48, left his house, headed for a nearby jogging track. Telling his family he would be back shortly, he climbed into his 1988 burgundy Chevrolet truck and left.

About 50 minutes later, Herlinda Estrada's concentration on the National Basketball Association's All-Star Game was shattered by every wife's nightmare: a stony-faced constable was at the front door.

"I have a 27-year-old son," Mrs. Estrada said, "so the first thing I thought was, 'He had a wreck.' But then the constable said, 'What is your husband's name?' And then, 'Does he have a red truck?' "

"When I said 'yes,' he said, 'I'm sorry ma'am, he's had a heart attack.' "

Told that Jose's condition was grave, Mrs. Estrada, who like her husband is Catholic, called a priest to administer last rites. Then, Mrs. Estrada "drove like crazy" to nearby Memorial Hospital Southeast, where she was ushered into a small consultation room, and told that she was too late; Jose Estrada had died.

The constable—the same officer who had come to Mrs. Estrada's house—escorted the grieving wife to a small room, where she identified the body. Then she signed the death certificate and returned to the waiting room, where she asked the constable to make the first few calls to family and friends. He did so.

Within minutes, family and friends began gathering to comfort the Estradas. Thirty minutes later, in walked a relative no one expected: Jose Estrada himself.

"At first it didn't register," Mrs. Estrada recalled. "and then I started screaming, 'You're alive, you're alive! They told me you were dead.' And he said, 'I'm O.K.—I was worried about you.' "

Jose Estrada had just rushed to the hospital after someone told him that his wife had a heart attack.

How did this all come about? Elementary, Watson; while Jose Estrada was jogging, another runner had a coronary. Emergency medics and the constable were summoned, but could find no identification on the man. The only clue was a set of General Motors keys, which the constable tried in the doors of G.M. vehicles in the area.

Despite 26,000-to-1 odds, the keys opened the wrong G.M. vehicle—Mr. Estrada's. A license check led the constable to the Estradas' house.

And the misidentified body?

"You just have to put yourself in that state of mind," Mrs. Estrada said. "There was tape on his eyes and mouth, so I couldn't tell if he had a mustache. He had the same shoes, same radio, same shorts as my husband. He even had the same kind of belt. So I said, 'Let me see the hands and feet.'" He had the same feet.

"What's so funny is I asked Constable Hernandez, 'Does he look Mexican?' And the constable said, 'Yes.'"

Jose Estrada, meanwhile, had returned from his jog to find the house curiously deserted. Then, the phone rang; it was his wife's boss, who had received a call from the hospital. "She said, 'Jose, you're alive!'" Mrs. Estrada related. "And then, she said 'Oh, my God—don't tell me it was Herlinda.'"

Mr. Estrada raced to the hospital, walked up to none other than the constable and told him he was looking for Herlinda Estrada. The constable pointed toward a consultation room filled with wailing friends and family. Expecting the worst, Mr. Estrada walked in.

After the Estradas' reunion, the constable returned to the track, where he found Mary Sammons looking for her husband, John. The constable broke the bad news once more and escorted Mrs. Sammons to the hospital, where she identified her husband's body.

"Let me tell you, we've changed some things since it happened," Mrs. Estrada said. For one, she said, they do not take each other for granted. And there were practical changes.

"We always look at what the other is wearing. He's put a silly yellow thing on the end of his keychain, so I can tell his keys. And he always takes an I.D. when he jogs."

Comment

Many of us "sleep-walk" through life. Sometimes we need a "jolt" to wake us from our apathy, our slumber, our automaton-like existence. This includes taking the people we love and need in our lives for granted. When such a jolt does occur, as in the jolt of coincidence that the Estradas experienced, we begin to look at our lives—and each other—with fresh eyes.

*M*ax left from New York City and had been traveling for several hours in the rain. His windshield wipers worked tirelessly as he headed toward a business meeting in Philadelphia. Sometime around midnight, Max got hungry and stopped at a roadside diner.

Max seated himself at the counter, alongside an elderly man with drooping shoulders, wearing tattered clothing. Max was moved by the presence of this individual, who looked as though he had walked too many miles in his lifetime. "Pretty nasty weather out there, isn't it?" said Max, attempting to make some conversation. The response was a grumble under the breath. The old man seemed to be too despondent to engage in dialogue. Max finished his meal and just before he left, he turned to the waitress and asked, "How much for a baked apple?"

"Two-fifty," she responded.

"Here," said Max, pulling out three singles. "This should cover the price of the apple and your tip." Then, pointing to the elderly man, Max said, "Now, please give it to that man and just say, 'It's on the house.' "

The waitress gave Max a warm smile and said, "Sure, will do." And with that, Max turned and left the diner.

As he traveled, Max thought about the gesture he had just made. "Why a baked apple?" he questioned himself. "Why didn't I buy him a cup of coffee?" Max pondered this seemingly illogical overture and delved into the workings of his mind until he came to a conclusion. "A cup of coffee from a stranger to a stranger may be a sweet gesture," he reasoned, "briefly noticed, but quickly forgotten. Whereas a fresh-baked apple might jostle the old man out of his stupor, even if only momentarily, and maybe even allow his spirits to be lifted." Max was satisfied with his reasoning as he continued on the long and narrow highway.

The night wore on. The endless white line became a challenge as Max struggled to stay alert and awake. He spoke out loud to the darkness but it was to no avail. His body was giving way, and despite all his efforts, the lull of sleep called to him. He was on Interstate 295 going south, when a huge Mac truck hit him on the side, pushing him off the edge of the road. Perhaps in the light of day, with different weather conditions, Max might have been able to handle the car and maintain his position on the highway. But now, Max's car skidded and slid into a ditch. At first Max was shocked. Within a few moments, he was unconscious.

In the dark of night, with torrents of rain pouring down, cars just zoomed by. No one seemed to notice the accident on the side of the road. Finally, after some time, a young man driving by spotted Max's car. He stopped and made his way towards the wreckage. The young man sized up the situation. He figured that with the weather being so bad, even if he managed to call 911, it would take a great deal of time for someone to arrive. Since he lived so close by, he decided to take Max, still unconscious, to his own home. There he would call for help.

Shortly after arriving in the stranger's home, Max regained consciousness. He opened his eyes to an unfamiliar face.

"My God," the stranger said, "that was some fall you and your car took! It was sure hard getting you out of that wreck and into this house, but I tell you, buddy, you were mighty close to death there! Now sit up and eat something my wife made for you." Max looked at the plate set down in front of him. Sitting on a glass dish was a fresh-baked apple.

Comment
Passing on a kind gesture, enabling another's spirits to be lifted—these are goodly deeds. The word God is contained in the word good. When good is done, God is present and when God is present, miracles occur.

The eminent psychiatrist Carl Jung had a lifelong interest in coincidences—an interest that was stimulated in part by his experiences during his therapeutic work with patients. In one such example, he was treating a fifty-year-old man whose wife had told him that following the deaths of both her mother and grandmother, a flock of birds had suddenly appeared outside the windows of the death chamber.

Jung's treatment of the man's neurosis was successful, and he was about to terminate the therapy when the patient suddenly began complaining about physical symptoms. Although the patient didn't appear to be in any imminent danger, some intuition led Jung to believe that the man was suffering from heart disease, and he immediately sent him to a specialist for a thorough checkup. After an extensive examination, the physician declared the man to be in good health, and wrote a note to Jung advising him of his diagnosis. On his way home from seeing the specialist, the man collapsed in the street.

As he was brought home dying, his wife was already in a high state of anxiety, because shortly after her husband had gone to the doctor, a huge flock of birds had alighted on their house. Remembering that, in the past, their sudden arrival had heralded the deaths of both her mother and grandmother, she naturally feared the worst—a fear that was justified and confirmed.

In a second instance of coincidence involving a patient, Jung was treating an extremely "resistant" woman, with whom he was unable to achieve any meaningful breakthrough. The difficulty lay in the fact that the patient—the beneficiary of an excellent education and a woman totally dominated by an implacably rationalistic spirit—thought she knew more than everyone else. Jung hoped fervently for an irrational and unexpected episode to occur that would pierce her intellectual armor. One day, the woman was in middle of reciting an odd dream to him—a dream in which she was given a costly piece of jewelry, a golden scarab (beetle)—when he heard a gentle tapping at the window. Turning around, Jung saw a strange-looking insect knocking against the windowpane from the outside. He opened the window and caught the creature as it flew in. It was a scarabeid beetle—an insect whose gold-green color makes it closely resemble that of a golden scarab. Jung handed the beetle to the patient with these words: "Here is your scarab." Years later, when he presented the case to other therapists, he noted that this startling coincidence had achieved what he himself had been unable to accomplish: it had broken down the patient's intellectual resistance and resulted in successful therapy. "But nothing quite like this has ever happened to me before or since," he declared.

So many other startling stories of coincidence were brought to Jung's attention during his lifetime that he dedicated enormous time and energy to studying this phenomenon, and coined a term to describe it. It was "synchronicity," a word common in our parlance today, which is defined as "meaningful coincidence of two or more events where something other than the probability of chance is involved."

ill and Jules ran an adult education school called the Learning Annex. While business was good, these two entrepreneurs wanted to expand, which meant getting lots more people to sign up for courses. But how could they make sure that everyone in New York City heard about their school? Breaking through all boundaries of thought and logic, they came up with a scheme that the city had never seen before. They planned on taking ten thousand one-dollar bills and affixing a sticker to each bill with information about the Learning Annex. The media alerted the public that on March 13, 1982, ten thousand one-dollar bills would be thrown off the Empire State Building, and whoever was standing at Fifth Avenue and Thirty-fourth Street at that time would be able to keep as much money as they could catch. This would make for sensational publicity.

The New York media loved the idea, and reported it with lots of fanfare. Unfortunately, the police were not as enthusiastic. They were given strict orders to stop the event from happening, believing that thousands of people expecting to catch dollar bills would wreak havoc with traffic and create nightmarish circumstances.

Despite the official disapproval, Jules and Bill left their uptown office on the appointed date with two bags, loaded with ten thousand one-dollar bills. As they cruised down Fifth Avenue, making their way towards Thirty-fourth Street, they were followed by a bevy of reporters eager to capture each moment as it unfolded.

As they approached Thirty-fourth Street, they heard sirens. The reporters following the lead car had police band radios and were monitoring police activity in the area. The reporters started shouting, "Hey! Those sirens are for you guys!" Bill and Jules gulped and stared at the enormous crowd that had turned out for the event.

Then the unexpected occurred. Just as Bill and Jules were getting out of their car, two other men walked into a bank inside the Empire State Building, fired a shot in the air, and screamed, "This is a stickup!" They grabbed all the money they were handed, stuffed it into two bags, and ran out of the building and right into the street—which was teeming with police officers, reporters, and cameramen. Instead of the quiet getaway they had planned, this became one of the most publicized bank heists of all time.

What we now have are two groups of men, both carrying bags of money, one group running to take money away, and the other running to give it away. Both were on the same street corner at the very same moment.

Nobody could figure out what was going on. The cameramen didn't want to film the wrong people, the police didn't want to make a false arrest. The rest of the crowd was eagerly looking to see which pair was about to throw them money.

Finally, the bank robbers were apprehended. Meanwhile, Bill and Jules attempted to make their way into the building, but crowds of people closed in on them, trying to grab their bags. The same policemen who caught the criminals now had to extricate these two men from a crowd that wanted its fair share of the money. Amid the pandemonium, and much to the chagrin of thousands of onlookers, Bill and Jules were quickly hustled away by the police.

One lady who was trying to figure out what all the mayhem was about walked over to a police officer and asked, "What exactly is going on?" to which the officer answered, "Lady, if I told ya, ya wouldn't believe me."

❧

Comment

God gives and God takes. The money comes and the money goes. It's all a circle. At times you want to take it and it's given to you, at other times you want to give it and you can't because it's been taken. We think we are our money and that our bank accounts state our worth. Money though, is like honey. It can drip into your life, and is sweet to behold. But its pleasure can be fleeting, leaving a taste for more. Money, now it's here, now it's gone. When you have some, pass some on.

In the winter of 1979, I began work with a Bowen coach (a family therapist) to change my position in a key triangle in my family. As a seasoned therapist myself, I understood that such a task was not to be taken lightly. Indeed, I fully anticipated encountering my own resistance to change, as well as my family's "change back!" maneuvers. Despite my intellectual sophistication, I was naive and ill-prepared for my venture. No one had warned me about cosmic countermoves.

What is a cosmic countermove? It is, in my opinion, nothing short of a "change back!" reaction from the cosmos itself. It is something different from, and greater than, the usual forms of resistance described in the literature on the family. A cosmic countermove issues from the gods themselves when we dare to disturb our universe or invite our clients to do the same. The case in point: my own family.

When I began working with my coach, my long-term goal was to establish an emotionally close relationship with both my mother and my father. Before this time, my relationship with my mother had been at my father's expense in that he had occupied an extreme, outside position in the family. In fact, fathers had occupied an outside position in my family for several generations, while mothers and daughters were bound together by unswerving loyalty. I simply did not contemplate having anything other than a distant relationship with my father.

Never did I so fully appreciate the power of resistance as when I proceeded to behave differently in this entrenched triangle. I vividly recall my starting point—a memorable visit from my parents in 1979, shortly after the birth of my second son. My mother was washing dishes in the kitchen, busily elaborating on my father's most recent manifestations of immaturity and insensitivity. My father was entertaining my husband, Steve, in the living room, undoubtedly making conspicuous displays of these same qualities. In the past, I would have joined forces with my mom. This time was different.

I still recall the terror in my bones as I told my mother that I didn't want to talk about Dad anymore. I went on to explain, with genuine warmth, that the older I became, the more I realized that I needed to have a relationship with *both* my parents—and that both of them were very important to me. When I was finished, my mother's anxiety was sky-high.

"You cannot know me," she said with uncharacteristic coldness, "if you are unwilling to hear the truth about your father!"

I put my arm around her and said, "Mom, I want to get to know *you* from my relationship with *you*—and I want to get to know *Dad* from my relationship with *Dad*." And so it went.

I had rehearsed the conversation in my head many times. Nonetheless, it felt like nothing short of treason.

"I'm going to give her cancer," I announced to my husband that evening.

My mother was not struck dead by my words, although she did have a predictably dramatic reaction, as she proceeded to test out whether I could be induced to reinstate the old pattern. The next morning, however, she appeared at the breakfast table looking cheerful and relaxed, having obviously enjoyed a good night's sleep. I, however, had not slept well at all, and when morning came, I discovered large red splotches on my arms. This new and colorful symptom was my first lesson in humility. My parents' resistance to change proved to be considerable—but less considerable, I confess, than my own.

So what's new? Any student of Family Systems Theory 101 knows that we can all be counted on to resist the very changes that we seek. I ask the reader to bear with me. This small slice of life is merely the historical backdrop against which I will illustrate a potent source of systemic resistance heretofore ignored in the family literature—the *cosmic countermove*.

Recently, I visited my parents in Phoenix, following news that my father—who prides himself on reaching the age of seventy-five without even a sniffle—had suffered a mild heart attack. This unexpected and unwelcome reminder of my father's mortality heightened my awareness that my parents were old and would not be around forever. During the visit, I felt especially loving towards them *both* and I was inspired to engage in a bold and courageous act.

Actually, bold and courageous acts were the name of the game since that first conversation with my mother in 1979. Of course, change occurs slowly, and rightfully so. But, as we will see, too bold a change may incur a *countermove* from the cosmos itself!

What, then, was my bold and courageous act? It was this: I asked my father if he would make me a gift of an old, prized Chinese bond. I told him that I would frame it and give it a place of honor in my home. This request may not sound particularly daring, or even noteworthy, to the reader. Nonetheless, the request and granting of this particular gift was a bold challenge to my family's long legacy of emotional distance between fathers and daughters.

My father carefully rolled the bond into a cardboard tube, so that I could hand-carry it safely on the airplane back to Topeka. His anxiety about this exchange was revealed only by the number of times he reminded me to keep it clean and frame it quickly, so that no harm would befall it.

As I boarded the airplane his final words were spoken with affection. "Now don't get chicken *schmaltz* (fat) on that bond, Harriet!" I had to smile at this reminder of my growing-up years in Brooklyn, and my father's chronic irritation at my habit of snacking while doing my homework, which sometimes led to chicken *schmaltz* finding its way onto my schoolwork.

I arrived home both pleased and anxious about this forbidden act of father–daughter intimacy. Where could I keep the bond until my schedule would permit a visit to the frame shop? I carefully removed it from the narrow cardboard tube and laid it flat on the carpeted floor of a remote attic room on the third floor of my large, old home. Our entire third floor is reserved for guests and this room is forbidden territory for the rest of the family. It is my private space and it has long been my custom to sort out my manuscripts and documents on the floor there.

Three weeks later, after receiving an inquiry from my father about the bond, I proceeded to retrieve it to bring to the framers. As I lifted the bond from its place, I could not register nor make sense of what my eyes saw. *The face of the bond was crinkled and stained.* But this was not possible! I examined the papers on the floor surrounding it and they were in perfect condition. I looked up at the ceiling directly above, half expecting to see a leak, but no leak was to be found. I stood staring at the bond in stunned disbelief and recalled my father's final words to me at the airport. Had the heavens dripped chicken *schmaltz* on his bond?

I rushed downstairs, bond in hand, where a friend was drinking tea in the dining room. She is almost thirty years my senior and wise in the ways of the world.

"What is this?" I demanded of her, as I thrust the stained bond under her nose.

My friend looked and sniffed—and then made her diagnostic pronouncement. "It's cat urine," she said blandly.

And so it was. My sons had left the front door open and one of the neighborhood cats that graced our front porch had made its way up two flights of stairs to find my father's bond and pee on it. How can we understand such an action! Did the cat not have 4,500 square feet of floor on which to pee, to say nothing of the countless papers that were spread about the floor of our attic rooms? How can we fathom such a choice? And how could I explain it to my father?

It was in contemplation of this event that I concluded that the concept of *cosmic countermove* should be added to the family systems literature. And yes, I believe there is a moral to my story: Dare *you* disturb the universe? Remember that multigenerational work is only for the boldest among us. Do not begin the journey, unless you are prepared to answer to the gods themselves!

As for my father, he took the news with surprising good humor. Perhaps—although I may be wrong—I detected a tad of relief in his voice.

Be it chicken *schmaltz* or cat pee . . . it is reassuring to know that some things never change!

— *Dr. Harriet Lerner*

Dr. Harriet Lerner is one of the foremost international authorities on women's psychology. She is the author of *The Dance of Deception*, *The Dance of Intimacy*, and *The Dance of Anger*. She is also a staff psychologist at the Menninger Clinic in Topeka, Kansas.

Tony Angelo* and his best friend George Petro* grew up in the Bensonhurst section of Brooklyn. The two dreamed about their future. "When I'm older, I'm going to join the navy," declared Tony, leaning against the banister in front of his house.

"And I'm going to join the army," said George.

It all seemed like wishful thinking at the time. But the years flew by and their boyhood dreams did become a reality.

Just before Tony entered the navy, George gave him a lavish farewell party and invited all their friends from the neighborhood. Everyone drank and danced for hours. As the party neared its end, George put his arm around Tony and said, "Buddy, I'm gonna miss ya." "Me too," said Tony. George was scheduled to leave for his army post within a few weeks. They recounted some of their better childhood memories, wished each other well, and said their goodbyes.

A few years passed. Tony's ship was docked in San Francisco. Like many of the other sailors, Tony wanted to take in the sights, but first he needed to tend to his wash. He found a nearby laundromat, but was disappointed to see that all its machines were in use. Wanting to explore the area in the small amount of time he had available, Tony wandered further into town. He found a laundromat in a cul-de-sac off a main thoroughfare.

Tony unloaded his clothing into the washing machine and then noticed that he didn't have the correct change. "Hey, buddy," he said, turning to the first person on his right, "got change of a dollar?" The stranger found the change, looked at Tony and said, "Here, that should do it." Tony thanked the stranger, and the two made eye contact. "GEORGE! IS THAT YOU?" shouted Tony. "TONY! IS THAT YOU?" came a resounding reply. They laughed and embraced each other warmly, in this place they had both found, far away from home.

Comment

The bonds we make in our youth are everlasting. They are patterned into the fabric of our lives. Time shifts, looks change, and much is left behind as we move along. But there are bits and pieces of our past that follow us through in life. Just like the woven threads of a tapestry that are integral to its design, friends from our childhood will continue to appear and reappear in our hearts and in our lives, because the bonds of youth remain.

Small Miracles

While attending Princeton University, Cathy shared a dorm room with three roommates. Each one had her fair share of male admirers. In order to maintain some semblance of privacy, the girls would occasionally make arrangements to meet their respective dates at some anonymous location.

One summer's evening, Cathy set out on a blind date. She didn't have much faith that it would turn out well, but having agreed to the date, she wanted to keep her word. Cathy walked to the corner of Nassau Street and Washington Road. Her date was expected to be there at 8:00 P.M. Cathy had been told to look for a blue car whose driver would be wearing a fraternity sweater.

Everything seemed to go as planned. At a couple of minutes past eight, a blue car driven by a young man in a fraternity sweater pulled up alongside the curb. "Sorry I'm a little late—I got caught in traffic," he said apologetically.

"That's all right," Cathy said, pleasantly surprised that her date was good-looking.

Sometime after the movie and before dinner, the young man turned to his date and said, "By the way, how do you know Bob?"

"Bob? Who's Bob?" said Cathy.

"What do you mean, who's Bob? Bob is the one who set us up!" the young man said, raising a bushy eyebrow that accentuated his questioning glance.

"What are you talking about?" Cathy sputtered. "Jim set us up."

"Jim!" the young man answered. "Who's Jim?" A few more whos and whats and what-are-you-talking-abouts, and the puzzle was solved. They realized that another couple must have made arrangements to meet at the same time and at the same place. Which meant that they were each out with the "wrong" date.

Without skipping a beat, the young man turned to Cathy and said, "Look, I'm having a good time—want to continue?"

"Sure," she said, glad that he asked.

It's now ten years later, and they are happily married with three beautiful children.

$\mathcal{I}$*n* 1969, amidst the turbulence of the Vietnam War, a young Thai woman and a 20-year-old air force sergeant fell in love, lived together and gave birth to a baby boy. They named their son, Nueng.

At the end of the war, John Garcia, the father, and Pratorn Varanoot, the mother, faced each other, uncertain about the future. Transferring back to the States together seemed remote since the air force discouraged John from marrying a native, and Pratorn's family discouraged her from moving away. John moved back to America, leaving behind his ex-lover and his baby boy. He tried to maintain contact with them, but as time wore on, it became increasingly difficult to do so. Pratorn had married another U.S. soldier who repeatedly returned John's letters, unanswered. John wrote the Thai government in an attempt to locate them and retain some contact with his son. He never received a reply. The ties that bound this father and son were ultimately severed.

In 1996, a man drives down a highway in Pueblo, Colorado in his restored 1970 Nova. He happens to peer at the gas gauge that indicates the tank is half full. For some unexplainable reason, he decides to stop at a Total service station, a place he does not usually patronize. When it comes time to pay, once again he does something that he ordinarily wouldn't do: Despite having 30 dollars cash in his wallet, he pays by check. The young man behind the service counter looks down and notes the name on the check. With raised eyebrows he looks up at the man standing in front of him and asks, "Are you John Garcia?"

"Yes," comes the reply.

"Have you ever been in the air force?" inquires the young man.

"Yes," replies John, not thinking too much of the question.

"Have you ever lived in Thailand?" he continues.

"Yes," John says, as he steps back, wondering what this is all about.

"Do you have a son there?"

With great puzzlement, once again a resounding "Yes."

Now with halting breath and a racing heart, the cashier poses one more question, "What was his name?"

"Nueng," comes the reply.

Amidst the sea of anonymous commuters on highway 50, the young man then looks into the eyes of the stranger standing before him and simply states, "I am your son."

Comment

People can leave each other, cross continents, sever ties. But if there are lessons to be learned from one another, if they are meant to be together, then time and distance dissolve and they are reunited once again.

$\mathcal{I}n$ 1991, Debra Robinson* was dating Ed Wilson. They had been seeing each other for over three years. Although he had "popped the question" several times, she had avoided giving him an answer. Fearful, conflicted, and anxious about "tying the knot," she kept stalling. As a result, she was tormented and miserable.

One night, Chuck Anton, an old friend of her deceased father, Wayne Robinson, had a dream. In the dream, Wayne Robinson said, "Chuck, do me a favor. My daughter Debra is going out with someone, and this person is her destined one. Please find her and tell her that she should marry him, and that she's going to have a wonderful life! This match has my blessing and, for once, she should listen to her father!"

Chuck Anton woke up with a muffled scream. He hadn't seen Debra Robinson since her father had died ten years before. Shaken, he roused his wife and recounted the dream. She told him it was ridiculous and advised him to go back to sleep. He followed her counsel and soon forgot the entire episode.

A week later, Wayne Robinson reappeared in a new dream. "Chuck!" he expostulated, wagging an accusing finger. "You didn't do what I requested! How many times do I have to ask you to tell my daughter to marry the young man she's seeing!" Once again, Chuck awoke with a start, but this time he resolved to consult his priest.

"Look," said the priest after Chuck poured out his heart. "Find the girl, and ask her if she's currently seeing anyone seriously. If she isn't, say nothing. If she is, you have a responsibility to deliver her father's message."

The following Sunday, Debra Robinson lay on her bed, weeping. The night before, her younger sister Susie had gotten engaged. Although she was happy for her sister, the engagement had undeniably served to accentuate her own sense of aloneness and her anxiety about her relationship with Ed. Debra was in agony, and cried out, "Please God, help me figure out what to do! I beg you . . . send me a sign!" At that precise moment, the telephone rang.

"Debra?" an old, familiar voice inquired. "This is Chuck Anton . . ."

Three months later, Debra and Ed were married, and they have been living a fairy-tale life ever since!

Comment

Many of life's decisions are painfully difficult to make, for none of us know what lies ahead. The jolt of coincidence can nudge us in the right direction. In this story, what was so comforting to Debra was not merely the wonderful message from her father, but that it arrived just when she needed it—and was most receptive to it. What impeccable timing! At the precise moment when Debra was feeling particularly lost, she received a loving, nurturing, supportive communiqué from her father that told her, "I'm with you! You are not alone!"

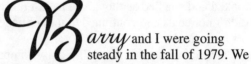

arry and I were going
steady in the fall of 1979. We
were on our way to a restaurant one day when Barry decided to change
course. He asked me if I would accompany him while he went to look at
an old tenement house that was for sale. "I may be able to buy the building at a very good price," he said, "but first I need to check it out. Is it
okay if we stop by for a quick look?" Though I was hungry, I agreed to
go along. Experience had taught me that following Barry's lead usually
led me down an interesting path.

After a short drive to the seedy part of town, we found ourselves in
front of a dilapidated building. The windows were sealed off with odd
pieces of iron and wood. The brick walls were covered with layers of
spray paint.

"Are you sure we're in the right place?" I asked.

Barry checked the address again. "Yes, this is the building," he affirmed. Then, looking at me with an adventurous twinkle in his eye, he
said, "Let's go inside."

"Are you serious?" I exclaimed, afraid to follow his dare. But my interest quickly got the better of my doubts and we ventured into the
building.

As soon as we pried the front door open, we were immediately struck
by an awful stench that permeated the hallway. "My God," I said, "are
you sure we should go inside?"

"Let's go for it," Barry said. The hallway led to a narrow staircase.
Together we climbed a flight of rickety steps. When we arrived at the
first landing, we stood and gaped at the rat-infested debris. "How long
do you think it's been since people have lived here?" I asked Barry.

Barry shook his head. "No idea," he said.

Thinking that the rest of the building must be very much like the first
floor, we decided to leave and began to descend the decrepit steps. But
we were stopped short when we heard what sounded like a muffled
voice emanating from above. "What was that?" we asked each other in
astonishment. "How could anyone be living here?" I wondered. Our curiosity aroused, we swallowed our fears and turned around to go check
out the situation.

As we approached the next floor, the voice became more audible.
"Uh, lets see," we heard a man muttering, "gotta get some milk and go
to the post office, well maybe I should go first to the post office and
then . . ." As we got closer, the stench became stronger. We proceeded

despite our revulsion until finally we were face to face with a man who looked and smelled as though he hadn't taken a shower in years. He didn't notice us and continued to mutter under his breath as he prepared for his errand.

"Hello, my name is Barry," said my companion, trying to establish contact. But the man continued to talk to himself, oblivious to our presence.

Barry and I were incredulous that he had been able to survive in these squalid conditions. We were even more surprised, though, when we heard a voice from one of the back rooms calling out the name "Fred." "Who's that?" we asked. He turned to walk away, and we asked if we could follow. He nodded.

Fear dissolved into concern and compassion as Barry and I passed the mounds of dust and heaps of garbage that led to the back recesses of the apartment. There we saw a woman lying in bed, under layers of covers. All that showed were her dark eyes. Just when we thought we had seen it all, the woman spoke up and said, "Poppa?" There, on the adjacent bed, under torn towels and army blankets, lay an ancient-looking man.

Barry and I tried to make sense of all this, but our rational minds could not comprehend what our eyes beheld. Our hearts weighed heavy as we gazed upon a state of humanity neither of us had known existed.

I leaned over to one bed and asked the woman her name.

"Dorothy," she responded, in a faint voice.

Barry and I explained to her why we were there and inquired about their situation. We learned that the elderly man was the father. Dorothy and the younger man, Fred, were sister and brother.

"What about your mother?" we inquired.

"She passed away a few years ago" was Dorothy's response.

"We would like to help you," Barry said. "Is that all right with you?" Dorothy nodded but wouldn't say much more.

We tried to find out how they had been able to sustain themselves and persevere in these conditions. It proved to be very difficult to obtain answers. The father appeared to be too weak to converse. Dorothy seemed lost in her thoughts. As for Fred, he was unable to engage in the simplest conversation.

Barry and I were utterly moved by this encounter and we vowed to help the family in any way we could. Over the next few months, Barry used all his contacts to help them. As a result of his efforts, the father was placed in a nursing home. The daughter, Dorothy, received treatment from an outpatient mental health facility, where she was placed on antidepressant medication. This enabled her to hold down a job that Barry was instrumental in obtaining for her. Both Dorothy and Fred were relocated to an apartment that was subsidized by the city. And Fred was placed under the care of a social service agency.

Standing in those squalid conditions on that autumn day, I promised myself that I would help those people in any way that I could. However, seeing that Barry was doing so much for them, I figured that there wasn't much more that I could contribute.

Twelve years later, their haunting image came to mind. I wondered about what had become of them and I pondered the many changes that had taken place since that time. As I sat in my office, I thought about Barry and recalled that he did indeed buy the building. For him, the deal worked out well. Our relationship though, did not. We were both fortunate to go on and find our respective mates and I had since become a psychiatric social worker. Memories came flashing back but were then interrupted when the door opened and the next patient walked in. And there he stood. The man I had vowed to help twelve years ago stepped right into my life.

I was one of thousands of social workers in the great metropolis. Fred counted as just one among the thousands of poor souls. "Will you help me?" he asked. He hadn't recognized me.

"Yes, Fred," I said, "I absolutely will." I became Fred's social worker and was able to fulfill the vow I had made long ago.

— *Judith Frankel Leventhal*

❧

Comment

When you have a strong desire to perform an act of kindness, the universe assists in mysterious ways.

$\mathcal{A}$ $\mathcal{Q}ueens$, New York woman leaned out of her eighth-floor tenement window and screamed for help. She was trapped in her bathroom. The inside knob had fallen off when her youngest child, age two, had closed the door from the other side. Two of her other children, ages four and five, were in the kitchen, alone, as supper cooked on the stove. The woman alternated between trying to break down the door herself and shouting to be heard. Both courses seemed futile and she was beginning to give up hope.

Meanwhile, a young man who lived twenty miles away happened to be visiting the neighborhood that day. From the street below, he heard the woman's pleas. He waved his hand to catch her attention and then screamed out, "I'm coming up to help you!" A short time later, she heard his voice from outside the bathroom door. "Listen closely," the young man instructed. "Put your fingers in the hole where the knob should be, pull it up, lift the door slightly, and then quickly pull it open." The woman followed the stranger's instructions, and within moments the door was open.

Once freed from her temporary prison, she ran to check on the children. In response to their mother's screams, they had become upset and needed some coddling to soothe their cries. When all three children were safe within her view, the woman turned to the young man and asked in amazement, "How could you possibly have known how to get into my apartment, and how did you know how that door opens?"

"I know very well," he answered with a smile crossing his face. "I was born here. I lived in this apartment for fifteen years. I know how to get in the front door without a key. And the bathroom knob? It would always fall off, and we learned to open the door just the way I showed you!"

Comment

Sometimes we need to walk back over routes we've already traveled in order to help someone cross a path we've crossed before.

In his book *Journey to my Father*, Israel Zamir recounts how his father, Nobel laureate Isaac Bashevis Singer, frequently incorporated real-life material into his "fictional" works. Dramatic episodes and mysterious encounters that happened to friends, relatives, and neighbors eventually all worked their way into one of his mystical tales. Singer was often considered the master of the magical and the supernatural. Ironically, many of his most eerie stories were actually drawn from true life.

Zamir was in his father's house when the phone rang one day. The caller was an acquaintance of Singer's to whom a strange coincidence had just occurred. As the woman poured out her tale, Singer interrupted her remarks with repeated exclamations—"Really?" "Indeed?" "You're sure?"—shaking his head in amazement.

The woman caller, who lived on Long Island, had been out shopping and sometime during the day had lost the key to her apartment. It was her only key, she lived alone, and no one had a duplicate. Desperate, she wandered the streets for hours, hunting for the lost key. Retracing her steps, she returned to all the shops she had patronized that day and conducted thorough searches of the premises. Her tenacity, however, was not rewarded with success. As evening drew near, she decided to abandon her inquiries and travel to her sister's home in Brooklyn, where she would stay the night. She went to the local station of the Long Island Railroad to catch the next train. As she stood in line to buy a ticket, something on the floor next to the ticket booth—a shiny metal object—glinted and caught her attention. She bent down and picked up her key!

She had been nowhere near the train station that day, she told Singer, excitedly demanding an explanation from the man who filled his books with demons, sorcerers, and ghosts. His answer was that an "entity" had "made sure" that she would find what she was looking for, in order to protect her from having to travel to the wilds of Brooklyn at night! Finding the explanation perfectly acceptable, the woman thanked him and hung up.

The tale was avidly digested by Singer and became the basis for his story "The Key."

oincidences don't happen only to adults. They can happen to children, too. Just recently, my nine-year-old son reported the following story to me, in a tone filled with awe at the marvels and mysteries of the universe. "Last Thursday in school," he said, "I ate my snack during morning recess and it was salty, so I got very thirsty. We have a soda machine in the hallway and I wanted to buy a soda. But I was worried that recess might be over, so I asked a kid what time it was. 'It's 11:05 exactly,' he told me. I had five minutes to spare, so I ran down the hall to the machine. I have a habit of looking at each quarter before I put it into the machine, because I'm always hoping that somehow I'll get an old one that's worth a lot of money. So, as usual, I looked at each quarter before I inserted it. My teacher is very strict and gets very angry when we come into class late. I was so afraid that I was going to miss the recess bell that I made a mistake and put in an extra quarter. I put in four quarters instead of three. When I looked at the last quarter, I saw that the date written on it was 1980. I also saw a nick that I had made on that quarter during class, when I played with it and scratched a nickel across its surface. As soon as I put in the fourth quarter, I realized my mistake. I pressed the coin return and banged on the machine, but the only thing that came out was the Sprite. I noticed the principal walking by and asked him if I could get my lost quarter back.

" 'Yeah, yeah, sure, sure,' he said absentmindedly. I could tell he didn't think my lost quarter was important. I ran back to class and later that day I went over to the principal again and asked for my quarter back a second time. 'Soon, soon,' he said. He seemed impatient. All week long, I asked him for my quarter and all week long, he repeated 'soon, soon.' But he never gave it back to me.

"Exactly one week later, also on a Thursday," my son told me, excitement rising in his voice, "during the first morning recess, I again wanted to buy a Sprite from the soda machine. Again, I was nervous about being late, so I asked a kid for the time. 'It's 11:05,' he said, 'exactly.' This time, I was very careful to be sure to put in only three quarters. I put in the three quarters and out came a Sprite. I was about to race down the hall to my class when I heard something drop into the coin return slot. I put in my fingers and pulled out a quarter. That's strange, I thought. So I looked at the quarter closely. It was dated 1980 . . . and it had a nick on it. It was *my* quarter . . . the exact same quarter I had lost the week before in the machine . . . at the exact same time . . . on the exact same day of the week. Can you imagine that!"

"So what do you think all of this means?" I asked my son, curious to hear his interpretation.

"Hey, mom," he said with a wide grin, "this lesson's easy to figure out!"

"Really," I said, bemused, "and what exactly is the lesson here?"

"When it's coming to you . . . it's coming to you!" he yelled exuberantly, triumph glinting in his eyes.

— *Yitta Halberstam Mandelbaum*

Comment

What a blessing for my son that, through the coincidence, he fortuitously learned that justice *is* indeed served in this world. Obviously losing a quarter is not a major tragedy, but still he might have come away from the experience a bit soured on the universe's sense of fair play. Perhaps, on a small scale, this experience might have given rise to a child's speculation that God cheats little kids. But given the startling symmetry between the two events, he came away with the perception that just the opposite holds true.

*O*n a cold day in 1942, inside a Nazi concentration camp, a lone young boy looks beyond the barbed wire and sees a young girl pass by. She too, is moved by his presence. In an effort to give expression to her feelings, she throws a red apple over the fence—a sign of life, hope, and love. The young boy bends over, picks up the apple. A ray of light has pierced his darkness.

The following day, thinking he is crazy for even entertaining the notion of seeing this young girl again, he looks out beyond the fence, hoping. On the other side of the barbed wire, the young girl yearns to see again this tragic figure who moves her so. She comes prepared with apple in hand. Despite another day of wintry blizzards and chilling air, two hearts are warmed once again as the apple passes over the barbed wire. The scene is repeated for several days. The two young spirits on opposite sides of the fence look forward to seeing each other, if only for a moment and if only to exchange a few words. The interaction is always accompanied by an exchange of inexplicably heartening feelings.

At the last of these momentary meetings, the young boy greets his sweet friend with a frown and says, "Tomorrow, don't bring me an apple, I will not be here. They are sending me to another camp." The young boy walks away, too heartbroken to look back.

From that day forward, the calming image of the sweet girl would appear to him in moments of anguish. Her eyes, her words, her thoughtfulness, her red apple, all were a recurring vision that would break his nighttime sweats. His family died in the war. The life he had known had all but vanished, but this one memory remained alive and gave him hope.

In 1957 in the United States, two adults, both immigrants, are set up on a blind date. "And where were you during the war?" inquires the woman.

"I was in a concentration camp in Germany," the man replies.

"I remember I used to throw apples over the fence to a boy who was in a concentration camp," she recalls.

With a feeling of shock, the man speaks. "And did that boy say to you one day, 'Don't bring an apple anymore because I am being sent to another camp'?" "Why, yes," she responds, "but how could you possibly know that?"

He looks into her eyes and says, "I was that young boy."

There is a brief silence, and then he continues, "I was separated from you then, and I don't ever want to be without you again. Will you marry me?" They embrace one another as she says, "Yes."

On Valentine's Day 1996, on a national telecast of the *Oprah Winfrey* show, this same man affirmed his enduring love to his wife of forty years. "You fed me in the concentration camp," he said, "you fed me throughout all these years; now, I remain hungry if only for your love."

Comment

The darkest moments of one's life may carry the seeds of the brightest tomorrow.

In 1939, Japanese diplomat Chiune Sugihara, who was stationed in Lithuania during one of the darkest times in human history, saved thousands of Polish Jews from the Nazis by issuing transit visas to them. Defying his own government, he wrote visas day and night, even scribbling them by hand and passing them through a train window as he departed Lithuania.

His bold and extraordinary act of heroism was largely unknown and unsung in the immediate aftermath of the war. For many years he occupied an obscure footnote in history—until survivors who had been rescued by Sugihara began to emerge from the silence of their post-Holocaust shock and started telling his story. Soon, his courage and greatness were being celebrated all over the world, catching the attention of the mass media and inspiring several authors to write books describing the actions of the "Japanese Schindler."

Meanwhile, the Israeli government was gathering names of "courageous rescuers," whose efforts it wished to repay. One of the ways the Jewish state attempted to acknowledge its debt was by giving rescuers and their families sanctuary and lifelong pensions. Another, more symbolic way, was by planting trees in their honor. When Sugihara's valor came to light, Israeli officials immediately made plans to plant a cherry grove, as was customary, in his memory. But suddenly, in an uncommon move, officials rescinded the order. They decided that, in keeping with the breathtaking scope of Sugihara's actions, cherry trees were an inappropriate symbol. They opted instead for a grove of cedar trees, deciding that cedar was sturdier and had holier connotations, having been used in the First Temple.

It was only after they had planted the trees that the astonished officials learned for the first time that "Sugihara" in Japanese means . . . cedar grove.

Comment

Does a name confer a certain destiny? Is our fate formed by the name we are given at birth? While many people scoff at this concept, there are others who are quite careful, indeed even fanatical, about the names they select for their offspring, believing that sufficient evidence exists to strongly suggest just such a link.

In 1995, Susie Henderson* was forty-five, had never been married, and was stuck in a dead-end job. Dispirited as well by the failure of traditional psychotherapy to create meaningful change in her personal life, she decided to terminate her longstanding relationship with her psychologist and explore other, more unconventional avenues of help. She enrolled in a "personal growth" weekend series, took up meditation, prayed, studied at New Age retreat centers, even consulted with a psychic or two.

None of these brought the metamorphosis she hoped for, until she was directed by a friend to a "spiritual counselor" who incorporated "spiritual principles" into the psychotherapeutic process. Now, Susie finally began to experience the personal transformation she was seeking. She encountered fewer difficulties with men, formed more stable relationships with them, and was finally able to break free of the shackles that were binding her to a stifling job.

One of the techniques that Susie's spiritual counselor successfully taught her was to ask the universe for whatever it was she *truly* wanted. In session, Susie had often complained that God had failed to meet her needs. Her therapist had stopped her short: "Well, did you ever really *ask?*"

"What do you mean, ask?"

"The universe is abundant and plentiful," the therapist had replied. "You simply have to ask God for what you want. But there is a technique to it." The therapist taught Susie the art of affirmation-making and stressed that one had to be extremely specific when articulating one's request. One had to tell God exactly what one wanted, and precisely when, how much, and for what purpose. Initially skeptical, Susie discovered to her own surprise that most of the time, asking God for what she wanted . . . worked.

One day, in her new job as residence manager of a home for the developmentally disabled, Susie was conducting a "goal-setting session" with the counselors on her staff. They were enormously overtaxed by the tremendous stresses of working with the profoundly dysfunctional and, using the session as a vehicle with which to let off steam, were complaining vigorously. Susie went around the room and, replicating the stratagems her own therapist had taught her, coached the counselors on how to achieve their goals. Although they ridiculed the exercise, Susie asked them to suspend their disbelief.

"Let's discuss what you would like to alter in your work environment," Susie began. "What changes could possibly increase your job satisfaction? What would *you* like to see happen? If you had a magic wand, what new scenarios would you want to create?" she challenged Denise, a sullen and disgruntled employee.

"What would I like to see happen?" shouted Denise, glad to have a chance to vent her rage and frustration. "Well, I am so tired of watching one of my patients, poor Karen, wait at the window day after day for relatives who never show up. No one in her family comes to visit. Her mother hasn't been here in six months. It breaks my heart . . . I can't take her pain anymore!"

"Okay," Susie said, nodding encouragingly. "So what exactly do you want?"

"I want her relatives to come visit!"

"Fine, let's articulate this wish in precise terms," Susie coached.

Susie worked with Denise for a few minutes, until Denise was able to stand up in the middle of the room and articulate her wish in the language of Susie's therapist: "I hereby make a commitment that Karen's mother and other relatives will come to visit her more often."

"*How often?*" Susie drilled. "You have to be precise."

Denise restated her request. "I hereby determine that her mother will come every two months."

"Perfect!" clapped Susie. "Okay. Now let's see what happens."

The very next evening, Karen's mother showed up at the home for the first time in six months. Susie's eyes sparkled when Denise told her the news. "Why do you think she came?" Susie asked.

"Uhh . . . someone probably called her to come," Denise mumbled in disbelief.

"Go ask her if that's what brought her here tonight," Susie directed.

But when confronted with the question, Karen's mother shook her head emphatically. "No, no one called me. I just happened to be in the neighborhood and decided to drop in."

Two days later, Karen's grandmother, who hadn't come to visit in four years, put in an appearance. "Did somebody call you to come?" Denise asked, startled to see her.

"No," said the grandmother. "I just started thinking about Karen, that's all. Something . . . I don't remember what . . . made me think of her."

The next day, Karen's aunt came and the day after that, her first cousin. "My God," said Denise to Susie, as a whole procession of relatives began to parade through the home to Karen's room. "Karen's had more visitors in one week than she's had all year!"

"So, what do you make of it?" Susie asked with a smile.

"Oh, it's very clear to me," Denise said with utmost certitude. "It's a . . . coincidence!"

⎯⎯✦⎯⎯

Comment

This story vividly portrays the power of belief and its reverberations . . . on two entirely different levels. On one level, we have the dawning spiritual consciousness that our beliefs create our realities—the lesson that Susie's spiritual therapist taught, and that she in turn transferred to her staff. On another level, we learn from Denise's reaction the essential truth that basically most of us see what we want to see in life, and that ultimately the eye sees from the heart.

*W*hen Jimmy Haggerty*
lived in New York, he won
the state's ten-million-dollar lottery. Then he moved to New Jersey,
where he collected an impressive eighteen million as the solitary winner
in that week's draw. Then he moved to California, where for the third
time in a row, he beat the odds, collecting twenty million from that
state's lottery. When reporters frantically descended on him to interview
him about these amazing coincidences, he shrugged his shoulders and
said nonchalantly, "I didn't need to win any of them. I was wealthy from
the start."

Comment

In a society driven by the work ethic, we sometimes find it hard to
concede that a major component of success is sheer "luck" or "divine
providence." In a way, though, it's a relief to accept that there's just so
much we can do, and the rest is up to God.

$\mathcal{L}$*inda* Valentine* was a famous model. Yet despite her money, fame, and glamour, she felt a gnawing emptiness inside. There was a sense of unease she could not cast off, a restlessness of spirit that filled her with unspeakable anxiety and dread. At night, she was plagued with insomnia. She began to ask her friends what they thought of taking prescription drugs like Xanax and Valium.

While many of them obligingly described the relative merits of each, one friend looked at Linda with genuine concern and took her aside. "That's not what you need," she whispered in distress. "Popping pills will only do you harm. And they only mask the symptoms, they don't address them. Are you free this weekend?"

That weekend, Linda's friend took her to a program called "Impact" that promised to help participants articulate and accomplish their goals. It delivered. Incredibly, within a short week of taking the seminar, Linda achieved career breakthroughs and won contracts she had been dreaming about for years. But despite the sudden fulfillment of her greatest ambitions, her general angst lingered. Her soul remained in torment.

One morning, she was taking her usual route to work, driving down La Brea, the main thoroughfare, when traffic came to a standstill. A water main had broken, and traffic was being diverted to a small, obscure street, one that she had never driven down before. As she inched her car along the unfamiliar street, she noticed a small storefront church with a handwritten sign in its window that proclaimed: "No God, no peace. Know God, know peace. Everybody welcome." "Hmm," she thought, as she drove slowly by, "how quaint!"

The next morning, Linda was on her way to work again, driving down La Brea, when, for the second day in a row, traffic came to a halt. A fire was blazing out of control in one of the shops lining the boulevard, and fire trucks were converging on the scene from all directions. Policemen blocked off the area, and diverted traffic to the same obscure street as the day before. "Oh, no!" she groaned, "not again!" Once again she drove by the small storefront church. This time, the sign seemed compelling, not quaint. She thought for a moment that it was summoning her inside. "What an imagination I have!" she laughed, scolding herself for her penchant for melodrama. Still, from her car window, she squinted at the storefront church, trying to catch a glimpse of its interior. Her gaze was wistful.

The next day, she thought of changing routes, but told herself that she was being foolish. After all, what were the odds of another calamity occurring on the same street three days in a row? "This will be a test," she chuckled to herself. "If there's some disaster on La Brea again, and traffic gets diverted down that same street again, then I'll know for sure it's a sign!"

When she turned down La Brea, she was thunderstruck. Traffic was backed up for blocks. A major car accident, explained an apologetic cop, diverting traffic again, for the third time in a row, down the same small street. "That does it!" she exclaimed. She parked her car and entered the church, which was empty except for a young priest sitting behind a desk. He looked up at her and smiled. "What took you so long?" he asked.

He had seen her car pass by all three days, and had absorbed her wistful gaze. They spoke for a long time, and she joined the congregation. That was eighteen years ago, and she's been there ever since, having found the peace and serenity that had eluded her elsewhere. Just as the sign promised, what she had really needed in her life was God. And wasn't it, after all, God who had sent her there in the first place?

Taylor Caldwell was a best-selling author in the 1950s and 1960s. For decades, her historical romances had dominated the bestseller charts. In terms of sales and excitement, she was the midcentury's equivalent of Danielle Steel.

Her devoted husband, with whom she had a long and wonderful marriage, preceded her in death. His death came after a protracted illness, and both had prepared for it. Just minutes before his death, Taylor Caldwell clutched her husband's hand and pleaded, "If there *is* life on the other side, I beg you, send me a sign. Let me know you are with me."

Her husband nodded his assent.

"Promise?" she begged.

"I promise," he pledged.

The next morning, overcome by her grief, Taylor Caldwell stepped out into her garden, seeking solace from nature as she always did. "Oh, darling," she cried out to her husband, "if you would only send me a sign that you are with me, I could try to go on. My pain is so wrenching and my grief so strong, I fear I cannot survive otherwise."

Just then, Ms. Caldwell approached a section of her garden where the ground had always proven stubbornly infertile and had never flourished like the surrounding area. As her gaze absently swept over this section, she gasped.

In the center of this section stood a rosemary bush that had not been productive for thirty years. Just the day before, when she had walked these same grounds seeking respite from her death watch, she had commented to herself how sorry she was that the bush had never thrived. But one day later, it was inexplicably in full bloom. Staring in shock and awe at the bush, Taylor Caldwell stood motionless for a long time, absorbing its message. "Thank you," she whispered fervently, "thank you. I will be able to go on, now that I know you are with me."

She had clearly been given the sign she was seeking, she told interviewers later. "You see," she explained, "rosemary means . . . remembrance."

Comment

When love is strong and runs deep, it pulsates with an energy that cannot be stopped, not even by death's grip. When two souls are connected and one departs from this world, the separation may seem final, but in truth the relationship transcends time. Love, like a river, flows eternal, and it embraces all those who swim in its streams.

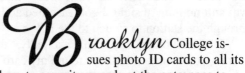**_Brooklyn_** College is-
sues photo ID cards to all its
students, which they must show to security guards at the entrances to
various buildings on campus. Thus, I was utterly dismayed one evening
when, at the entrance to the library, I reached into my wallet for my ID
card, and discovered to my shock that it wasn't there! Although I begged
the guard at the door to let me in because I had a paper due that required
extensive research, my pleas fell on deaf ears and I was turned away.
Fuming, I berated myself for having lost the ID card, and wondered how
and where it had gone astray. I seemed to recall having taken my wallet
out of my pocketbook sometime during the day, probably en route to
work in Manhattan, but after that I drew a blank. I was annoyed at myself, because the process of applying for a new card was a bureaucratic
nightmare, with hours of waiting in line for the application, for the photograph to be taken, for the ID card to be validated, etc. Worst of all,
since the semester was already underway, the offices where I would
need to go for help were only open during the daytime. I was an evening
student and worked full-time. I would have to take a day off from work,
and I had just started a new job.

I returned home later that night, still in a bad mood, still chastising
myself, still wondering how I would approach my supervisor about a
day off. As I walked through the door, the phone rang. It was my best
friend, Toby.

"Guess what I found today at a subway station in Manhattan?" she
crowed. "You're going to get a kick out of this!"

"Oh yeah, what?" I asked, uninterested, grumpy, and still obsessing.

"Your ID card!"

"What!" I screamed. "That's incredible! Where'd you find it?"

"At the Thirty-fourth Street station of the B train. I saw a piece of
paper lying on the floor, and something just made me bend down and
pick it up. Imagine my astonishment when I saw that—of all things—it's
my best friend's picture!"

We both agreed that her retrieval of my ID card had been a minor
miracle, and chalked it up to one of life's undeniable mysteries.

Just as she was about to hang up, I suddenly had a thought.
"Toby . . . wait a second . . . it just dawned on me . . . You don't usually
take the B train to Manhattan, do you?"

"No," she said, "but there was some mechanical trouble on the
N train that I was originally on, and it was taken out of service. I waited

around for another one, but when twenty minutes had passed and there was still no train in sight, I got frustrated and lost patience. So I walked through the station to switch to the B."

"Toby, do you realize," I said excitedly, "that if you had waited for the N train you would never have found my card?"

— *Yitta Halberstam Mandelbaum*

Comment

A missed plane that crashes . . . an object that mysteriously finds its way back to its owner . . . a friend's unexpected phone call precisely at the moment when we're undergoing a crisis or feeling especially blue. These are whispers that can awaken us from our stupor and remind us that the hand of God is always there, guiding us through our days.

My mother, a widow, is practically destitute, and relies on me for financial help all the time. As I am not particularly well-off myself, this represents a tremendous pressure. Most of the time, I seem to be able to bear this burden with equanimity and good humor, but every now and then, the strain wears me thin. Such was the case last month, when my mother's air conditioner went on the blink during the worst heat wave of the summer.

For the preceding few months, she had been particularly needy. There had been unusual expenses to carry, in addition to the regular ones. Doctors' bills, summer clothes, a brief trip to the seashore . . . It seemed as though no day had passed that she hadn't called me about a new bill she wanted me to pay. So when she called and told me she needed a new air conditioner, I snapped. "Not now!" I screamed, slamming down the phone hard.

That night, I came home late from work, and found that my apartment resembled a steam bath. As soon as I opened the door, the hot air hit me instantly, and beads of sweat began pouring down my face and body. "Thank God I have central air conditioning!" I said to myself, as I moved the dial on the meter to turn it on.

I waited for the cold air to come pouring through the vents, but nothing happened. I suddenly realized that the slow, steady vibrating hum that always signified the functioning of the central air conditioner was missing. "I can't believe it!" I muttered to myself in dismay. "The central air conditioner—which has never given me a minute's trouble—is broken . . . on the hottest night of the year!"

It was eleven o'clock at night and too late to call a repairman. I would literally have to sweat it out till the next morning.

I was so uncomfortable that night that I couldn't sleep. I tossed and turned, showered repeatedly, gulped down cold drinks. But nothing helped. It was unbearably hot outside, and I was in misery.

Suddenly, I sat up in bed. "Oh my God!" I thought guiltily. "My poor mother! If I, a healthy forty-year-old, am experiencing such tremendous discomfort, what is she going through? How could I have been so insensitive, so uncaring?"

I felt overwhelmed with shame and remorse at my callous behavior the day before, at my lack of compassion for my mother. But perhaps I was not entirely to blame. Perhaps I had not really understood how oppressive the heat could be. I had finally gotten a glimmer of what she had been experiencing when my own air conditioning broke down. "First thing in the morning I'm going to buy her an air conditioner!" I immediately resolved. "I won't even go to work until I make sure the air conditioner is installed in her bedroom. No, better yet, I'm not going to buy her one air conditioner . . . I'm going to buy her one for every room in the house!"

Satisfied with my envisioned act of expiation, I settled back into my pillows and closed my eyes. Suddenly, I heard the most welcome noise in the world: the whir of the air conditioning motors and a reassuring hum.

Cold air blasted through the vents. I gasped in wonderment and disbelief at the impeccable timing. And then I knew: my penance had been accepted.

— *Celia Robbins**

Comment

We think that concrete physical actions are the only possible manifestations of our benevolence. But in fact, just the *thought* of doing a good deed is powerful enough to effect a change in the universe.

For years, my family had made a tradition of traveling to the Pine View Hotel in the Catskill Mountains every spring for the Passover holidays. We had been doing this for over ten years, and during this time had made many close friends with other "repeats." My parents had become especially close to a lovely couple from out-of-state who were also frequent guests at this popular resort. Although they didn't keep in touch with one another over the course of the year, when they did meet at the Pine View, they all shared an unusual camaraderie.

By now, my parents had known this couple—Eve and David Stern*— for over a decade and considered them one of the most happily married couples they had ever met. They looked forward to their yearly reunions. Thus, one Passover, as my parents were checking in at the registration desk, they were shocked to encounter Eve standing in the lobby, clinging to the arm of a different man, whom she immediately introduced as "my new husband." My parents nearly fainted.

As soon as she could, my mother drew Eve aside and asked what had happened over the last year. Eve shrugged her shoulders in a parody of bewilderment and said that, to tell the truth, she was as astonished as my mother about the unusual series of events that had occurred. She herself was still reeling, she said, from the peculiar twists of fate she had experienced in recent months. She didn't know what to make of it all, she told my mother, but she would gladly recount the sequence of events that defied reason.

"About eleven months ago," she related, "my husband stormed into my room one day and dropped a bombshell into my lap. He told me, without any explanation or apology whatsoever, that he wanted a divorce. I was stunned. I had always been quite content in our marriage, and I assumed he was too. There had never been any previous difficulties, and no plausible cause for his sudden outburst. As much as I tried to beg him for a reason, a motive, a basis for his abrupt request, he wouldn't give me any. He insisted that he had always been unhappy, and wanted to make a change in his life now before it was too late. I was devastated and heartbroken, but after several weeks of trying to get him into counseling or change his mind, I succumbed. I had my pride; I didn't want to live with someone who didn't want to live with me. So I gave him the divorce, and we went our separate ways.

"Six months later, I met and married the man whom I introduced to you in the lobby. He's a wonderful man, and I'm deliriously happy. In fact, I'm much happier than I was in my first marriage. Everything has gone exceptionally well.

"There's only one jarring note," Eve said slowly. "One thing that kind of gives me the willies, and for which I can find no possible rational explanation.

"You see, my second husband is also named David Stern—same as the first. Well, you could argue that both the first name David and the surname Stern are fairly common, so that's not what gives me the creeps. What I do find eerie is that both my second and my first husband were born on the exact same day, month, and year. They were both born on September 8, 1931.

"Now, how," she said, turning to my mother, "do you explain that?"

— *Shira Freedman*

Comment

There are markers that set us on a course for life. We are born under a certain star and we are given a specific name. These point us in a direction that we may not understand. For often it is too difficult to step back from ourselves and gain enough distance to see how the markers all play out in the greater scheme of our lives.

*W*hen Miri Fabian, an Israeli stage actress, won a small role in Steven Spielberg's film *Schindler's List*, she felt mixed emotions. "I had auditioned on videotape," she recalls, "and didn't know what it was for—only that it was for Spielberg. I had seen *The Color Purple* and *Empire of the Sun*. Then I found out I got the part and what it was. I was happy but also very sad. I had been born in a Slovakian work camp in 1944 and was cast as one of the women saved by Schindler. Here was something my mother had saved me from—Auschwitz—and here I was going back of my own free will. It was poignant.

"To help me prepare for the part, I was given the name and number of the daughter of the character I was playing and called her. When I phoned, I said, 'I'm playing your mother in *Schindler's List* and would like to know everything about her. Can I visit you?' I did, and the daughter graciously showed me old photographs of her mother as she had looked then and current photographs as she looks today.

"I practically leaped to my feet in astonishment. 'But I know your mother!' I shouted. 'She lives in the house opposite me. I see her every day on the street!' "

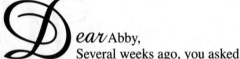
Dear Abby,
Several weeks ago, you asked readers to share their experiences of suicide attempts that failed or were aborted. I know you've already printed many, so I hope you don't mind printing one more.

Ten years ago, everything hit me from all sides. I became depressed and suicidal. I attempted to kill myself once in a motel, but a cleaning lady saved me.

I came out of the hospital still determined to end my life. I began saving prescription pills. When I went to church in search of answers, I would look around to see if there was a way I might hang myself from the ceiling. Two months later, I tried again. I headed for a small town and took 300 prescription pills with me.

A friend traced me to the motel. Three other friends talked me into going to the hospital. I walked into that hospital with the 300 pills, determined to kill myself there.

While seated in the lobby, I picked up a *Reader's Digest* and randomly opened it without looking at the index. Here is the unbelievable part: The page I arbitrarily turned to contained an article entitled *Before You Kill Yourself.* It gave several powerful reasons to choose life over suicide.

I called a nurse and handed her all the pills I had hidden. You should have seen her face!

That *Reader's Digest* article saved my life. That was ten years ago, and I am doing just fine now!

— *From a September 1995 column*

Comment

Sometimes all that may be needed to salvage the soul and mend the heart is a kind word and a message of hope and inspiration.

Gerry drove a big red Cadillac. It served as a multi-purpose vehicle. On weekends, the whole family enjoyed the use of the car, and during the week, Gerry used it to cart his wares. Gerry was a salesman and he kept samples of his electronic merchandise in the car's trunk.

A typical workday for Gerry involved making various sales calls at different locations. On August 15, 1994, Gerry made a stop at Bob's Electronics, with the hope of making a substantial sale. Through the store window, he was able to see Bob, the storeowner, walking to the cash register. Rather than parking the car for what he assumed would be a two-minute exchange, Gerry left the engine running as he walked up to the store. "Hey, Bob!" Gerry called while holding the door ajar, "need anything?"

"Not today, Gerry," came the reply. "But try me again at the end of the week."

"Will do," said Gerry, and headed quickly back toward the car.

But there was no car. That two-minute exchange had given someone ample time to get behind the wheel and drive off. Gerry was aghast. First, he called the police, and then he called his good friend Mike. "Mike!" he cried into the phone, "they got my Cadillac!"

"What do you mean?" asked Mike.

"What do I mean?!? I mean MY CAR WAS STOLEN!!" yelled Gerry.

Mike was concerned. "Where are you?" he asked. "I'll come right over."

Gerry gave him the address and then waited anxiously for help.

The police were the first to show up. Moments later, Mike arrived. The police took down all the necessary information and assured Gerry that all efforts would be made to retrieve his car. Having completed their preliminary work, they left.

Mike turned to Gerry and in an overly optimistic tone, said, "C'mon, let's go look for your car ourselves."

Gerry was incredulous. "The thief might be anywhere by now!" he barked, "Brooklyn is a VERY BIG PLACE! Where would we possibly begin to look?"

"I guess you're right," responded Mike, his spirit dampened. "It *is* a ridiculous idea. Listen," he went on, "I need to buy a pair of pliers from Rickel's Home Center. Think you can wait in the car for me while I run in and get it? It'll just be a minute."

"No problem," said Gerry. He was feeling extremely down on his luck and welcomed the opportunity to be with his close buddy, regardless of where they were going or what they were doing.

Twenty minutes later they arrived at Rickel's massive parking lot. "I don't think I'm in the mood to go inside," said Gerry. "Let me wait out here for you."

"All right with me," responded Mike as he left the car. "Like I said, it'll only take a few minutes."

Gerry sat slumped in the seat, looking out at all the hundreds of cars in the parking lot. It was a hazy day. The gray clouds mirrored his gray mood. Suddenly, for a fraction of a second, the clouds parted and a strange light shone from the sky.

Gerry was mesmerized by this single ray, which was shining on one car. It was as though a laser beam had pierced through the clouds and settled on this one automobile. "How strange," thought Gerry. He craned his head out the window to take a better look at the ray of sunshine dancing on the hood of the car. Then his head shot up. It was *his* car.

Parked among the thousands of cars in the vast parking lot was his very own red Cadillac. Gerry called the police again. This time it was to reclaim his property.

A certain homeless man who walked the streets of our neighborhood had become a fixture in our household over the years. My husband, Good Samaritan that he was, had seen "Bert" scavenging in our garbage cans one day, and stopped to speak with him. Learning that he was homeless, he took pity on him, and invited him inside for a hot meal. Since he was dressed neatly, and spoke in educated, well-modulated tones, I never suspected a thing. His breadth of knowledge was far-ranging and extensive, and during dinner he regaled us with intelligent and witty comments about politics, medicine, and urban affairs. My husband had deliberately refrained from telling me Bert's background, and by the time dinner was over and the truth was out, my prejudices about "street people" were shattered forever.

Bert was in and out of our lives over the course of the next fifteen years. I learned that he held a master's in physics from City College and had experienced a nervous breakdown in his twenties after his mother, father, and fiancée all died within a three-month period. At first I tried to help Bert. I spoke earnestly to officials at several social service agencies about trying to enroll him in welfare, getting him an apartment or at least a room, and finding him a job. I even made arrangements with a local senior citizens' center to give Bert a free hot lunch every day. But he never kept a single one of the appointments I excitedly but naively made for him—never even put in an appearance at the senior citizens' center, where all that was required of him was that he show up. Eventually I gave up. There was something wizardlike, secretive, and hidden about him, and it seemed as though he possessed a mysterious past that he was trying hard to conceal. In time, I began to accept Bert for what he was. I always opened our home to him and shared our meals with him, giving him cash and clothing whenever I had some to spare. But I no longer tried to change his life.

Bert was pleasant company, jovial and witty, and I always marveled at his optimistic spirit. Despite his bleak circumstances, he seemed to be perpetually in a good mood. It was therefore never any kind of effort or sacrifice to have him around, even though my friends remarked constantly on my so-called "altruism."

After fifteen years of hosting Bert without incident, I was startled one day to receive a visit from a neighbor who said she had come to warn me about him. She couldn't help but notice his comings and goings, she said, and she wanted me to know that he was nothing but a common thief.

"How do you know this?" I demanded in disbelief.

"Haven't you ever noticed anything missing from your home?" she asked with a sly look.

"No, never," I replied. "Well, you're so absentminded to begin with, you probably wouldn't even be aware if something was stolen from under your nose!"

"Why are you saying these things?" I demanded. "On what basis?"

"I saw him in front of a local store the other day. The police were frisking him. He had stolen something from the shop. And the store-owner, whom I personally know, said that all the shopkeepers on the avenue have learned to be wary of him. He has a reputation for pilfering, and he's also said to be violent."

"Are you sure we're talking about the same man?" I insisted, incredulous and shaken.

"It's definitely the same man," the neighbor answered with certitude. "I'd recognize him anywhere. So I came to tell you . . . beware!"

That evening, the doorbell rang, and with a sinking heart, I looked out the window and saw that it was Bert. My husband had taken our two sons to a baseball game, and I was all alone. For the first time since I had met him, I was suddenly afraid of Bert and didn't want him in the house. I stuck my head out the second-story window and yelled, "Hi, Bert! How ya doing?" He squinted up at me, brows knitted in puzzlement. This was not part of our routine; usually, I just opened the door and warmly ushered him inside.

"Uhh, Yitta," he stammered, confused by the obvious shift, "can you open the door? I'm starving!"

I felt anguished. "Oh, Bert, I'm so sorry, I was just about to leave the house this minute for a doctor's appointment." "Well, do you think you could wait just a little bit while I eat? It's cold tonight and I sure could use a warm meal." I thought of the four pieces of chicken and the mashed potatoes on the stove waiting for my family's return. Ordinarily, I would have given Bert my portion without hesitation, but after the neighbor's visit, I found myself gripped by fear. The jovial man who had graced our table for years as a friend suddenly loomed as a stranger whom apparently I had never really known at all. "So sorry, Bert," I hedged. "Really, I have to leave this minute. But tell you what, I'll pack a shopping bag for you with stuff you can eat."

I raced around the kitchen, pulling out cheese, fruit, and hardboiled eggs from the fridge, crackers, sardines, seltzer, and paper goods from the pantry. When I opened the door and handed the bag to him, his face had a hurt and bewildered expression. I felt ashamed. "Well, thank you for this," he said gesturing towards the bag as he strode down the walkway. "But I sure could have used a hot meal tonight," he threw over his shoulder, before he disappeared.

As I waited for my husband and children to return home from the baseball game, I wrestled with tumultuous thoughts, besieged by self-doubt. "You did the right thing," comforted one voice. "What are you, crazy?—to let a thief into the house! Charity is one thing and stupidity is another."

"You were wrong to turn him away!" strongly rebuked another voice. "He's been in your home for fifteen years, and nothing ever happened. You let yourself be swayed by a vicious gossip. How can you know for sure it was really Bert she was talking about, anyway?"

On and on it went all evening, the verbal sparring between my two inner voices never ceasing, my despair, remorse, and guilt growing with each passing minute. Had I done the right thing? Had I been wrong? How would I ever know the truth?

Finally, my family came home from the baseball game starved, and I began to concentrate on serving dinner. Holding my husband's plate, I began walking towards the dining room table, when I stumbled over a toy on the floor. The plate crashed to the floor, and food flew in all directions. "Don't worry, I have plenty to go around," I lied, planning to give my husband my portion.

The second plate heaped with food had been safely navigated onto the table, when the phone rang. It was for my husband, and he left his place at the table to answer the call. When he returned to the dining room, he stared in astonishment at the sight of our beagle, Flash, perched on her hindquarters, gobbling up his food from the plate. She had been with the family for five years and had never done anything like this before. "Is there enough food to go around now?" he asked, scowling angrily at Flash. "Sure, sure," I lied, wondering how I was going to stretch the remaining pieces of chicken three ways. Just as I approached the stove a third time, the light bulb in the overhead hood inexplicably exploded, scattering shards of glass all over the burners and into the pot of food, which I had left uncovered. Hearing the pop of the exploding bulb, my husband came into the kitchen to investigate, and immediately flung the pot's contents into the garbage can. "Is our dinner jinxed tonight?" he joked good-naturedly.

I began to cry. "Why are you crying?" he chided. "It's not your fault."

"Oh, yes, it is," I sobbed, and I explained what had happened with Bert.

As my husband and boys left the house for the nearest restaurant, I thought of Bert, who didn't have that recourse, who didn't have hot food in his belly to keep him warm through the cold night.

Before the "coincidental" mishaps with the food had occurred that evening, I had wondered long and hard about whether I had done the right or wrong thing about Bert. Had I canvassed my friends for their opinions (which I typically do whenever I'm faced with a moral dilemma), I am sure the answers would have been conflicting, indeterminate, and confusing. Some friends would have reassured me that I was justified in closing both my house and heart to Bert, while others, I know, would have scolded me rigorously for listening to gossip and not giving Bert the benefit of the doubt. My soul-searching would have remained tormented, my quandary unresolved.

But attuned to the message of the mishaps, I knew that I had made a mistake. For in the coincidences, I had found the incontrovertible truth.

— *Yitta Halberstam Mandelbaum*

Comment

The universe provides the answers to our questions. We can hear them if only we open our hearts and tune in our souls.

$\mathcal{B}$*lanca* was born in Satmar, a small town on the outskirts of Hungary. She was the third in a family of ten—seven girls and three boys. As part of a large family and in a community bustling with children, Blanca was somewhat lost in the shuffle. She was not an exemplary student. She did not exhibit exceptional talent, nor was she especially popular with her friends. No one took particular notice of her.

No one except for Sergi.

He was a young boy who lived down the block. From the time that they were both very young, Blanca and Sergi played together in the courtyards of their homes and in the fields on the edge of town. Long after all the others had outgrown childlike games, they continued to delight in frivolous play. When he was fourteen years old, Sergi spoke to his mother about his plans for the future. "I'm going to marry Blanca one day," he said over dinner.

"Sure you will," replied his mother, and then encouraged him to finish his meal. Blanca knew how much Sergi cared about her, and it made her feel special.

Sergi's admiration for Blanca grew, as did the years. On the evening of her fifteenth birthday, Sergi came to celebrate. "Blanchuka!" he called to her from the back window of her house. Blanca peered out. There Sergi stood, serenading her with love songs, accompanied by a band of gypsies playing violins and guitars. "You are so special to me," he called up to her. "Sergica," she sighed. As Blanca leaned out the window, listening to Sergi sing, she felt cherished and loved.

For the two budding sweethearts, life was good but it didn't last too long. Shortly after their special night, World War II broke out. In anticipation of the worst, Blanca's parents prepared to move the family to America. Blanca was devastated. "How can I leave Sergi behind?" she thought. "But how can I not?" At fifteen years of age, Blanca did not imagine that she had any choice but to follow her parents' lead. "I will miss you," Blanca said to Sergi between tears.

"Write to me," Sergi implored. The two promised to stay in touch and meet again someday soon.

For Blanca, the move to America was difficult and unsettling. Though she longed to stay in touch with Sergi, the war made it impossible to do so. When Blanca turned eighteen, her parents arranged for her to meet a young man who had a fine reputation. Blanca's heart still yearned for Sergi, but she was persuaded to leave the past behind. She married the young man and together they raised a family of five. Despite various challenges, their marriage was good. As time wore on, the memory of Sergi faded somewhat but was never totally forgotten.

In 1995, Blanca returned to her homeland. She was now a grandmother of ten. She had heard from a distant relative that Sergi was still living in Satmar. This information awakened in her a desire to go back to her native land. She yearned to tell Sergi how much he had meant to her through the years. She wanted to tell him that he had remained a sweet memory, that she had never stopped loving him with the innocent love she had for him as a child.

Blanca walked the streets of Satmar, surprised by how small it seemed compared to the way she remembered it. She recalled that when she was a young girl, a horse and buggy was a familiar sight. Now taxis, buses, and cars were everywhere. She hailed a taxi. "Please," she said in her native tongue, "could you take me to this address?" Blanca showed the taxi driver the street name and number where Sergi reportedly lived.

"Ah, my dear friend Sergi," the taxi driver said, "you want to see him?"

"Why, yes," Blanca said, surprised that the driver knew him.

"You did not hear?" the taxi driver said in a lowered voice. "Why, yesterday, Sergi passed away."

Blanca never did get to say what was in her heart. Instead, she visited his cemetery plot, laid a wreath on his tombstone, kissed it gently, and walked away.

Comment

We think there is always a tomorrow, so why expose our feelings today? Why risk being vulnerable? Why take the chance? Because today, what we love, what we feel, what is real, is what we have. Tomorrow, it may all change.

Nature calls to me as I am walking down Lexington Avenue in New York City. I decide to do what I have always done, which is a version of the following: I saunter into an upscale restaurant. Typically I am stopped by the maitre d', who asks, "How may I help you?" I glibly reply, "Oh, I'm supposed to meet someone—do you mind if I look around to see if they are here?" An affirmative response always follows. "Sure, go ahead." I then pretend I am surveying the tables for a familiar face. When I am out of clear view of the maitre d', I find my way to the ladies' room and proceed to take advantage of the facilities. On the way out I mumble something to the maitre d' like, "Thanks, but I couldn't find the person I was looking for," and hastily exit.

That's the way it has always been. So one day, I proceed with my usual routine. I walk into an unfamiliar restaurant. I follow the usual protocol. I get as far as the bathroom, and then for some unknown reason, I am suddenly struck with pangs of guilt! My conscience decides to take a stand for honesty. Right there and then, in the bathroom, I begin having a major philosophical debate about the ethics of lying. "A lie to a total stranger doesn't count," I argue.

"A lie is a lie!" my conscience retorts.

After much deliberation, I decide that the truth must prevail and that I must repent. Then I hear a stern command from my superego: "Tell the maitre d' that you lied. Once you do that, you will have purged yourself of the wrongdoing you have committed and you will never, never do it again."

With my conscience in command and my morals high, I walk bravely over to the maitre d', steeling myself for a prickly situation. I clear my throat, readying myself to tell him that I really wasn't expecting to meet anyone. And then suddenly and unexpectedly, an old friend walks through the door, gives me a great big bear hug and says, loud enough for the maitre d' to hear, *"Hi! So glad to see you!"*

Just as I was about to lose respectability in a stranger's eyes, I was found by a friend who returned my dignity to me intact. As I left the restaurant, I looked over my shoulder and took note of its name. Appropriately enough, it was called "The Lost and Found."

~~~

Comment

The path of truth is paved with a light that burns through darkness and dispels shame.

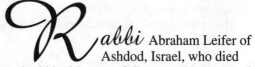 *Rabbi* Abraham Leifer of
Ashdod, Israel, who died
five years ago, was a celebrated rabbi with many followers. When one of
his faithful flock married off a child in Antwerp, Belgium, Rabbi Leifer
took an entourage from Israel with him and flew to the wedding. They
were nine men in all.

When they were only one hundred miles away from Antwerp, the
pilot suddenly announced that the plane was low on fuel and they would
have to make an unscheduled stop. They landed at a small country airport.

Everyone deplaned, and the rabbi and his followers decided to look
for a solitary spot where they could conduct the evening prayer service.
The rabbi approached an airport worker, and asked him if it would be
possible to open up a room where they could pray privately. The request
was couched in ordinary terms, in English, but the man blanched as if he
had been punched. He stared at the rabbi in disbelief and then answered,
"I'll grant your wish . . . provided that you allow me to chant the *kaddish* (the Jewish memorial prayer for the dead) for my father!"

"You are a Jew?" the rabbi asked in bewilderment. The man nodded
yes. "I didn't know any Jews lived in this part of Belgium. What are you
doing here?" The man rejoined, "Better yet . . . what are *you* doing
here . . . today of all days, just when I need you?"

As the man opened the door of the private room the rabbi had requested, he said: "Let me tell you something, which you may find difficult to believe. But I promise it is true."

"I broke with my family years ago and fled to this small village. Although I originally come from an extremely Orthodox family, I myself
have not been religious for decades. I have not said *kaddish* for my father in years.

"Last night, I had a dream in which my father came to me and said:
'Yankele, tomorrow is the anniversary of my death and I want you to say
the *kaddish* for me!' 'But father,' I protested in the dream, 'you need a
minyan (a quorum of ten men) in order to say kaddish. I'm the only Jew
in this village. I can never hope to find a *minyan* here!' 'Yankele,' my father answered, 'if you promise me you'll say the *kaddish*, I promise you
I'll bring you a *minyan*!'

"When I awoke from the dream," the man told my uncle, "I was trembling and in shock. But I soon told myself it was only a dream, and reassured myself that it had no significance. It was ridiculous, really! After

all, how would a *minyan* ever find their way to a remote Belgian farming village where no other Jews reside?"

The rabbi draped his arm around the man's shoulders, and said gently, "Come my friend, let's pray!"

In September 1995, my eight-year-old son came home from school one day to report excitedly that a new kid from overseas had just joined his class. This kid, he told me happily, "is just like me in every way. It's really cool, Mom," he said. "Josh loves basketball, he's great at sports, he's mischievous, he's funny, and he knows how to play great tricks on the teachers!" (Terrific! Now the poor souls would have to contend with a devilish duo instead of just one menace who had previously operated solo!) Sure enough the two fun-loving, spirited imps teamed up for a series of hijinks, innocent pranks, and frolicking escapades that had the school staff reeling. My son was ecstatic about his new friend. "It's amazing how much he's like me," he constantly commented, in a tone of wonderment and delighted surprise.

One day, my son came home with Josh to work on a school project together. Since he lived in a different neighborhood, Josh asked if I could drive him home when they were done, and I readily agreed. When I pulled up at his address, he asked if I would like to come in and meet his mother. The hour was late, but never one to rebuff a child, I obligingly climbed out of the car. Josh ushered me into the living room and went to find his mother. "Eli's mother is here!" I heard him call to her. "Come meet her . . . you'll love her!"

Quick, light footsteps danced down the stairs and I turned to meet Josh's mother. She blinked. I blinked. Her jaw dropped. My mouth gaped open. Her eyes filled with tears. I tried hard to muffle a sob. Then we simultaneously ran towards each other and embraced for a long time.

Josh stood staring at this scene transfixed and perplexed. "What's going on?" he asked.

"Oh, Josh!" his mother exclaimed laughing, wiping away a tear. "Eli's mother and I were best friends in high school. After graduation, I moved abroad and I met Dad and lived overseas for years. I haven't seen Yitta for twenty-two years!"

Of course, I hadn't had an inkling. How could I have known? It was his father's surname—"Goodfriend"—that Josh used, not his mother's maiden name, although perhaps, on second thought, the name should have provided me with a slight suspicion, if not a telltale clue!

— *Yitta Halberstam Mandelbaum*

Comment

The legacy of love and friendship spans and is transmitted by the generations, perhaps even genetically imprinted upon us in some mysterious and unfathomable way. Invisible lines of connection link us all, and the heart always returns to its source. Once attachments are formed, they never truly disappear, but continue to live on, in our thoughts, our deeds, and our children's lives.

In the 1950s, when it was unacceptable for a woman of breeding to work, Eppie Lederer of Chicago was faced with a quandary: how to direct her dynamism and energy, and what to do about her growing restlessness.

She had one teenage child who was away in school all day, and a busy executive husband who traveled much of the time. Having relocated to the big city in 1954 from Eau Claire, Wisconsin, where she had been active in civic affairs, she thought of entering local politics but had been warned away. "The Chicago machine is not manned by La Follette Democrats, let alone women," an old friend cautioned. "If you try your hand at local politics, you just might wind up in Lake Michigan wearing a cement ankle bracelet."

"I have to do something," she thought. "I must have a calling!" She didn't know what it was, but surely she would know it when she found it.

In August 1955, Eppie was reading the *Chicago Sun-Times* when a certain feature captured her attention. She read the column over and over again, once, twice, three times, with mounting interest. It was the advice column, penned by a woman named Ann Landers. At the bottom of the column, there was a note encouraging people to send their problems to Ann Landers, with the promise that all letters would be personally answered, even if they weren't used in the paper. "That columnist must be swamped," thought Eppie. "I bet she could use an assistant. Now that's something I'd like to do: help Ann Landers answer her mail!"

She promptly picked up the phone and called an executive she knew at the paper. "I've figured out what I'd like to do," she announced to Will Munnecke. "I'll help Ann Landers answer her mail."

There was a long pause on the other end. "Now this is odd," said Munnecke, "that you should be calling me now. Ruth Crowley, our 'Ann Landers,' just died suddenly . . . I'll call you back."

But by the time Munnecke had returned her call, Eppie Lederer had already revised her plans: since there was no one to be an assistant *to*, she would simply take over the entire column herself!

She knew it was a reach, but she had a feel for this kind of thing, she told Munnecke. In response, the executive laughed. "My dear," he chuckled, "the newspaper business is not about granting wishes to ladies with sudden inspirations and nothing to do!" When he sensed that Eppie's feelings had been hurt, he tried to cushion the blow by gently explaining that this column called for training that she simply didn't have. Crowley had been both a newspaperwoman and a nurse. And there was the added complication that "Ann Landers" wasn't just a local feature, but was syndicated in forty papers throughout the country.

But Eppie Lederer was not deterred. She asked how the new Ann Landers would be selected. "By competition," Munnecke answered. "All the contestants will be given the same letters so their answers can be compared for substance and style. Twenty-one contestants—most of them writers and reporters, a few of them executive's wives—have been lined up." "Well, now you have twenty-two!" answered Eppie feistily. Munnecke saw no point in arbitrarily keeping Eppie out of the contest. She would soon realize of her own accord that she couldn't cut it, he thought. "Fine, you're in the contest," he said.

Eppie Lederer had never written a line for publication, and had never held a paying job. But she had other qualifications that were important: common sense, motivation, energy, a clear idea of right and wrong—and tremendous self-confidence. The competition stretched over the course of many weeks and she kept knocking out sample columns that were entertaining, authoritative, and easy to understand. The judges at the *Sun-Times* were impressed—but they didn't know by whom, because each contestant had a code number. This bit of blind justice was necessitated by the presence of the executives' wives in the contest.

Week by week, more would-be Ann Landerses were eliminated, until the final decision was made. The numbers were decoded and the winner was . . . Eppie Lederer? There was a small meeting with Eppie and a few executives. They gave her a less-than-ringing vote of confidence.

"You'll never last," they said.

Comment

This story teaches us the importance of acting on impulse and being spontaneous, rather than being restrained by logic and reason (which many of us seem to feel is the higher good). It's important to be able to simply seize the moment, and be mindful of opportunities when they present themselves.

$\mathcal{H}$*enry* was pushing the speed limit, going northbound on Ocean Parkway in Brooklyn, New York. He was headed to a business meeting and he had no time to spare. His eyes darted around as he surveyed the other cars, and he quickly maneuvered his way through the traffic like a rattlesnake in the rocks. Just as Henry was about to enter the Brooklyn Queens Expressway, he was cut off by a vehicle turning in from the service road. Henry opened his window and bellowed out some hardcore profanities. Sam, the other driver didn't want to take that lying down. He was in a rush as well. So Sam put his anger into action and cut Henry off at the next turn. Henry's escalating tension now turned to anger at this nervy driver who had now ticked him off twice. Within seconds, Henry cut him off, leaving only inches between the two cars. The heat escalated as the two guys drove like manic daredevils. Just as Henry thought he had left the other car in a cloud of dust, he looked in the rearview mirror and there it was again. Sam stepped on the gas, opened his window, and matched Henry's profanities and then some. This only added fuel to the fire in Henry's eyes, and the chase took on an even more perilous angst.

But just as suddenly as it had all begun, it came to an abrupt, screeching halt. Henry stopped and got out of his car, and was surprised to see Sam pull up right alongside him. The two men marched right into the same building. Then into the same elevator. There were raised brows as they glared at one another. Both were utterly bewildered as they walked out of the elevator and through the same door.

The truth became apparent as they began to speak in civil tones: Henry the supplier and Sam the customer were running late to meet each other.

Comment

Be kind to the people you meet on the highways and byways of your life because paths cross, lanes merge, and you never know where or when you may meet some of those very same people once again.

In 1900, while writing his famous book on the atmosphere, the French astronomer Camille Flammarion was working on the chapter on wind force when a sudden, unnaturally strong gust of wind swept all his papers off the table and blew them out of the window. As they fluttered to the ground several yards away from his home, an acquaintance of Flammarion's walked by and saw the pile of papers heaped on the ground. Looking them over, he discerned immediately that they were Flammarion's work and assumed that he had dropped them on his way to his publisher's. Hoping to avert an alarm being raised for the missing chapter, the man decided to personally deliver it to the publishing house. The editor, however, was absent from his office (which boasted huge windows that were open at the time), so Flammarion's friend simply placed the chapter on his desk, without leaving a note of explanation. The next day, Flammarion was astonished to learn from the editor that he had in his possession the missing chapter, and both concluded with growing excitement that it must have been blown in by the wind—completely intact! It was only several days later that the friend would meet Flammarion and disabuse him of this dramatic notion.

Despite his disappointment with the more pedestrian truth, Flammarion's interest in the subject was piqued, and became heightened by another true story of coincidence that was recounted to him by a friend:

When he was a young boy in Orléans, France, a certain Monsieur Deschamps was once given a piece of plum pudding—an uncommon delicacy and luxurious tidbit—by a Monsieur de Fortgibu, a middle-aged neighbor. Delighted by the treat, the young boy ate it slowly and with relish, savoring every tasty morsel. He did not encounter this rarity again until ten years later, when he saw a lone plum pudding sitting in a showcase in a Paris restaurant. With great elation, he excitedly entered the restaurant and asked if he could purchase the pudding, but was told that it had been ordered and specifically made for an elderly customer—Monsieur de Fortgibu. Many years later, Monsieur Deschamps was invited to a dinner party where the pièce de résistance was a singular extravagance—plum pudding. After years of hunting unsuccessfully for the delicacy, Monsieur Deschamps delightedly took a generous slice and casually remarked to the company that the only thing lacking now was the presence of Monsieur de Fortgibu. At that very moment, the door opened and a very old man, frail and disoriented, walked in. It was Monsieur de Fortgibu, who had gotten hold of the wrong address and had burst in on the party by mistake!

The starry Jerusalem sky seemed to portend all kinds of possibilities. Like many people, I had come to Israel on a personal pilgrimage to find something that was sorely lacking in my life. But unlike many others, I was not embarked upon a mission to find God, religion, or transcendence. I was here to find a mate.

Back in the States, all leads toward finding a spouse seemed to have fizzled out. I had been to singles parties, singles weekends, bars. Every possibility had been explored and exhausted.

My parents were frantic at having a twenty-nine-year-old unmarried daughter. I was equally unhappy.

One day, a friend told my parents that in Israel I could easily find a professional matchmaker who could help find me a husband. "Oh, but that's for the religious crowd," my parents demurred. "We're not observant."

"Don't worry," my parents' friend insisted, "there are matchmakers there for everybody! Let her give it a try."

My older single brother had been living in Israel for several years now, and he promised my parents he would look out for me. So I was shipped off by my anxious parents before I could murmur even a single word of protest.

Arriving for my first appointment with the matchmaker, I expected to find either a haggard crone or a wizened, wheezing, bent old man with a long graying beard—like a character out of *Fiddler on the Roof*—and I was not disappointed. My matchmaker wore a shapeless black dress, a fading babushka, and a toothless grin. I had to suppress a giggle when she announced her name as "Yenta." Communication was difficult, because she was not fluent in English and I spoke only a smattering of Hebrew. However, it seemed to me that the basics had been properly communicated, especially when her eyes lit up and she shouted exuberantly, "Have I got a match for you!" (really!)

"So, tell me about him," I asked eagerly.

"Well, honey," she answered, "he actually reminds me a little of you. Also American, very smart, professional, comes from a secular Jewish background like you. Let me get in touch with him and I'll call you later."

That evening, she reached me with the news that he was interested and wanted to see me right away. "Go to the little park behind the Israel museum," she said, "and he'll be waiting for you."

I gasped my astonishment at the breakneck pace of events. "Isn't he going to call me first?"

"American ways!" she retorted. "The first phone call makes only *tsuris* (trouble). You get *meshugga* (crazy) from the person's voice and then you're disappointed! Believe me, this way is much better!"

"Okay," I sighed, "what's his name?"

"His name?" she shrieked incredulously. "We don't give out names. We just tell you to meet."

"Okay," I sighed again, partly exasperated, partly overcome by the hilarity of the whole adventure. "Why can't you give me his name?"

"The Jewish world is very small!" she scolded. "If I give you his name, first thing you'll do is call a friend and ask, 'Do you know so and so?' and they'll say, 'Oh, him, are you crazy, he's not for you!' and the whole thing is spoiled. No, it's better that you shouldn't know his name until you meet him!"

"Okay," I sighed a final time. "How will I know it's him?"

"This I can tell you!" Yenta the Matchmaker shouted happily. "He'll be wearing a navy blue pinstripe suit with a red tie. He's about six feet tall and broad-shouldered. He'll be waiting for you in the Japanese Sculpture Garden."

I dressed quickly, giggling to myself as I applied my makeup in smooth, swift strokes, promising to wring my parents' necks when I saw them next. Yet, even as I chuckled over this escapade, my heart pounded just a little bit faster than usual, my eyes gleamed with an unusual brightness, and my cheeks were flushed with an uncommon glow. My skepticism was tempered by hope, an aching wish that miraculously, this unknown man would turn out to be my soul mate.

I grabbed a cab to the museum and saw the tall figure in the navy pinstripe suit waiting in the distance. His back was turned to me, but my heart lurched. He was muscular and well-built and wore his clothes with confidence. My hands trembled as I paid the taxi driver, and my knees almost buckled as I made my approach. The Jerusalem evening was cool, but small beads of sweat began to form and trickle down my face. My pulse raced. "Excuse me!" I shouted towards the figure as I advanced. "Hello . . . hello?" I called.

He wheeled around and I saw him for the first time. I had come face to face with . . . my brother!

—*Sarah Perlstein*

"**L***ittle* children, little troubles . . . big children, big troubles!" goes an old aphorism, and ever since my teenage son began driving, I have unfortunately seen both the wisdom—and the applicability—of this timeworn saying. He's already on his second car, the first having been stolen when he forgot to lock the doors. And just last week, he called me from Long Island, where he was visiting his girlfriend, and said, in a slightly puzzled tone, "Mom? I don't know how this happened . . . but my car's been towed!" He had parked the car so that it was blocking a neighbor's driveway, and the irate man had called the police. I sighed, and advised him to call his father immediately at both his office and beeper number, and inform him of the news. He promised that he would, but clearly he hadn't, because just ten minutes later, I got a call from my husband.

Instead of sounding irate, however, he sounded oddly triumphant. Something was clearly wrong. "Honey?" he said buoyantly. "You won't believe this! I'm here in Manhattan, driving near the pier, when suddenly—of all things—I see Joey's car sailing by me—stolen by a private tow truck! Well, I said to myself, no way are you getting away with this, mister! No way am I going to let Joey's *second* car be hijacked in clear sight of me! So I quickly flagged down a police car, who called in reinforcements, and the tow truck is now surrounded by swarms of cops! Yup, I sure nailed the bastards this time!" he concluded proudly.

— *Anna Lam*

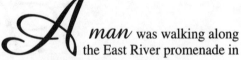 *man* was walking along the East River promenade in New York City in a very dejected state of mind. Actually, he was more than dejected—he was suicidal, and was seriously contemplating climbing over the railing that separated the promenade from the river and throwing himself in. Life felt empty, meaningless, hollow. He felt that the writing he had devoted himself to for decades had no real value, and didn't amount to much. What had he really accomplished in life?

As he stood staring at the dark, swirling water, trying to summon up the courage to do the deed, an excited voice interrupted his thoughts. "Excuse me," said a young woman, "I'm sorry to impose upon your privacy, but aren't you Christopher D'Antonio,* the writer?" He nodded indifferently. "I hope you don't mind my approaching you, but I just had to tell you what a difference your books have made in my life! They have helped me to an incredible degree, and I just wanted to thank you."

"No, my dear, it is *I* who have to thank *you*!" D'Antonio said as he wheeled around, turned away from the East River and headed back home.

Comment

It doesn't cost much to do a good deed. Benevolence does not have to be performed on a heroic or grandiose scale. The effect of a simple good word or a compliment can go a long way—longer than we may ever know. Sometimes, it can even save a life!

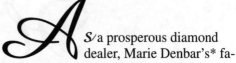

*A*s a prosperous diamond dealer, Marie Denbar's* father had outgrown his old office on Forty-seventh Street in Manhattan and had decided to rent larger quarters down the block. She was helping him move one day, when she met a neighboring merchant in front of the new place, who said casually, "Oh, it's your father who's moving in now? Well, I certainly hope he has better luck than all the previous tenants!"

"Why, what happened to them?" Marie asked, alarmed.

"Never saw a place so cursed," he muttered. "Everyone who moves in there stays one, maybe two years, then goes bankrupt. It's happened at least a dozen times."

Marie ran towards her father, who was unpacking a carton in the back of the store. "Dad, you mustn't rent this place; it brings bad luck!" And she recounted what she had just been told.

"Don't be ridiculous," Marie's father scoffed. "There's no such thing as a place having bad luck! I'm a successful businessman, and an empty space can't affect my fortunes. I'm ashamed I raised such a superstitious child."

Two years later, her father abandoned his new office, having lost, for the first time in his long career, hundreds of thousands of dollars that he was never able to recoup.

Comment

The coincidences *could* have served as an effective warning, but unfortunately the businessman chose not to heed them. As a result, he was forced to suffer the painful consequences.

There do seem to be places that pulsate with "bad energy," whether they are homes where a terrible tragedy or act of violence took place, or storefronts that are repeatedly vacated. One would probably be well-advised to avoid these places at all costs. It is only inviting trouble and tempting fate to ignore the messages of these "coincidences."

*H*e could easily afford the air fare, but David Brody* preferred instead to drive from Montreal to New York City, which he did, on a monthly basis. Ever since an acquaintance had been killed in a small-plane crash, he had avoided air travel whenever possible. Business brought him to New York frequently, and he knew the Montreal-to-New York route by heart. He loved to drive, and often made the entire seven-hour trip in one lap, bypassing rest areas, diners, and pit stops. He drove at night, when the highway was empty and he could speed undeterred towards his destination. He had been driving effortlessly to New York for ten years now and had never once encountered any problem with the commute. He always napped on the eve of his departure, guaranteeing that he would be wakeful and alert during the journey. He adhered faithfully to this practice and often joked to friends that when he drove to New York he was "on automatic."

But one evening in May 1996, an hour into his journey from Montreal, something unusual happened to David Brody. He suddenly felt inexplicably, overwhelmingly exhausted. Every bone in his body ached with weariness, and his eyelids felt heavy with sleep. He opened the car windows, hoping that a blast of cold night air would revive him, and took a long swig of coffee from the Thermos bottle nestled on the seat next to him, but neither did the trick. He felt utterly sapped, completely enervated, totally drained. And he was puzzled, almost alarmed, by this uncommon state of affairs: In all the years he had been driving to New York, he had never once experienced difficulty. He was only an hour into his journey and, besides, he had just woken up from a four-hour nap. This overpowering weariness didn't make any sense at all. Could he be ill?

Unable to drive any longer, David pulled off at the nearest exit, heading for an all-night gas station. He found himself in a small, obscure village in upstate New York which he had never heard of and had never noticed, even in passing. "Hi, how ya doing!" a jovial gas station attendant greeted him. "What can I do you for?"

"Any motels or hotels nearby?" David asked.

"You bet," answered the attendant. "I have a list with their phone numbers. Can I get it for you?" he offered graciously.

"Thanks a lot," David answered gratefully. But when he called all the lodgings on the list, he was disappointed to learn they were all solidly booked.

"Hmm, that's real unusual!" exclaimed the helpful gas station attendant. "Tourist season doesn't begin for another two weeks!"

"Well, how about places a little further away?" David asked anxiously.

"Here's a list of motels within a fifty-mile radius," said the attendant. "I'm sure you'll find a room in one of these places."

But to the attendant's surprise and David's consternation, these too were solidly booked. "Well, I'll be darned," muttered the attendant. "That's strange!"

"Listen," David said tensely, "I'm really desperate for a place to sleep. Is there maybe a sleep-away high school or college dormitory around here that might rent me a room for the night?"

"Nope, sorry," said the attendant, "can't say there is."

"Well," David said, feeling frantic for sleep and grasping at straws, "what about an old-age home?"

"Hey, you know," said the attendant happily, "there *is* one right down the road. And the owner, Patrick Riley,* is a real nice guy. Let me give him a call for you. I'll explain the situation and if he has an empty room, I'm sure he'll rent it out to you for the night." Sure enough, there was a spare bedroom in the home and it was made available to David for a modest fee.

In the morning, refreshed and renewed from a good night's sleep, David paid Riley, thanked him profusely, and turned to leave. Almost out the door, he suddenly wheeled around and made a U-turn back to the reception desk. "I've just had a thought," he told Riley. "Since I'm here already, maybe I could do a good deed. In addition to being a businessman, I also happen to be an ordained rabbi. Are there any Jewish residents in this home whose needs I might be able to minister to?"

"You know," Riley answered with a bemused look, "it's kinda strange you should ask. There *was* one Jewish patient here, but he died last night. Just about the same time you arrived here, as a matter of fact."

"So what are you planning to do about a funeral and burial?" David inquired.

"Well, Samuel Weinstein* was close to a hundred and outlived all his relatives. He had no next-of-kin listed on his documents, and he died without a nickel to his name. There's no Jewish cemetery around here and I think the closest one is in Albany—a good hundred miles away. So we just figured on burying him in our local Christian cemetery, which has a pauper's field reserved for these situations."

"Listen," David said urgently, "that's very nice of you, but since he was Jewish, I'm sure he would have wanted to be buried in a Jewish cemetery. I happen to have taken my station wagon with me this time— usually I drive to New York in my Corolla—and I have room in the back for a coffin. Maybe you could arrange to release the body to me, and I'll take it to New York with me for a Jewish burial."

Later that day David arrived at the offices of a prominent Jewish burial society in Brooklyn. "So terribly sorry," murmured the director. "We could gladly do a free funeral for the man, but we don't own any cemetery plots where we can bury him. Why don't you try the Jewish burial society in Queens?" But in this other heavily Jewish borough of New York City, David encountered the same problem. Here, too, the director shook his head mournfully and said, "You know, we just never anticipated a need like this before and we never made provisions for this kind of situation. I could try to raise funds from charitable organizations or individuals to buy a plot, but it might take days. I wish I could help you." But as David turned to leave, the director shouted, "Hey, wait a minute! I just remembered that someone once told me that the Jewish burial society in Washington Heights in Upper Manhattan has just such a fund. Why don't you try them?"

In Washington Heights, David finally met with success. "Yes, indeed!" exclaimed an ancient-looking man whom he found in this cluttered, dusty office. "We do have a special charitable fund that provides free funerals *and* burials for the destitute. About fifty years ago, a wealthy Jewish philanthropist in our community was concerned that the occasion might arise when Jews would die paupers or without next of kin. To address that situation, he endowed a special fund that bought burial plots for this express purpose. We have in fact several plots set aside in our cemetery that we use. I'll take care of everything," he assured David. "First things first, though—there's some paperwork that has to be done," he said, pulling out a sheaf of documents.

"What's the deceased man's name, please?" he inquired, pen poised in the air.

"Samuel Weinstein."

"Hmm," said the director, "that name sounds familiar. Mind if I take a look at the body?" he asked, heading for the station wagon.

When the director returned to the office, David noticed a small tear trickling down his cheek. "My dear friend," he announced to David, "not only will we be happy to give Samuel Weinstein a plot in our cemetery, we will give him the place of honor! God's ways are indeed mysterious, my friend. The man in the back of your station wagon happens to be none other than the very same philanthropist who originally established the Free Burial Fund. He will be laid to rest in the cemetery plot he himself purchased. . . . Your journey was long and arduous, Mr. Brody. But through your most commendable efforts, Samuel Weinstein has indeed been returned to his rightful place!"

Comment
Our actions are like a stone thrown into the river. The impact of their effects ripples on and on.

*A*llen Falby, an El Paso County highway patrolman, and Alfred Smith, a businessman, met for the first time on a hot June night when Falby crashed his motorcycle.

He was racing down the road to overtake a speeding truck when the vehicle slowed down to make a turn. Unaware that the truck was slowing, Falby slammed full throttle into its tailgate. The crack-up demolished the cycle and nearly amputated one of Falby's legs. As he lay in agony on the pavement, a pool of blood began to form beneath his shattered limb. He had ruptured an artery in his leg and was bleeding to death.

It was then that fate brought Falby and Smith together.

Smith had been driving home along the road when he saw the accident. Shaken but alert, he was out of his car and bending over the badly injured man almost before the sound of the impact died on the night air.

Smith wasn't a doctor but could see what had to be done for the dying patrolman. Whipping off his tie, Smith quickly bound Falby's leg in a crude tourniquet. It worked. The flow of blood slackened to a trickle and then stopped entirely. When the ambulance arrived a few minutes later, Smith learned for the first time that he had saved Falby's life.

Five years later, around Christmas, Falby was on highway night patrol when he received a radio call from headquarters to investigate an accident along U.S. 80. A car had smashed into a tree. A man was in serious condition, and an ambulance was on the way.

Falby reached the wreck well before the ambulance. Pushing his way past a group of frightened bystanders, he found the injured man slumped unconscious across the torn car seat.

The man's right pants leg was saturated and sticky with blood. He had severed a major artery and was bleeding to death. Well trained in first aid, Falby quickly applied a tourniquet above the ruptured artery. When the bleeding stopped, he pulled the man from the car and made him more comfortable on the ground.

That's when Falby recognized the victim. He was Alfred Smith, the man who had saved his own life five years before.

Fate had brought the two men together again—and both meetings had been for the same purpose: for one man to save the life of the other in exactly the same way.

"Well," Falby told Doug Storer of the *National Tattler,* who first reported the story, "you might say, it all goes to prove that one good tourniquet deserves another!"

⸙

Comment

When passing someone in need of help, people frequently think: "I'm busy, let someone else stop; it doesn't have to be me."

But what if the person who needs the help is really *you*, only the time hasn't come yet for you to see that so clearly?

$\mathcal{O}n$ a glass-enclosed case in Philadelphia's Maritime Museum lies a yellowing, tattered, frayed copy of a novel published in 1898 by Morgan Robertson. The novel, a work of fiction, recounts the story of the sinking of a big, fast, and luxurious ship, delineating all the details and events leading up to what the book describes as the greatest ocean disaster in history.

In the novel, Robertson describes a colossal ship, practically a behemoth, believed to be unsinkable, embarking on its maiden voyage in the month of April. It is out to set a record, and some of the wealthiest and most influential society figures from both Europe and America are on board. It is speeding along the northern lanes of Atlantic travel when it suddenly crashes into an iceberg and goes down swiftly. An inadequate number of lifeboats—only twenty-four—are on board, and consequently there is an enormous loss of life.

The name of Robertson's fictional ship? . . . the *Titan.*

Fourteen years later, in April 1912, the world-famous *Titanic* went down. The details of Robertson's story (called *The Wreck of the Titan*) paralleled the actual events of the sinking of the *Titanic* with uncanny faithfulness.

The fictional *Titan* had 3,000 persons aboard, the Titanic 2,207. Both were considered unsinkable because of their allegedly watertight compartments, and both made their maiden voyage in April. The length of the *Titan* was 800 feet, the *Titanic* was 882.5, and both used three propellers. The *Titan*'s speed at impact with the iceberg was 25 knots; the *Titanic*'s 23. The displacement tonnage of the *Titan* was 75,000 while the *Titanic*'s was 66,000. And while there was a grossly inadequate number of lifeboats aboard the fictional *Titan*—an appallingly meager twenty-four—the *Titanic* had even fewer—only twenty in all.

For two years they worked in the same section at the post office. "Just another new person," she said when he transferred in.

Many nights they'd find themselves working next to each other on one of the belts, sorting envelopes in the main Philadelphia office at 30th and Market. They'd make small talk—the weather, the job—then go their own ways.

But never did the environment get personal. It took a mutual friend's questioning for postal workers Yvette "Cookie" Richardson and James Austin to realize that they were long-lost brother and sister—who had not seen each other in more than 30 years.

When he was an infant and she was a toddler, their South Philadelphia family dissolved. Since then, they have traveled separate but similar paths, going to school within blocks of each other, both studying accounting, both eventually landing among the 1,825 postal employees who work the 4 P.M. shift at 30th Street, culling Philadelphians' mail.

"Working in the same department side by side," Richardson says, shaking her head. "The same place, the same time, every day. What are the odds of that?"

Their paths started to cross one night in June, at the beginning of the shift, as Austin, 33, was talking to a fellow shop steward about the movies. They got into how Austin never cried, and the steward mentioned that he was just like her friend Cookie.

The steward, Barrie Bowens, told him she even cried at funerals of people she didn't know. Austin started talking about how his father died young and he never knew his mother.

For some reason Bowens asked Austin his mother's name, and he said, Veronica Potter.

"That's Cookie's mom's name," she replied.

He told her he did have a sister, although he hadn't seen her since he was a baby. Her name was Yvette.

"That's Cookie's name," Bowens replied.

Talk to her, Austin urged Bowens. For the next several hours, his head spun as he moved the mail. He was seven months old when his father, James Austin Sr., left his mother. He was sent to live with his father's parents, who raised him in North Philadelphia. The girl, 14 months older, stayed with their mother in South Philadelphia.

Several times he had looked through the phone book under Potter for his mother, whom he met once again when he was 14. But she wasn't listed. He figured it wasn't meant to be.

About 6 P.M. that night in June, Bowens approached her friend Cookie and told her they had to talk.

According to Richardson, who is 34, Bowens managed to tread delicately around the subject, not wanting to upset her. Did she have a brother? Did she have any idea where he might be?

"I met someone," Bowens finally told her. "Would you like to meet him?"

"I'm thinking, 'Yeah, sure,'" recalled Richardson.

"Where is he?"

"He's close."

"How close?"

"In Cancellation."

"Cancellation?"

Austin was getting off early that night, about 9:30 P.M., so the two women hurried down one floor. "We were jumping, running through Cancellation," Richardson said. Austin was walking behind a counter, when she saw him, sturdy and broad-backed with deep brown eyes and full cheeks, a kind face.

"Oh, my God! It is him," she said. She had an old picture of their father and the resemblance was suddenly startling. Austin was named after his father, and Richardson remembered how he had been called Little Jimmy.

They grabbed each other and wouldn't let go. Neither brother nor sister cried. Bowens did.

Since then, their story has moved like priority mail around the post office, where 4,100 people work. Yesterday they were standing next to each other again, posing for pictures, giving interviews above the din of metal carts rattling along concrete floors.

On a Saturday last month, in scorching heat, Richardson and her mother drove to Southwest Philadelphia, where Austin lives with his family. The three were together for the first time in more than 30 years.

His wife entertained graciously, Richardson said. Austin found the reunion to be easier than he had anticipated. "I thought it would be real awkward, but it wasn't," he said.

He said he and his mother talked for a long time, dealing gently with difficult subjects. "She did tell me she was young at the time and already had one child," Austin said.

He and his sister caught up on their lives, and they realized they had a few more things in common. She was at Girls High School the same time he was next door at Central. Both have studied accounting. They have similar senses of humor and like the same sort of movies, their co-workers tell them. Co-workers see it more than the brother and sister do.

In fact, about a year ago, one of the 30th Street workers asked Austin if Richardson was his sister. He said no, never thinking twice about it—until a few weeks ago.

"We're still getting to know each other," Austin said. They take their breaks together and talk.

"We're basically trying to establish a friendship," she said. "He's a nice person." She had never sought to find her brother, figuring he had a right to his own life. "You hope he's happy and say, 'Maybe one day . . .'"

Comment

That which we hope for, dream about, long for and seek, may not be far off from ourselves. Finding it may simply require a mere look over the shoulder, a glance into our very own backyard, a deeper knowledge of the person standing by our side.

*A*s/the owner of The Better Half, a plus-size specialty shop in Brooklyn that has been in existence for thirteen years, I have come to know and love my customers, most of whom are "repeats." Even though they often vow to me that this is the last time they'll be shopping for large sizes because they're enrolling in a gym . . . starting a new diet . . . beginning therapy . . . working with a hypnotist—almost all of them come back regularly. I say this, not with disdain, but tenderly, with affection. I myself am a large-size woman and know the struggle.

Susan Bailey* was a "repeat" customer. An executive with a big real estate company in Manhattan, she would dart into the store twice a year (always in a big hurry), throw suits over her arm (she never tried them on, asserting that she was a perfect size 20 and knew already which cuts of which companies fit her), dash up to the counter to pay, and sprint out to a waiting car. She always went for the best: Jones New York and Harve Benard were her favorites, and she consistently ran up a tab that totaled well over a thousand dollars. Needless to say, I would get an adrenaline rush whenever she would hurtle through the door (thousand-dollar customers are not easy to come by these days) and would give her my devoted attention. Even though it was hard for me to keep up with her frenetic pace as she sped through the store, I faithfully followed her and serviced her every need, panting for minutes after she had made her hasty exit. Despite the fact that she created a hurricane in her wake, I was always delighted when she arrived. I was gratified that a big-time executive from Manhattan would patronize my humble store, even though I knew it was my huge discounts on designer clothes that were the draw, and not my sparkling personality. I was flattered anyway.

One day, I was reflecting about the customers I hadn't seen for a while, when I suddenly realized that Susan Bailey hadn't been around for a long time. A *very* long time, I thought with a start. Maybe even two years. I wondered what had happened to her. Had she been one of the minority who had gone on a successful diet and maintained her weight loss? Had she moved away? Had someone in the store insulted her unknowingly? Was she shopping somewhere else? I thought of calling her, but didn't want to be pushy. Nonetheless, I sent her a postcard announcing a special sale. It came back marked "Addressee Unknown." I felt a twinge of loss when the postcard was returned—where had Susan disappeared to . . . and why?

Every now and then, I leave the store to check out the competition. I make the rounds of all the plus-size stores in Manhattan, trying to spot trends, see which designers are hot, discover new labels. I make these forays two or three times a year. I was on just this kind of expedition one day, and was peering into the windows of Jeanne Rafal, a large-size specialty shop opposite Lord & Taylor on Fifth Avenue, when I heard a plaintive voice behind me. "Please, Ma'am, can you spare some change?" I wheeled around to face my petitioner. My jaw dropped open in astonishment and disbelief. It was Susan Bailey.

Gone were the Jones New York suit, the chic haircut, the flawless makeup. In the place of the woman I had known stood a stranger, disheveled, unwashed, and disoriented. "Susan!" I shrieked. "What's happened to you?"

She didn't seem to recognize me. "Please Ma'am," she repeated piteously, "can you spare some change?"

I pulled out all the money in my wallet and gave her forty dollars. As she stood looking at the bounty in her hand with delight, I gazed at her, stricken. "Susan," I said gently, "let's go somewhere to eat and talk." She shook her head no. "Susan," I said again, "don't you remember me . . . The Better Half of Brooklyn?"

For a moment, the cloudy eyes cleared. "Oh, yeah, sure," she said.

"Susan . . . what's happened?" I asked softly in what I hoped was a matter-of-fact manner, trying to conceal my shock and pain at her condition.

"Oh . . ." she muttered vaguely, "the real estate market went bust . . . I lost my job . . . my mother died . . . my brother stole my inheritance and kicked me out of our house . . . all kinds of terrible things."

"Where are you living now?"

"In a shelter," she mumbled, embarrassed. Then, just as suddenly as it had appeared, the spark of intelligence that had gleamed briefly in her eyes dimmed, and she became muddled and confused again.

"Susan, would you like to come stay in my house for awhile? I have a finished basement where you could live comfortably," I offered.

"No, no, no," she said, starting to back away, looking at me with suspicion. "I have to leave now; I have an appointment. I have to go!"

"Susan!" I pleaded, running after her. "I want to help you. Here's my number—please call me." Apathetically, she took my card.

"Susan," I pressed, "will you call me?"

"Sure, sure," she muttered, retreating quickly.

But she never did.

— *Yitta Halberstam Mandelbaum*

Several years ago, I treated my two grandchildren to dinner at a fast-food restaurant on Avenue J in Brooklyn, in a thriving shopping district. Although it is now closed, at that time a movie theatre adjoined the restaurant, and my grandchildren happened to notice the marquee as we passed by. It was displaying the name of a popular Disney movie, one my grandchildren hadn't yet seen. Needless to say, almost as soon as they began tearing into their burgers, they began campaigning to see the movie. Unfortunately, I had spent all my money on dinner, and literally didn't have a penny left. I tried to explain this to them, but they were very young and didn't understand. In fact, they began to wail in such a heartrending way that I had to take them out of the restaurant because they were disturbing the other diners.

On the street corner, I went through my pocketbook over and over again, checking every zippered compartment, shaking out every paper, hoping against hope that I would find a ten-dollar bill hidden somewhere, which is all that I required to get us into the movie. But not an extra penny dropped into my waiting palm. As the children's persistent crying rose to a shrill crescendo, I frantically turned every pocket of both the coat and suit I was wearing inside out, but again my efforts were in vain. Nothing. The cacophony of cries issuing from the children was now high-pitched and intense. I bit my lips in distress and muttered to myself in quiet desperation, "Oh, God. If I only had ten dollars. What I wouldn't give for ten dollars right this minute!"

Suddenly, to my shock and astonishment, dollar bills started floating down—seemingly from the sky—fluttering and landing at my feet. Stunned, I looked up at the second-story windows of the store buildings on the street, certain that someone holding the money had looked out a window and inadvertently dropped it. However, no anxious face peered out of any window, and no hastening figure hurried out of any building to retrieve the cash.

Stupefied, I bent down to pick up the dollars, which totaled ten in all—exactly the amount I needed for the tickets—one adult, two children!

I waited for about fifteen minutes to see if anyone would appear to claim the money. When nobody did, and I had satisfied my moral impulse to try to see that the money was rightfully returned, I took the children in tow and headed for the movie. In my head, I thanked my unknown and mysterious benefactor. I paid for the tickets, and went into the theatre. The movie was just about to begin.

— *Ettie Grossman*

Comment

With God, we are co-creators of our existence and destiny. When we declare for ourselves what we want in life, this declaration somehow goes into a law of mind and comes back to us as experience. Spoken words are the foundation of what we continually create in our own lives. We should never underestimate or limit their tremendous power.

*U*nrelentingly logical, I have always been a math-science person. I graduated high school in 1970 as a math major and went to UCLA, where I received a Bachelor of Arts in Theoretical Mathematics in 1974. Then, being a practical sort who aspired to employment, I entered UCLA Dental School and graduated with a Doctorate of Dental Surgery four years later. At that time, I had fully intended to pursue a career as a dentist. One doesn't usually attend dental school for self-actualization.

That was twenty-two years ago. And during those past twenty-two years, I've never picked up a drill—euphemistically known as a handpiece—nor have I scraped a single tartar-coated tooth. Instead, I am now a writer of detective fiction, choosing to explore the human condition instead of oral hygiene.

I couldn't pinpoint the metamorphosis, but I am glad it worked out that way. I could list several factors that steered me toward mystery writing—a desire for justice, a suspicious nature, an overactive imagination, and, of course, a penchant for the bizarre. All of the above can be summed up by what transpired the day I nabbed a mugger.

On that particular morning, my then four-year-old son—now a strapping lad of eighteen—had chosen to come down with a high fever and a burning sore throat. I suspected strep throat. My mother was at the house, lending a comforting hand while caring for my year-old daughter. Rather than drag the entire crew to the pediatrician, I suggested that my mother take a walk with the baby to the corner bakery while I ran my preschooler to the doctor's. It was a fine LA day—sunny, but not too hot. Yes, I thought, a walk would be refreshing for both Grandma and baby. Not to mention the fact that the soft-hearted bakery lady was always good for a couple of extra cookies for my tyke.

Grandma, baby, and stroller left first. I followed a few minutes later, and I could see them easily about a half-block up. As I pulled out of my driveway, I noticed a car near them but on the opposite side . . . slowing . . . then stopping. A young man got out of the front passenger's seat and started walking. And walking. And walking. Across the street from my mother and daughter, about twenty feet behind them.

But keeping pace with them.

I straightened the wheel of my automobile and shifted into drive. The car up the street was still there . . . creeping by . . . slowly.

And the man kept walking. Still across the way from my mother and child, still keeping pace.

That is odd, I thought. When I let someone out of the car, that person usually goes into a house. He doesn't keep walking for a block or two.

I'm being paranoid, I decided. Nevertheless, this was my daughter, this was my mother. I drove down the street, pointedly behind the creeping car. And then it drove away.

Just like that.

And I felt a little better.

Meanwhile, the man across the street kept strolling aimlessly, not doing anything suspicious. I waved to my mom and she waved back. Then I drove off.

But something nagged at my gut.

I turned the corner, made a series of right turns and circled around the block. Then I caught up with my mother, who was blithely ambling in the sunshine. Again, we exchanged waves, although she did have a puzzled look on her face. It said, "Why did you come back?"

And the man across the street continued to keep pace with my mother.

Too much TV, I chided myself.

Too many detective novels.

I drove off. One block, then another.

But this was my daughter, this was my mother.

Again, I retraced my steps.

By the time I returned, my mother was down on her knees, her hand gripping her head. The stroller had been tipped over. My heart raced as I pulled over, screaming, "Are you all right?"

"He took my purse," she shouted hysterically.

Frantically, she pointed around the corner.

Again, I asked if she was all right. Was the baby all right?

Yes, my mother answered. Despite the fact that she had two scraped knees from her fall, she was fine.

Anger coursed through my body. This was my *baby*, this was my *mother*!

With my son firmly ensconced in his car seat, I gave chase. Admittedly, not the brightest decision I've made. But I reacted rather than considered.

The French Connection it wasn't. I was in a car and he was on foot, so I caught up rather handily. Leaning on the horn, I rolled down the window and screamed at the top of my lungs, "Drop the purse, now!"

"Drop the purse, now!" my son imitated from the back seat.

But the sucker kept running. In retrospect, I think it was more in fear than in obstinacy. He pumped his legs hard and fast, racing with the wind. *Chariots of Felony.* But even Jesse Owens wouldn't have had a chance against a V-8 engine. I kept honking the horn, shrieking at him to drop the purse.

"Drop the purse, now!" my son aped.

Up ahead was a pedestrian. Two of them. I don't remember much about them. Except that they were male and one of them was wearing a yellow plaid sports coat. I don't know why that particular fact registered, but it did. And it was the one in the plaid coat who pulled out the gun . . . pointed it at the runner and yelled "Freeze!"

And the man froze.

Just like in the movies.

I jerked the car into a driveway, not really understanding what was going on.

Plaid Coat instructed the runner to drop the purse. "Drop it," he shouted. "Drop it, drop it, drop it!"

The runner had that deer-in-the-headlights look on his face. He dropped the purse.

Plaid Coat told him to hit the ground.

Just like in the movies.

I bounded out of the car, spoke to Plaid Coat. I pointed to the runner, pointed to my mother's stolen handbag and angrily said, "That's not his purse!"

Neighbors began filing out, offering to call the police. Which was kind of redundant.

Because Plaid Coat had turned out to be an off-duty policeman who had been visiting his father, heard me leaning on the horn, and came out to investigate.

Now he took off his belt and began to secure the suspect. At that point, I went back to my mother. She was upright and so was the stroller. I pulled the car over, loaded them both inside. Her palms were sore, her pants were ripped at the knees. But as promised, both she and my baby were all right.

"He took my purse!" my mother sobbed.

"We caught him, Ma," I said.

"You what?"

"We caught him. We have your purse!"

"Oh, that's good," my mother answered. "That's very good."

"Very good," my son coughed from the back seat.

We returned to the scene of the crime, now thick with patrol cars. I explained my story as I held my baby, and my mother explained her story from inside of my car. The uniformed police officers were amazed.

"We never catch these guys," one of them told me.

My mother was required to come down to the station to claim the purse. It would be there waiting for her. The police only needed a couple of hours to process the paperwork.

"She can't just take it now?" I asked. "Save us both a trip?"

"Nope. Evidence."

"Fine," I said.

They congratulated me. I took my mother and baby home. We were all pretty shaken, but life does go on.

I loaded my son back into his car seat and zipped him over to the pediatrician. A good move on my part.

Indeed, it was strep throat.

— *Faye Kellerman*

Comment

This story by bestselling author Faye Kellerman vividly exemplifies the maxim "God helps those who helps themselves." It is probably correct to assume that many people finding themselves in the exact same situation would have been far more passive than Ms. Kellerman, who admirably assumed a proactive stance here. Although other people would have undoubtedly turned their attention towards helping their mother and child off the sidewalk and uttered a silent prayer of thanks that both had escaped harm, they probably would not have doggedly pursued the mugger until he was tagged by the undercover cop. Was the sudden and miraculous appearance of "Plaid Jacket" a mere fluke, or was it God coming on board to assist Faye, to repay her for her determination that the miscreant who preyed on elderly ladies and helpless toddlers be brought to justice? Thankfully, through her tenacious efforts, he was!

Permissions

"Reunited Vets Find Third Lost Buddy," written by Karen Henderson, appeared in the April 20, 1996 issue of the *Cleveland Plain Dealer*. Reprinted by permission.

"Twists of Fate Take a Family From Grief to Joy," written by Christine Biederman, appeared in the March 4, 1996 issue of the *New York Times*. Reprinted by permission.

The Networker. Excerpt by Dr. Harriet Lerner. Reprinted by permission of the author.

Incredible Coincidences: *The Baffling World of Synchronicity*. Copyright ©1979 by Alan Vaughan. Reprinted by permission of HarperCollins Publishers.

Excerpt from *Journey To My Father, Isaac Bashevis Singer*, by Israel Zamir, copyright ©1994 by Sifriat Poelim, translation copyright ©1995 by Arcade Publishing. Reprinted by permission of Arcade Publishing, Inc.

Excerpt from *The Net of Dreams*, by Julie Salomon, copyright ©1995 by Julie Salomon. Reprinted by permission of Random House, Inc.

Excerpt from "Dear Abby" column, copyright ©September 1995. Reprinted by permission of Universal Press Syndicate.

Excerpt from Chapter 13, *Eppie: The Story of Ann Landers* by Margo Howard, copyright ©1982. Reprinted by permission of The Putnam Publishing Group.

"Postal Coworkers Learn They're Siblings" by Dan Rubin, August 3, 1995. Reprinted by permission from the *Philadelphia Inquirer*.

Acknowledgments

We have been blessed with the most wonderful editor, Pamela Liflander, whose expert advice, gentle wisdom, and intelligent counsel greatly enriched our experience. Virginia Rubens, copy editor par excellence, did a superb job with our material. Elise Bauman's editorial contributions were also extremely valuable. We are very grateful to all three, whose combined efforts produced this work. We also want to thank our agents, Carol Mann and Channa Taub, for bringing our book to Adams and helping turn our dream into reality.

Judith would like to thank her father of blessed memory, Harry B. Frankel, whose broad intellect, robust humor, and richly colorful personality left a lasting impression. Her mother, Rose, lent her creativity, devotion, and uncompromising love. Her older sister Hedy and husband, Myer Feiler, and their children provided great warmth and a generous spirit. Her younger sister, Estee, has been a partner throughout this adventure. Isser and Malku Handler are like a second set of parents and have contributed generously. Anne Leventhal defies the stereotype of mother-in-law, and provides a profound sense of support. Pessi Dinnerstein has continuously pointed onward and upward with her insights and encouraging words.

Yitta would like to thank Charles Mandelbaum, who was extremely generous, especially for repeated intrusions into his law office to use his computer, copier, and fax. Rabbi Meir Fund graciously spent time discussing the theological implications of coincidences. Miriam Halberstam, world traveler and devoted sister, scouted coincidence stories for us wherever she went.

Lastly, we wish to thank our husbands, Mordechai Mandelbaum and Jules Leventhal, who added their deep wisdom, extreme patience, kindness, and generosity of spirit, which gave us the love and support we needed to grow and complete this project.

Small Miracles, Volume II

Introduction

Throughout our journey in life we encounter many teachers and signposts that lead us along our way. They whisper words of wisdom and encouragement to us as we struggle and yearn; they invite us into new spheres of Being and Existence. They let us know that in our existential loneliness we are not alone—that Spirit surrounds us always.

Chief among these signposts and teachers is none other than the phenomenon that some choose to call coincidence, but that we—the authors—recognize and firmly believe are nothing more and nothing less than "small miracles."

And it is precisely at this moment in time that we need "small miracles" in our lives—now more than ever before.

Why is the identification of coincidences as "small miracles" crucial to our spiritual and personal growth?

When a person dismissively shrugs off a "coincidence" as merely a random event or pure happenstance, he is doing himself—and the universe—a grave disservice. He is failing to apprehend a divine moment that was gifted to him by God, a ripe and full moment that comes in the great flow of energy in which he is a spark. Had he recognized the coincidence for what it truly is—God's gentle tap on the shoulder or God's veritable shout: "Hello from Heaven!"—his spark would have united with other scattered sparks and ignited into one giant flame. He would have entered a corridor into a different dimension, and his days and nights would have been illuminated by a brilliant light. But the opportunity for endless transformation is lost when "coincidences" are perceived in pedestrian terms as simply "luck" or "chance."

How much more fortunate is the individual possessing enough awareness to recognize coincidences for what they truly are—mysterious, magical, and awe-inspiring testimonials to God's presence in our ordinary, everyday lives. This graced individual will most assuredly be filled with what we like to call "spiritual optimism." She will believe that the events in her life have purpose, that the "coincidences" in her life have purpose and that—most important of all—her very life is hallowed by sacred purpose. She will see the holiness of day-to-day existence, the holiness of herself. And, in a world where nihilistic forces threaten at times to submerge us, this is the greatest blessing of all.

To believe that nothing is an accident, but that everything is foreordained, fills us, paradoxically, with both vigor and serenity. It makes us examine our lives more closely; makes us more attentive to detail. And, as the saying goes: "God is in the details." Cultivating consciousness about the "coincidences" that come into our lives fills us with excitement and gratitude. We feel that we are truly God's children and that He is with us, always.

During our book tour for *Small Miracles* last year, we were continuously made aware of the amazing role that the power of belief plays in choreographing the flow of our lives. We saw with tremendous clarity the workings of the spiritual principle that *thoughts create realities,* and that *vibrating a certain energy attracts a like energy to it.* What do we mean by this?

When you believe in coincidences, they pour into your life at an exhilarating, almost dizzying rate. When you require something from the universe, and you truly believe that the universe is responsive, then you most assuredly will receive its full bounty for the asking.

Here are just a few examples that vividly illustrate this point:

On book tour, we lived, breathed, dreamed, ate, and spoke "coincidences." Our consciousness was clearly in alignment with the universe's. As a result, strange things happened almost every day.

We had talked incessantly about approaching one of the most famous spiritual writers of our time to discuss *Small Miracles.* Since we were not personally acquainted with him, we faced a challenge. How to meet the man and humbly submit our request? We explored many avenues, and finally it was decided that Yitta would enroll in a one-night course that the "guru" was giving. Surely at some time during the three-hour class there would be a window of opportunity that Yitta could seize to our advantage. However, a day before the course was scheduled, we were disappointed to learn that it had been canceled due to the teacher's unexpected illness. Now what? It was a setback, but we were not discouraged. We both vibrated an intense need to meet this man. The very next week Judith flew to Washington, D.C., on book tour, sat in the airplane seat that had been "randomly" assigned to her, and discovered . . . to her shock and delirious joy . . . that her seatmate was none other than the spiritual guru we had resolved to meet! Not only did they engage in animated discussion during the entire plane ride, but after swapping personal biographies they discovered that they had lived in the exact same house in Crown Heights, Brooklyn, when Judith was a toddler and the spiritual leader was a college student, and that the spiritual leader's parents had been Judith's parents' landlords many years ago!

During Yitta's book tour to Brookline, Massachusetts, she wandered early one spring morning through the maze of leafy residential streets in search of a restaurant where she could have breakfast. Finding herself hopelessly lost, she approached the first person she saw walking down the street and asked for directions. She explained that she was from New York and didn't know her way around the neighborhood. The man smiled pleasantly and said that he too was originally from New York, and asked her name. When she introduced herself, the man's smile froze, and he took a few steps back and stared at her in incredulity. Then he recovered his composure and introduced himself. "I am Yitzhak Halberstam," he said simply, "your long-lost cousin!"

One of our favorite stories in the first *Small Miracles* book came from the *Oprah Winfrey Show*'s Valentine's Day special of 1996, which featured an elderly couple who had been married for over fifty years. We wrote the story based on the transcript of the show, but were unable to track down the individuals themselves, a fact we greatly lamented. We often spoke of our great desire to meet them personally, but they had asked Oprah's producers for privacy, and their whereabouts were shrouded in secrecy. We had no idea where they lived. One evening, Judith was delivering a talk at the Barnes and Noble bookstore in Bayside, Queens, and during the question and answer period that followed, a hand shot up from someone sitting in the back. "Page 129," he announced proudly. "Ex-excuse me?" Judith stammered, confused. "You wrote our story on page 129 of your book," the man repeated genially. It was the Valentine's Day couple from the *Oprah Winfrey Show*—the couple we had yearned to meet for so long!

During another question and answer period—this one following a talk we gave to eight hundred people in Baltimore—a woman stood up and announced her validation of the perspective on coincidences that we had just offered. "Whenever I need something," she stated confidently, "I just talk to God and tell him what it is I require, and then he gives it to me." She went on to say that she constantly won door prizes at parties—and she always won items that she had a specific need for. After this woman spoke, the question and answer period was wrapped up, and the second part of the program—a raffle—was begun. When the Grand Prize raffle winner—chosen randomly onstage by a blindfolded Yitta, who plunged her hand into a box containing hundreds of tickets—was announced, a collective gasp was heard throughout the auditorium. Guess who the winner was???

When we pray, we are speaking to God. When "coincidences" occur, it is God speaking to us. To be attuned to these moments is truly to be awake to the Divine that calls us every day.

But beyond providing us with testimonials to God's presence in a spiritually barren landscape where there are few useful clues, "coincidences" also contain within themselves precious moral lessons and profound teachings. Many of the stories in this book revolve around the concept of what some people call "karma," a certain payback the protagonist receives from the universe, a manifestation that "what goes around comes around." Other stories illustrate how the universe answers— through a seeming coincidence—a question or prayer the protagonist has articulated; still other stories demonstrate the age-old wisdom that we always reap the harvest of seeds that we sow in life.

When "coincidences" happen and we are aware of the messages we are being sent, a delicious sense of communion, of harmony with the universe, unfolds. We sense that everything is One, and that if we can only integrate these messages—these little bulletins from God—we can grow as moral and spiritual beings.

We are exhilarated when coincidences come into our lives, for we see them as blessings and gifts. Many people bemoan the lack of open, revealed miracles in the late twentieth century, maintaining that their absence makes the sustenance of faith that much harder. Seas don't part; God doesn't appear in a pillar of flame to talk with us; recalcitrant humans are not transmogrified into columns of salt. And it *is* true—the more grandiose, apocalyptic miracles of yesteryear do seem elusive. Nonetheless, we staunchly maintain that "small miracles" are everywhere, and that awareness of their existence can lead us to renewed faith.

Many people have written and told us that after they read *Small Miracles,* momentous changes began to occur in their lives, and that as soon as they opened their hearts to "coincidences," the coincidences came flowing in. Or they began to examine the past with a different eye and recognized that miracles had been happening all along, but they simply hadn't identified them by their rightful name! We hope that a newfound awareness will develop in your life after reading this book, and that you, too, will begin experiencing the wonders, the bounty, the splendors of life that resonate with those who believe in "small miracles."

"There are only two positions you can take," Albert Einstein once said. "Either you believe that nothing in life is a miracle, or you believe that *everything* in life is a miracle."

It is clear that the individual whose journey in life is more joyous, more meaningful, and more sublime, is the individual who subscribes to the second view.

By opening the pages of this book, you have already begun the voyage.

Travel with us into the Light, as we bless and receive the joy that "small miracles" always bring.

$\mathcal{S}he$ wanted to live out in the country, where the poet in her could find its muse, and be inspired.

I was a hard-nosed reporter whose pulse quickened at the sound of a police siren or the wail of an ambulance—who liked the fast tempo of city life, the energy it sizzled with, the babble of different tongues, the gritty noise of survival. Besides, I was a rising young star in the world of broadcast news, and I couldn't give up my job now at the big station where I worked. There was nothing for me out there in the country, and a long commute to the city was unappealing.

As always, she was the one asked to make the sacrifices in our marriage, the one who deferred a dream.

"At least," she sighed with resignation, "a big yard with lots of trees and bushes and flowers and birds."

I promised her that and I kept my word.

The house was small but it came with a wraparound deck that overlooked magnificent and sprawling grounds. There was a large expanse of lush grass dotted by majestic trees, evergreen bushes, a rose garden, even a vegetable patch.

"Perfect!" she breathed. "It's a little oasis where I can retreat. Where *we* can retreat," she corrected herself, stealing a sidelong glance at me.

"Promise me you'll sit out here with me every now and then and just inhale the beauty of the scene," she begged.

I laughed. I had married a nineties hippie, into meditation and alternative health, whose soul was stirred by a verdant expanse of rolling lawn. We were so different—but she brought a kind of music into my life that I had never quite heard before.

I kept that promise, too. Every now and then, I would join her on the deck and, despite myself, be moved by the idyllic scene. Sometimes we moved our chairs together from the deck into the yard itself, where branches from the old oak trees were entwined and formed a canopy over our heads.

It was a month after we had moved into the house that we first saw them. A pair of cardinal birds, hidden in one of the evergreen bushes, suddenly alighted onto the ground—a dash of vivid and warm color only a few yards from where we sat.

"Look!" she exclaimed, with the delight of a young child. "It's husband and wife!"

"Cardinals get married?" I teased.

"They mate for life," she said.

"I didn't know that," I answered.

"You never, ever see a female cardinal without a male. And what's nice is he always defers to her. He always lets her feed first. I really find that very sweet."

"But how can you tell which is the male and which is the female?" I asked, confused.

"Oh," she laughed, "you don't know anything about birds at all, do you? There is no bird more easily recognizable than the male cardinal, almost entirely red except for the conspicuous black mask on his face. And see? The female cardinal's overall color is buff-brown and yellowish-olive."

"You never cease to amaze me with all the stuff you know," I said.

"Wait till you hear them sing!" she enthused. "They are proud musicians. Their notes are very distinctive and beautiful, kinda like the quality of a small bell being rung. They sing different songs, too. The song they sing in the winter sounds something like "pretty, pretty, pretty," but their spring ballad is more piercing and poignant: a series of sounds that sort of descend into a kinda 'sweet slurring' and that some people describe as 'cheer, cheer' or 'dear, dear.'"

"When they look at you," I said lovingly, "they're clearly singing 'pretty, pretty.'"

"Oh, you!" she giggled, planting a tender kiss on my cheek.

For months the cardinals came, visiting us on a regular basis. She knew that they loved sunflower seeds, and she kept a huge bag stored in the pantry. As faithful as they were to each other, they became equally devoted to us. Every day they became more and more emboldened, until they were only a few feet away. They always sat opposite us—like mirror images—the female opposite my wife, the male opposite me. They watched us carefully, and we watched them, and my wife fancied that the pair of cardinals were metaphors for life, or at the very least, for *our life*. We felt we were all connected in some great cosmic way. Even I, the entrenched cynic, was beginning to feel some bond that was bigger than all of us combined.

And then something strange and mysterious and anomalous began to happen—something that, according to my wife the expert, definitely deviated from patterns of typical cardinal behavior.

Whenever my wife would sit out alone in the yard, only the female cardinal would come to visit. And when I had occasion to unwind in the garden and sat by myself in the lounge chair, only the male cardinal would make an appearance. But when we both sat outside together, the cardinals would come to call as a pair, and would sit opposite us side by side, as they always did. It was as if the two birds were beginning to mirror our lives more and more.

And then the day came when we sat outside together no more.

It was galloping leukemia, the doctors said, and it took her very fast. Six weeks after the diagnosis, she was gone.

At first, I couldn't venture into the yard at all. It held too many memories of our best times together, the times when I held her close and she melted my heart. But then I wanted to be in the place where her memory was the strongest—and it was there in the yard, surrounded by the nature that touched her spirit so.

So I hazarded a few steps into the garden, looked around at the lush foliage that had entranced her soul, and sat down in the lounge chair that remained where it had been left. I leaned back in the chair and covered my face with my hands, and the tears began to fall.

It was then that I heard it . . . a beautiful vocalization, a full-fledged song. I raised my eyes and saw the male cardinal . . . alone . . . sitting opposite me, a few feet away. I fancied that he looked mournful and had come to pay a condolence call.

The female cardinal was nowhere to be seen.

And just as my wife had once told me, the song in the spring *was* different from the one in the winter. In the winter, it was just one note, but now it was a series of sounds that descended into a sweet slurring.

And I could swear on my life that what I clearly heard that day was the cardinal's commiseration, a vocalization that sounded like "cheer, cheer" or "dear, dear."

Now I always retreat to the chair in the yard, which has become both my sanctuary and my mourning stool, and the male cardinal faithfully returns to keep me company, day after day, alone.

—*Steven Richards**

Comment

There is a melody that pulsates through the universe, and its song is that we are all one.

$\mathcal{A}ll$ his life, Andy Golembiewski was known as both a mischievous prankster and a warmhearted Good Samaritan. As owner of Andy's Bar and Grill, a tavern in Lawrenceville, he was a neighborhood fixture with a reputation for playing pranks on his customers but also lending them money when they were short. He believed that helping another human being in time of need was the greatest good a man could do. He provided well for his family members in life—and they believe he worked in mysterious ways to provide well for them in death too.

At the age of eighty-three, Andy contracted prostate cancer, and in the summer of 1997 his condition took a noticeable turn for the worse. One night in August, he fell into a coma, and his grieving family gathered at his bedside, braced for the inevitable. When hope for an improvement in Andy's condition had all but vanished and he had been unconscious for hours, his eyelids suddenly fluttered. His fingers began to quiver, and his body trembled. Then his eyes flew open, and they darted around the room with a gleam of intelligence and lucidity. He propped himself on his arms, looked his granddaughter Debra White in the eye, and said loudly and clearly, "1 . . . 6 . . . 9 . . . 5." And then as suddenly as he had stirred, he fell back onto the bed unconscious, and a few hours later he died.

His relatives didn't know what to make of it. They all agreed that Andy had appeared perfectly rational and clearheaded when he had uttered the four numbers. But what did these numbers mean? They had clung to the hope that he would awaken from the coma to bask in their love and receive a last embrace. In turn, they had yearned for some final words of love from Andy, or some crowning and climactic nugget of wisdom that would cap his life and serve as a departing testament. But . . . numbers? What kind of message from the grave was that?

"Those were the very last words he uttered," said his daughter-in-law, Millie Golembiewski. "Nobody could figure out the significance of this number. It wasn't anybody's birthday, phone number, address. Nothing connected."

For the next several hours, the relatives puzzled. They could not shake their conviction that Andy's words held import, and they tried to make sense of his communication. What could those numbers mean?

It was Andy's son, Tony, who finally suggested that they play the Big Four Lottery, which was being held the next day.

The next evening they were celebrating a very bizarre and bittersweet lottery win of $23,500.

"Andy!" his widow screamed, as the numbers were called up. "You're so concerned about your family, you even paid for your own funeral!"

The win was ironic, his family told reporters later, because during his lifetime Andy was opposed to gambling and had never even once played the lottery.

"He was a prankster," said his granddaughter. "I think he's up there laughing that we only put a dollar on the number."

"He was so kindhearted," another relative told a TV crew, "that he had to look out for his family even after he was gone."

*O*ne hot summer day, a young couple and their four-year-old daughter, Tzippie, were on their way to the mountains for a few weeks' vacation. Suddenly, a huge truck in the oncoming lane collided head-on with the family's small car. The couple was injured seriously, and little Tzippie sustained many fractures. They were immediately taken to the nearest hospital, where Tzippie was brought to the children's ward and her parents were taken to the intensive care unit. As can well be imagined, Tzippie was not only in great pain, but she was also very frightened because her parents were not nearby to give her comfort.

Martha, the nurse who was assigned to Tzippie, was a single, older woman. She understood Tzippie's fear and insecurity and became very devoted to her. When Martha finished her shift, instead of going home, she would volunteer to stay with Tzippie at night. Of course, Tzippie grew very fond of her and depended on her for her every need. Martha brought her cookies, picture books, and toys; she sang songs to her and told her countless stories.

When Tzippie was able to be moved, Martha put her in a wheelchair and took her to visit her parents every day. After many months of hospitalization, the family was discharged. Before they left the hospital, the parents blessed Martha for her devoted and loving care and invited her to visit them. Tzippie would not let go of Martha, and insisted that she come to live with them. Martha also did not want to be parted from her little Tzippie, but her life was in the children's ward of the hospital, and she could not think of leaving. There was a tearful parting as Tzippie and the loving nurse said good-bye to each other. For a few months the family kept up a close relationship with Martha—through phone calls only, since they lived quite a distance from her. When they moved abroad, however, they lost contact with each other.

Over thirty years passed. One winter Martha, who was now in her seventies, became seriously ill with pneumonia and was hospitalized in the geriatric ward of a hospital near her home. There was a certain nurse on duty who noticed that Martha had very few visitors. She tried her best to give the elderly lady special care, and she saw that she was a sensitive, clever person.

One night when the nurse was sitting near her elderly patient and they were chatting quietly, she confided in her as to what had prompted her to become a nurse. When she was four years old, she explained, and her parents had been injured in an automobile accident, there had been a wonderful nurse who had brought her back to health with her loving, caring devotion. As she grew older, she determined that one day she, too, would become a nurse and help others—from the young to the old—just as that nurse had done for her.

After she graduated from nursing school overseas, she had met a young man from America, and when they married, they moved to the States. A few months ago they had moved to this city, where her husband had been offered a very good job, and she was happy to get a position as a nurse in this hospital. As the nurse's story unfolded, tears flowed from the elderly patient's eyes, as she realized that this must surely be her little Tzippie, whom she had cared for after the accident.

When the nurse had finished her story, Martha said softly, "Tzippie, we are together again, but this time *you* are nursing *me!*" Tzippie's eyes opened wide as she stared at Martha, suddenly recognizing her. "Is it really you?" she cried out. "How many times I have thought about you and prayed that someday we would meet again!"

When Martha recovered from her illness, Tzippie—this time—did not beg her to come and live with her family. Instead, she just packed up Martha's belongings and took her home with her. She lives with Tzippie to this day, and Tzippie's husband and children have welcomed her like a most special grandmother.

—*Ruchoma Shain*

Comment

In the circle of love, we are all givers and receivers. First we are one, then we are the other . . . the circle keeps turning around and around.

We live in a rural town in Montana—small enough for everyone to know his neighbors. At best the census taker might clock us all in at one thousand residents. The winters here are cold and deep. When some friends in Southern California invited us to visit them, my brother Steve and I decided to take that "once-in-a-lifetime" trip. For a week we could enjoy the warm climate and just relax with our wives and four children during the Christmas break. The kids were especially excited about visiting Disneyland.

We started planning the trip two months in advance. It made economic sense, we felt, to travel together in a recreational vehicle that was large and comfortable enough to accommodate us all. Our mother, a first grade school teacher, was also on her Christmas break and asked if she could join us. In fact, she insisted. This struck me as odd, since my father showed no interest in our plans and, understandably, preferred to stay home. No lengthy journeys in a crowded van for him. But I saw the gleam in her eye, and of course, we had to say, "Yes, come along."

We drove for two days before reaching our friends' home south of Los Angeles. The following day we were all basking in the sun at Disneyland. It surpassed our children's wildest dreams. The next two days we visited other tourist spots in the area.

For the final day of the vacation, the family voted to make a return trip to Disneyland. I, however, had a quite different idea—at least for myself. I told my family that I wanted to venture out on my own to see Los Angeles. I would get there on the city bus and see the sights—a stunning contrast, I knew, to our small home town.

My host was most helpful the evening before. Together we made a plan so that I could make the most of my few hours in Los Angeles and—importantly—my host gave me a map of downtown to keep me from getting lost. I went to bed excited about my upcoming adventure.

The next morning when my host was about to drive me to the bus stop, I saw my mother running toward the car. She had originally planned to go with the others, but now, suddenly, she wanted to spend the day with me. I said: "Mother, that's not a good idea. More than likely we'll get lost and accidentally end up in some rough part of town." We continued to argue, but she would have none of it. There was no changing her mind. I had to concede, and she jumped into the car.

The first part of the bus trip into the city was very pleasant. Mother and I had a lively conversation about family and friends. Proceeding to the "inner city," the bus made stops about every two blocks to let passengers on and off—passengers of every conceivable nationality, color, and income level. Suddenly, mother and I were a minority of two. This didn't bother us. Our hosts assured us we would be perfectly safe.

However, as we approached a rundown part of town I became apprehensive. Although it was the middle of the day, I sensed that I had made a big mistake taking my mother into this area. When we reached the last stop the bus driver noticed our concern. "You'll be all right," he said. "You're only five minutes from downtown. Any of the drivers can give you additional directions."

Stepping off the bus, we were surrounded by old, dilapidated buildings. Street people were all around us. We were rather scared. Before approaching anyone for directions to another bus, we thought we might find some spot to rest and let our blood pressures settle down. We stuck closely together and started around the block in search of a store or restaurant that might possibly have a restroom. We had no desire to spend any time or money in the area. Canvassing both sides of the block we found a store that suited our temporary needs. We kept watch for one another while we used the restrooms.

Upon leaving the store we turned to the right and—quite suddenly— we came face to face with the shock of our lives. Before us was a homeless man. His hair was long and dirty. His beard nearly reached his belt. His stained clothes hung loosely on his thin frame. I couldn't look at him. But I had to. He was my brother, Doug. He was my mother's first child. Gone was the star high school athlete. Gone was the college graduate. Gone was the Vietnam veteran. He had never recovered from that terrible experience. He was now a schizophrenic. His only words to us were: "Hi, what are you guys doing here?"

There was really nothing to say. My mother embraced him. She brushed the hair from his face. I brushed the tears from my eyes. Two years ago Doug had boarded a Greyhound bus on a warm summer day without telling any of us. His destination was Los Angeles—a city of 13 million. He rented an apartment for a couple of months until his money ran out. Since then, he had been living on the street, begging for food, and sleeping in doorways under cardboard blankets.

This unexpected encounter was our first contact with him in two years. Now I realized why my mother had to come with me on the bus that day. She had a mission, and she completed it.

When my mother and I left Doug in the middle of that sad street, we both felt, understandably, that we would never see Doug again. Happily that did not prove to be the case. Doug, on his own, returned a few months later to Montana, where I helped him get situated at the Rescue

Mission in my town. For the last ten years I have met him every Sunday afternoon for coffee and pie at the mission, where he now is able to work a few hours each day in the mission's thrift shop. He tells me about his personal discoveries as he walks endlessly around town. In short, he has come to have a life of his own that he considers satisfying and useful.

Although they live some two hours away, Mom and Dad visit Doug every other month or so. About twice a year he boards a bus—not to drop out of sight as he originally had done—but to go back home again and spend a few days with them. Because Doug is at peace with himself and his special world, I now realize that this never would have happened but for the fact that on one cold December day my mother and I boarded that fateful bus to Los Angeles.

—*Dave DeBoer*

Comment

The universe provides its own system of transportation to carry us to the places we most need to be.

In 1919, my grandfather Aaron Lazer was a struggling young scholar, newly married, with a pregnant wife and no viable means of support. He worked part-time at his mother's shop in the town of Koscive, Czechoslovakia, but the wages he brought home were meager, and the store's earnings were not adequate to sustain two families. Regretfully, his mother advised him that it was time for him to strike out on his own, and Aaron took her counsel to heart.

Indeed, Aaron *wanted* to be on his own—self-sufficient and independent—and he felt he possessed both the initiative and the savvy to become a successful businessman. So he began to cast about for something to do that would launch his career.

World War I had just ended, and Czechoslovakia was experiencing many serious shortages, both in food supply and in other sectors. The leather goods industry was particularly hard hit, and good, sturdy shoes were difficult to come by. At that time, most shoes were of necessity being fashioned from cardboard and paper, and they did not hold up well. My grandfather decided that this was the opportune time to open up a shoe business that would fill an important vacuum and offer strong, solid footwear.

Aaron borrowed 5,000 kronin—a princely sum in those days—and traveled to a large city to seek out an agent who brokered shoes. He returned home after several days weary but elated. His mission had been accomplished. In the back of his wagon were several cartons of heavy military shoes. He had used all his money to buy five hundred pairs—a risk, to be sure—but he was convinced they would be eagerly snapped up by the local townspeople and that he would make a veritable killing. Imagine Aaron's despair when he opened the cartons to proudly display the merchandise to his family, and found that instead of five hundred pairs, he owned a thousand right-foot shoes only!

Heart-rending sobs tore from him as he stared in shock at the row of right shoes lined up in a long, mocking procession. Not a single left shoe among them!

His merchandise was utterly worthless, and he now owed huge sums of money to relatives, neighbors, and friends who had lent him, at great personal sacrifice, the kronin they had frugally hoarded for years.

How was he ever going to recoup his losses? How was he ever going to repay his loans? How was he going to support his wife and new baby? How was he going to save face in a town that had placed its collective trust in him? No, no, it was too much to bear, and the almost inhuman, unearthly wails that Aaron emitted testified to his anguish.

Everyone urged him to return immediately to the big city, find the unscrupulous broker from whom he had bought the merchandise, and demand a refund. But when Aaron backtracked to the marketplace where he had originally encountered the man, he found that he had vanished. No one seemed to know anything about him—who he was, where he lived, where else he did business. All leads to him ran cold. It was as if he had never existed. Aaron wondered whether he had hallucinated the whole deal. But no, the nightmare was real enough: he had a thousand right shoes in his wagon, and all his money was gone.

He returned home despondent and inconsolable. His wife looked with concern at his pale, wan face and urged him to visit the wisest person they knew, a holy man who lived in Koscive and was renowned for his gentle wisdom and spiritual greatness. "Don't give up!" she exhorted her husband. "This man has helped many people. Maybe he can help you too."

Aaron tried to put on a brave front as he was ushered into the wise man's office, but as he stepped across the threshold, he burst into a torrent of tears. As he described the terrible fraud that had been perpetrated upon him, the great sage's face became suffused with sympathy for Aaron's downcast spirit. His words were sincere and kind.

"This is what you must do," the holy man murmured softly. "Go and pray, recite psalms and God will help. Have faith. All will be well."

Dutifully, Aaron followed the wise man's advice and sequestered himself in prayer in the synagogue. For several days, he wept and prayed, prayed and wept, focused only on his torment, unable to distill other forms of reality. Rivulets of tears flowed down his face and wet his cheeks. He had surrendered completely to his pain and was oblivious to his immediate surroundings. Aaron was so consumed by his misery that he was completely unaware that sympathetic congregants were tiptoeing softly around his sobbing figure, or that his compassionate wife was bringing him hot plates of steaming food, which he ate heedlessly. He had become so preoccupied, in fact, by the obsessive thoughts of failure and ruin that tortured him that he failed to observe a stranger quietly enter, retreat to a reclusive corner, and begin to sob himself. But when the man's heart-rending cries had escalated to ghastly shrieks, even Aaron's armorlike oblivion was pierced.

The man's cries tore at him and woke him from his days-long stupor. He didn't know the man, but he recognized the timbre of the cry. The man was in great emotional pain, that much was clear. Laboriously Aaron rose from his seat and crossed the room to approach him. He didn't know whether or not at this point he possessed the emotional resources to help the man, but he was the only one in the synagogue and the man clearly needed help.

As Aaron approached, he noticed a Book of Psalms on the stranger's lap, from which he was reciting in between sobs.

"Welcome," Aaron said, extending his hand. "I heard you crying and my heart goes out to you in your pain. Is there anything I can do to help?"

The stranger shook his head mournfully. "No one can help," he cried out in dejection. "I borrowed a lot of money to buy merchandise for a business. Alas, it was my terrible misfortune to be cheated by a dishonest merchant. I thought I was buying five hundred pairs of military shoes, but it turned out that the carton contained no pairs at all, but only a thousand shoes for the *left foot!*"

The stranger with the red-rimmed eyes looked sadly into my grandfather's red-rimmed eyes and was bewildered by the happy gleam that suddenly began to dance in them.

"My dear friend," my grandfather said as he draped a consoling arm around his soon-to-be partner, "I have very good news for you."

My grandfather and the stranger paired up the shoes (they were perfectly matched), sold them, and made a tremendous amount of money. Consequently, my grandfather became a very rich man, and this incident secured his position, both in the financial world of Czechoslovakia and in the annals of our family lore.

—Chayke Lobl

❧

Comment
In any enterprise, God is the silent partner.

$\mathcal{R}$ichard Fleming,* a retired businessman, was doing paperwork at home one Monday afternoon when the phone rang.

"Mr. Fleming?" a cool, crisp voice said. "This is Lauren from Dr. Brown's office. I just wanted to confirm your appointment with the doctor tomorrow morning at nine o'clock."

"An appointment with Dr. Brown?" Mr. Fleming repeated slowly, dully. He knitted his brows in puzzlement and turned to his wife with a perplexed look.

"What's the matter?" she whispered urgently, moving quickly to his side.

"Did I make an appointment with Dr. Brown that I totally forgot about?" he asked her, befuddled.

He had been to see Dr. Brown, a renowned Manhattan cardiologist, half a year before, and had been given a clean bill of health. He had no recollection of being advised to come in for another checkup in six months, nor did he recall making such an appointment.

"Can you just hang on for a minute, please?" he asked the doctor's secretary, while he hunted for his calendar. He was usually so careful about recording all his engagements, but the doctor's appointment wasn't penciled in.

"Oh, no!" he mouthed to his wife. "Am I beginning to suffer from Alzheimer's?"

"Are you sure about the appointment?" he asked the nurse, returning to the phone.

"This *is* Richard Fleming?" she asked, more brusquely this time.

"Yes, of course it is."

"Well, Mr. Fleming, I have you down for a nine o'clock."

"Lauren," he confessed, "I don't remember making this appointment."

"Listen, Mr. Fleming," she snapped, all traces of civility now gone. "Dr. Brown is one of the busiest and most important cardiologists in New York. Appointments with him have to be booked months in advance. I have a long list of people waiting for a cancellation. If you don't want to come in, just tell me, and I'll call one of them. But you have to tell me right now whether you're coming or not, because this is a very busy office, and I don't have all day!"

"What should I do?" Richard mouthed to his wife.

"Go!" she shrugged. "If you made an appointment, it's not nice for you to cancel at the last minute."

"OK," he told Lauren, "I'm coming; I'll be there tomorrow morning."

"Fine," she breathed, sounding friendlier and less hostile. "See you tomorrow morning, then. You'll get the usual battery of tests. Just take it easy today and relax."

But Richard Fleming was unable to heed the secretary's counsel. All day long, he fretted over his apparent slip-up. A close friend had recently begun to experience serious memory loss and had been diagnosed with possible early Alzheimer's. Of all the terrors he associated with advancing age, Richard Fleming was most afraid of losing his mind. Was his inability to remember the appointment an impending and ominous sign?

The next morning, he underwent a grueling series of tests in Dr. Brown's office. "When they're all over," he kept vowing to himself, "I'm going to bring up the subject of Alzheimer's."

But he didn't have the opportunity, because after Dr. Brown had begun to evaluate the results, he returned to Mr. Fleming's room, a grim expression on his face.

"Not a moment too soon!" he exclaimed. "You're a lucky man, Mr. Fleming. You have a serious cardiac problem, and you'll have to go in for surgery immediately. It's fortunate that you had an appointment today," the doctor added. "Had this problem not been detected soon, you would surely have been in serious trouble within a month or two."

Meanwhile, at the secretary's desk in the reception room, an irate man was causing a minor commotion.

"What do you mean, Richard Fleming is already in the doctor's office? *I am* Richard Fleming!"

One young nurse rolled her eyes meaningfully at the secretary, as if to say: "What some brazen people won't do these days to get an appointment." But the older secretary's eyes clouded with consternation, and her face grew pale when the man withdrew an official appointment card that had been issued to him from the doctor's office.

"Here!" he shouted, shoving the appointment card under her nose. "See for yourself. It's today's date, and it says nine o'clock." He started flinging various forms of identification from his wallet. "And here is my driver's license and several credit cards, which I assume," he screamed, "will prove that I am none other than Richard Fleming!"

"Then who," the young nurse asked, bewildered, "is the man sitting in the doctor's office right now?"

"Wait a second," said the secretary slowly, "let me check my records." And there she found two separate files for two different Richard Flemings—one who lived in Manhattan and was currently fuming in the reception room, another who lived in Brooklyn and was currently being given a serious diagnosis together with the prescription for cure.

The wrong Richard Fleming had been called by the secretary.

Only it was really the *right* Richard Fleming—the one who needed the coincidence to happen in order for his life to be saved!

Comment

An event can be seen as a mistake or a miracle depending on the prism through which you view your life.

*N*othing is purer than the joy in a child's smile. Nothing elicits that smile more than love . . . and sometimes, the perfect present. That is what Louisa knew as the days approached until her daughter Stephanie's tenth birthday.

What she would give to make her precious daughter smile! For each day was a challenge to little Stephanie, who had been born deaf. She lived in a virtually silent world. Not an echo, not a buzz, not a sound. Louisa was trying her best to raise her daughter with love and instill a feeling of self-confidence in her. She provided Stephanie with everything she possibly could.

So of course, the child's tenth birthday should be something special. And yet the sky was not the limit, in terms of birthday gifts. In fact, the bank account was nearly empty. Louisa's marriage to Stephanie's father had gotten increasingly worse over the years and finally, in the past year, Louisa had felt that it would be best to split up. The divorce left Louisa strapped financially and anxious about expenses.

"Mommy," Stephanie signed one day, "I know what I want for my birthday." Louisa took a deep breath, worried that she would not be able to accommodate her daughter's wishes.

"Yes, honey," Louisa signed back, "what is it that you would like?"

"A white cat," Stephanie signed. A great big smile came over her face, just thinking about it. "A white female cat with long hair."

Louisa gulped hard. The divorce was still something that Stephanie had not fully understood. Plus, they had recently moved, and Stephanie was adjusting to a new environment and a new set of schoolmates. Any child would have been challenged; Stephanie had almost more than she could bear. It broke Louisa's heart to watch her daughter holding up with such grace and strength.

And yet, a long-haired cat? Louisa had an immediate sense that such an exotic animal would be costly. Over the next few days, she struggled with the dilemma every time she looked into her daughter's eyes. Just the idea of it seemed to give Stephanie a happier countenance. Never had Louisa seen her daughter want something this badly. In the end, Louisa was so moved by her daughter's deep desire for this cat that she resolved to find one.

Her first move was to look through the newspaper classifieds. Maybe someone was selling a cat that would fit Stephanie's dream. Maybe it wouldn't be that expensive. She found four ads for cats for sale, and circled them in red ink. She called the first number.

"Hi, I'm responding to your ad in the paper," Louisa said to the stranger who answered the phone.

"Yes, I am selling a cat," came the reply.

"What color is it?" asked Louisa, fingers crossed.

"It's a beautiful, all black, male cat."

Louisa's heart sank a little. The exact opposite of what Stephanie had asked for! "Oh . . . I'm sorry," she said. "I was looking for a white cat . . . female . . . thank you," she said and hung up. There were still more numbers to call. Louisa tried the next number. "Hi, I'm calling about the ad in the newspaper about a cat for sale?"

"Yes," came the reply, "I'm selling a beautiful short-haired white male cat." Once again, Louisa's heart sank as she thought about her daughter's bright eyes, her animated signing, her reluctance to hear of anything but a pure white, long-haired, female cat. "No, I'm sorry, that's not what I was looking for," replied Louisa.

Louisa continued to make phone calls for the rest of the afternoon. She found people selling orange tabbies and gray Siamese, but no long-haired fitting her daughter's specific description. Frustrated in her efforts, Louisa decided to ask her daughter if she might want a different type of cat—or even another birthday present altogether. But as she approached Stephanie's room, she caught a glimpse of the child signing to God. "Please God," she saw Stephanie pray, "please help my Mommy find me a white female long-haired cat. It's all that I want. Please. I know you have lots of those kind of cats. Please give my Mommy one." Louisa couldn't move. She just stood in the doorway, watching her child, tears welling up in her eyes. Then, slowly, she turned around, went back to her own room, and said her own prayer.

The next day Louisa was on the hunt again. She called yet another number listed in an ad from a different county newspaper. But all she got was the answering machine, so she left her number and waited to hear back.

That night she got a call. "Hello," said a woman on the other end of the line. "I'm returning your call about the ad I had placed in the newspaper."

"Yes," Louisa said, "would you please describe the cat to me?"

"Sure," said the woman. "The cat is pure white, long-haired and female."

Louisa jumped out of her seat. "I'll take it!" she screamed.

"Great," came the response, "that will be five hundred dollars."

"*What!*" shouted Louisa, "five hundred dollars?"

Trying to contain her disappointment, Louisa tried to explain the situation to the woman. "You see," she began, "my little girl is turning ten, and this is all that she had wanted. I can't afford much. I was hoping that maybe, somehow I would be able to give this to her. But five hundred dollars is too much. It's an amount I can't afford to spend."

Nevertheless, the woman could not be dissuaded from her price. Louisa thanked the woman anyhow for calling her back, and they both hung up.

Louisa felt more hopeless than ever. "Dear God," she implored, "my little girl is so alone in her deaf world, with her father gone and in a new home, I really want to be able to give her the gift she wants so badly. Please, help me find the kind of cat she's looking for.

Just as Louisa was completing her prayers, the phone rang. The woman with the white cat had been moved by Stephanie's story, she said, and she felt a change of heart. She was willing to reduce the price to three hundred dollars.

"Thank you so much," said Louisa sadly, "but even three hundred dollars is still way above and beyond what I can afford."

The woman must have sensed the sadness and despondency in Louisa's voice.

"You know . . . I do have another cat, a long-haired, perfectly white female cat that I can't seem to give away," she began.

"Oh? What do you mean? Why is that?" asked Louisa, perking up.

"Well, you see," said the woman, "this particular cat is deaf."

Louisa was speechless. After a moment of silence, she released a grateful sigh, and then came her exhilarated reply. "I'll take it," she said. "I will gladly take that cat."

Comment
The sound of magic rings loud and clear, even in a silent world.

harles Francis Coghlan was born on Prince Edward Island in 1841. He displayed exceptional dramatic ability as a boy and first appeared on the stage in London in 1860. In the years that followed he attained international fame as an actor and was considered one of the greatest Shakespearean performers of his day. Throughout his life, Prince Edward Island remained his home.

The actor was appearing in Galveston, Texas, when he died on November 27, 1889, after a short illness. His lead-lined coffin was placed in a granite vault in a Galveston cemetery.

On September 8, 1900, the great hurricane struck Galveston Island. The flood waters washed into the cemeteries and shattered vaults and disinterred the dead. The bodies of the long dead mingled with the newly dead. Coffins beat a dirge against uprooted tombstones, then floated out into the Gulf of Mexico to be scattered far and wide by the waves.

After the fury of the hurricane had been spent, a backwash carried the coffin of Charles Coghlan to the southeast. There it was caught by the West Indian current and carried into the Gulf Stream. It drifted around the tip of Florida and began moving north in the great oceanic river.

The Gulf Stream current moves rapidly, approximately seventy miles a day, and it is quite likely that the coffin moved with this current until it reached the vicinity of Newfoundland. There it was probably blown out of the current by a gale.

Once free of the Gulf Stream, it apparently drifted aimlessly off the eastern Canadian coast, subject to vagrant winds and waves. No one will ever know.

In October 1908, after a series of gales, several fishermen left Prince Edward Island to set their nets in the Gulf of St. Lawrence. They noticed a large box lying low in the water and drifting toward shore. They towed it to the beach.

Encrusted with sea mollusks and barnacles, it was obvious the box had been in the water a long time. They chipped away the thick crust of shells. It was a coffin containing the body of a middle-aged man. A silver plate gave his name as Charles Coghlan, a name well-known on the island.

Only a few miles away was the village where he had been born and raised. Only a few miles away was the home where he had rested between his extensive travels. With appropriate ceremony and honor, he was buried near the church where he had been baptized.

Across the trackless sea, Charles Coghlan had at last reached home to stay.

—*Alan Vaughan*

9n 1984, Gertrude Levine of Queens, New York, received a phone call from the administrator of an older adults' summer camp where, she thought, her mother was safely ensconced.

"Mrs. Levine," the administrator said in a subdued voice, "I'm terribly sorry to have to tell you the tragic news, but your mother, Sarah Stern, just had a heart attack and died in the hospital. I'm so sorry—please accept my deepest condolences."

The telephone slipping from her hand, Gertrude slumped in her chair, dazed and stricken. It was incomprehensible . . . her beloved mother, dead. Especially since she had always been so robust and alive, so high-spirited and feisty. In contemplating her mother's advancing age, she had often reassured herself that Sarah Stern would give the Angel of Death a good run for his money!

"Mrs. Levine, Mrs. Levine," came the administrator's faint voice from the telephone receiver on the floor. "Are you still there?"

Gertrude retrieved the phone in slow motion, still muddled and disoriented. "Y-yes, I'm here," she responded numbly.

"Mrs. Levine, I feel terrible to throw this at you so suddenly, but someone has to come to identify the body."

"I don't think I can bear to do it; I'll send a close relative instead."

"That'll be fine, Mrs. Levine. And again, please accept our deepest condolences. Your mother was a very fine woman. She loved you so much. She talked about you all the time, always telling everyone what a marvelous daughter she had."

Gertrude bowed her head in sorrow. She was shattered by the loss of her beloved mother. At the funeral and later, during the first hours of the *shiva* (the Jewish mourning period of seven days), her tears flowed unrestrainedly. She told the family members who sat on the low mourning stools with her that the shock was too much for her to absorb.

Several hours after the *shiva* had begun, the phone rang and someone handed Gertrude the receiver.

A crisp operator's voice announced: "Collect phone call for Gertrude Levine from Sarah Stern. Will you accept the charges?"

"Collect phone call from *whom?*" Gertrude asked, befuddled.

"Sarah Stern," the operator repeated.

"Is this someone's sick idea of a joke?" Gertrude asked. "I just *buried* her!"

"Gertrude!" A beloved and very real voice suddenly came over the line, fretting, "I can't seem to adjust my medicine . . . "

It was her mother, Sarah Stern.

There had been *two* Sarah Sterns at the camp, and the wrong family had been notified! The relative sent to identify the body had been sickened by the sight of a corpse and had given it only a quick, perfunctory look. "Yeah, sure it's Sarah Stern," she had muttered hastily, eager to depart. Because coffins are always kept closed during Jewish funerals and Jewish law prohibits viewing of the body, the mistake was never uncovered. Consequently, a stranger was now lying in the family plot!

"You cannot imagine the emotional trauma," sighs Gertrude Levine in rueful recollection as she recounts the saga. "Thinking my mother is dead . . . all the pain and suffering . . . the stress of the funeral and the burial *and* the commencement of the *shiva* that followed. I won't even talk about the expense or the public embarrassment. But of course, all this faded into insignificance when I considered that my mother was very much alive."

But the story doesn't end here. When Gertrude called the children of the other Sarah Stern to offer her condolences and ask that the family make arrangements to transfer *their* mother's body out of *her* mother's burial plot, they refused!

"She's there already," they said, "let her be! Why should we go to all the bother of digging her up, buying a burial plot, and giving her another funeral? One is enough."

Gertrude was aghast at the suggestion. How could she allow a complete stranger to remain in her mother's burial plot, lying next to her deceased father? She begged the children to remove their mother's body, but they ignored her appeals. She had community leaders call on her behalf, but they remained intractable. Finally, with no other recourse left, Gertrude had a local rabbi call the family and threaten to obtain a court order forcing them to comply. It was this approach that finally worked.

"So are you at least going to give your mother a decent funeral?" Gertrude asked the family when arrangements for the body's removal had been made. To her horror, the children replied that a gravesite funeral would be sufficient.

"In that case I'm coming!" Gertrude said passionately, having become drawn into the drama of the late Mrs. Stern's life, and feeling fiercely protective of her honor.

Besides the immediate family, she was the only one there.

Watching the pitiful proceedings unfold at the stark and lonely graveside funeral, Gertrude Levine felt engulfed by an overwhelming sorrow for the life and death of the second Mrs. Stern. At the same time, she also experienced an epiphany, one that illuminated God's plan.

"I always wondered how and why the bizarre mix-up with my mother occurred," she reflects. "At the dismal funeral that wrenched my heart, I suddenly understood the larger picture."

"You know," she said to the children after the funeral, "your mother must have really been a very special woman or, at least once in her lifetime, done something extraordinary. Because *three hundred people* came to her funeral—thinking she was *my* mother—and paid her homage. Look at what kind of funeral you gave her now, and think about what kind of funeral she had as a result of the strange coincidence. God *wanted* her to have an honorable funeral, one that she obviously would never have been accorded otherwise, so He arranged for the coincidence to occur."

Six months later, Gertrude's own mother—the first Sarah Stern— died. Once again, she was given a beautiful funeral, but this time only a hundred people came.

Why the stunning decline in numbers?

"People were tired of going to her funeral!" sighs Gertrude Levine.

Comment
When the dance of life confounds us and we're uncertain of the next step, we can pause and remember that the choreography of our existence is divine and purposeful.

*T*wice we had been burned by unsavory tenants living in the basement apartment of our home. The first miscreant robbed us of two thousand dollars, while the second rogue fled in the dark of night owing us back rent for several months. We also had a close brush with a third, who came to see the vacant apartment and expressed an immediate interest in taking it. Thank God for an inquisitive neighbor with a sharp eye and a loose tongue. As soon as he left, she raced across the street. "You know that man who just left your apartment?" she said. "He's wanted in Argentina for murder."

Alas, my husband and I are not wise in the ways of the world, and we are naive when it comes to people. This innocence, which has lasted long past our youth, has provided us with many unexpected blessings and interesting encounters, but it has also furnished us with an overabundant supply of trials, tribulations, and sheer unmitigated grief that we surely could have done without.

"Let's face it," I sighed one day to my husband, as we thought forlornly about the basement apartment, which was—surprise!—vacant again. "The basement is very small and dingy. It only attracts real problematic and troublesome individuals. Let's call it quits as a rental and use it as a playroom for the kids."

"No way," he shook his head adamantly. "We put in a lot of money to fix it up and we need the income it provides."

"It's not worth the trouble!" I argued. "The apartment doesn't appeal to nice, quiet, respectable people. I shudder when I think that we almost harbored a *murderer* in our very own home!"

"We need the income!" my husband replied stubbornly.

"Can you promise me you'll be extremely careful in checking out the next tenant? Ask for references and so on?"

"I promise. And I'll tell you what. Just to really be on the safe side, I'll try to rent the apartment to a woman rather than a man. Okay?"

"If it doesn't work out this time, I want you to promise me never again," I warned.

"No more heartache," he promised cheerfully.

When an elegantly dressed middle-aged schoolteacher appeared several days later and expressed an interest in renting the apartment, my husband excitedly gave her a lease on the spot and called the local newspaper to cancel the ad he had placed.

"You'll love her!" he assured me, when I expressed my dubiousness about the deal.

"I don't understand this," I said warily. "Why would a well-heeled schoolteacher choose *our* apartment? It doesn't make any sense. Did you ask her for references?"

"She's so respectable looking, I didn't want to insult her by asking for references."

"*What?*" I shrieked. "I don't believe this. You promised."

"I know people," he said confidently. "This is a fine woman. You'll see."

One week later, a moving van appeared in front of our house, and movers began heaving furniture into the basement apartment. I looked for the elegant woman my husband had described, but the person directing the movers with an authoritative air was a young man, neatly dressed in a decent suit. I approached him and asked if he was related to the new tenant.

"That's my mother," he said, flashing a bright, charming smile. "She went abroad for a few weeks, but she said I could use her apartment while she's gone."

The young man looked respectable enough, although I was a little unnerved by his long ponytail and his earring. However, always having given my children long-drawn-out lectures about the importance of looking beyond outward appearances, I was embarrassed not to try to practice what I preached.

"I guess it's OK," I responded. "When is she coming back?"

"Soon," he answered vaguely.

The woman never materialized.

After the first day, the suit never materialized again either. Instead, the new tenant began appearing regularly in torn jeans and tight-fitting T-shirts. A few weeks later, the T-shirt was replaced by an undershirt, and soon after that, he began walking around with a bare chest that exposed several ominous-looking tattoos.

Soon, bizarre-looking characters began drifting in and out of our basement apartment and raucous music could be heard late at night. My husband tracked down the mysterious woman, who confessed that she had tricked him into renting the apartment to her problematic son, Michael.

"I'm sorry," she said, not sounding sorry at all. "But nobody wanted to rent him an apartment, so I had to do it for him. He's a good boy, don't worry. He won't hurt you."

"Can't we get Michael out?" I wailed to my husband day in and day out.

"Even if we have legal recourse, it'll take months. Anyway," my Good Samaritan husband gently chastened me, "instead of focusing on

Michael's problems, maybe we should see the situation in a different context. Maybe it's no accident that he landed here, since we've worked with people like him in the past. See it as a test from God," my husband counseled. "Let's invite him for Friday night Sabbath dinner."

Friday night, Michael gleamed like the silver candlesticks on my resplendently set Sabbath table. He wore the first day's suit, and was buffed and polished handsomely. He wore a *yarmulke* out of respect for our Orthodox tradition. (He was Jewish but not religious.) He helped me serve dinner, engaged in witty, charming banter with my sons, told a few jokes, sang a few Jewish melodies in an enchanting baritone, and even recounted a few Hasidic tales that he remembered from his childhood days.

"Do you see the beauty in this boy's soul?" my husband pressed me after he left. "We can do good work here."

A few weeks later, we found out that Michael was a drug addict.

"Now what?" I sighed to my husband.

"Well, the challenge is *bigger* now, but I still believe we can help him. Now I really know his coming here was no accident. God sent him to us and we've got to help him."

Truly I felt conflicted. On the one hand, I agreed with my husband. On the other hand, I didn't feel that we were equipped to deal with a drug problem. Most important, I worried about my children's safety and the safety of the other children on the block. My husband had confronted Michael about his addiction and he swore he would hide his problem from them. He also gave my husband his word that he would enter a drug rehabilitation program and said that he had already applied to one in California. He also told my husband that as a result of our influence he had started attending synagogue and was thinking about becoming observant. He had even sent away for information about schools that specialized in returnees to Judaism, he said.

My husband was satisfied. He didn't entertain for a moment the thought of having Michael evicted, as I had half-hoped he would. Whether Michael was sincere about his intentions or fed my husband the lines he knew would push his buttons, I couldn't be sure. But his promises certainly kept the sheriff's men at bay.

One night, I drove to Brooklyn Heights, a neighborhood about thirty minutes from where I live, to take an adult education course. The class ended at eleven, and I asked the instructor for directions back to the highway. I was a trifle nervous about driving home alone late at night, but once I got onto the highway, I breathed a sigh of relief. It would be smooth sailing from here on, I thought.

My relief was premature. To my distress, I suddenly realized that I was on the wrong side of the highway. I was on my way to *Queens* instead of Brooklyn! I had no recourse but to get off the highway immediately. At the next exit sign, I pulled off the ramp and began searching for an entrance to the Brooklyn-bound side.

I was dazed and disoriented. It would have been a strain even during the daytime, but the misshapen shadows of the night played into my fears. These fears were heightened and compounded by my sudden realization that I was cruising along the streets of one of the toughest neighborhoods in Brooklyn.

"It's OK. Nothing's going to happen," I reassured myself, repeating the words like a mantra. "Just find a gas station and the attendant will give you directions."

A gas station appeared around a bend. Weak with relief, I pulled into it and honked my horn. Anticipating that the attendant would be out momentarily, I rolled down my window to talk with him. Instead, five menacing figures stepped out of the station's shadows and encircled my car. The attendant was nowhere to be seen.

"Need help, lady?" one man growled, as I cautioned myself to look beyond appearances.

"Hi, good evening, how ya doing?" I said brightly, deciding that the cool I'm-not-scared-of-you, you-are-God's-divine-creature-just-as-much-as-I-am approach might work here. "Could you please tell me how to get onto the BQE going west?"

"Sure, honey, I'll be glad to," the man said, and for a fraction of a second my fears were allayed. "But it'll cost you . . . " he added with a growl.

The menacing figures moved closer to the car.

Suddenly, a new figure detached itself from another throng of men huddled in a corner of the gas station and raced towards my car. "I recognize that voice. It's Mrs. Mandelbaum! Mrs. Mandelbaum, Mrs. Mandelbaum, how ya doin'!" the voice inquired serendipitously.

It was Michael.

He approached the men encircling the car and scowled at them threateningly. "What're you bothering this nice lady for? She's my landlady. Leave her alone! Scram!"

Reluctantly, the men walked away from the car, giving it and me one last lingering look.

"Mrs. Mandelbaum, what are you doing here?" my savior inquired blithely.

"Michael, what are *you* doing here?" I countered.

"Oh, I come here to do some business," he answered vaguely.

"Want a lift home?" I asked.

"Nah, thanks, but I'm not finished here yet."

"Michael, you probably saved my life. I don't know how to thank you."

"Well, you've been valiantly trying to save mine, so I guess we're even now," he said in a light tone.

A few weeks after the gas station incident, Michael left for a rehabilitation center in California. I haven't seen him since, but I pray that God will continue to protect the man who protected me the night I took a wrong turn off the highway.

—*Yitta Halberstam Mandelbaum*

In New York City, the police advise you not to take out your wallet when approached by a beggar—but you develop a sixth sense about these things. So I had no misgivings about the young black woman, shy and rail-thin and obviously homeless, her matted hair covered by a scarf, who approached me a few years ago in the nearly empty Times Square subway station while I was waiting for the train.

Could I give her some money for a meal?

I took a few dollars from my wallet. Then I noticed her feet. She was wearing threadbare sneakers and had no socks on. I asked her why. She had no money for socks, she explained as she turned to ask another commuter for spare change.

I had no more money to offer. But the vision of her sockless feet accompanied me home. I rummaged through my dresser drawers for a few pairs of nearly new, thick socks and put them in a plastic bag.

I waited for the woman for the next several days in the same place, at the same time, but she never showed up. Unwilling to give up, unable to linger on the platform, I brought my little package up a flight of stairs to the woman who worked in the token booth. Though we had never spoken, we did have a smiling relationship. I usually traveled to and from Manhattan before rush hour, and she knew my face.

I asked the clerk to open the booth's side door. I handed her the bag and an assignment: Please be on the lookout for a thin, black homeless woman who comes to the station in mid-afternoon and has no socks. And give her these socks.

My schedule kept me from that subway station for the next several weeks. When I finally went by her booth again, the clerk excitedly waved me over.

No, the young homeless woman had never showed up. But, the clerk told me, the day after I left the bag two homeless men knocked on the booth's door and said their socks were wet. Their feet were cold. Did she have any dry socks?

She gave the men my package.

She had never seen those men before, she said. She had worked at that station for several years, and no one had ever asked her for socks before.

"The Lord," she said, "sure works in mysterious ways."

—*Steve Lipman*

~~⁂~~

Comment
Our good intentions are powerful enough to set the wheel of miracles in motion.

John Donovan's* father was a cantankerous, ornery fellow whose querulous temperament had alienated many friends, relatives, and neighbors over the years, literally driving them away. His churlish manner had worsened with advancing age and chronic illness, and he was cross and disagreeable all the time now. Hence, John Donovan found it virtually impossible to find live-in help for his father—something that had become an absolute necessity since his mother had died two years before.

The city he lived in abounded in home-attendant agencies that catered to people like his father, and good, reliable help was easy to come by. But nobody stayed for more than a week.

The routine was always the same. The new prospect would arrive with shining eyes and a determined manner, and John would warn, cautiously, "My father is not an easy man." The home attendant would shrug, smile, and say something reassuring like, "No one who is sick and elderly is easy." But a week later, the smile would be wiped off, replaced by a grimace of pain, and the shining eyes would have become weary and bloodshot. "Sorry," they would say quickly, as they beat a hasty retreat. "But your father is just impossible."

John Donovan couldn't blame them. *He* couldn't wait to retreat from his father's presence, either. No matter what or how much he did for him, his father always grumbled and complained.

"There has to be someone who exists in this world who could have a magical effect on Dad!" John said in exasperation one day. "Someone like Mom," he added wistfully.

Indeed, his sweet, soft-spoken mother had always had a calming influence on his truculent father. People had marveled for years about the way he became transformed when she was around. "He's like a different person altogether," they would often remark.

If people had physical doubles in the world, why couldn't they have emotional ones? Why couldn't he find a home attendant with a serene temperament and a mellow nature, someone who mirrored his mother completely?

"Oh, Mom!" he cried at her grave one day. "I know this is the height of desperation, coming to ask you for help. But I'm at my wit's end. Please send me a home attendant for Dad—someone just like you!"

"I can't believe what I just did!" John thought as he walked away from the grave, rubbing his forehead in disbelief. "Praying at a parent's grave for good health or general success is one thing. But praying for a home attendant is downright ridiculous!"

Still, when the phone rang two days later, John couldn't help but wonder if there wasn't a connection.

"Mr. Donovan," chirped a pleasant-sounding voice. "Mrs. O'Reilley here. I think I've finally hit pay dirt. There's a young man looking for a home attendant position who fits the bill perfectly. I think you'll be very pleased."

His name was Charlie Edwards and he was planning to be a nurse one day. In the meantime, he was saving for his tuition by working as an attendant, and he had walked into the agency for the first time that morning.

Although easygoing and placid in temperament, Charlie possessed a wicked sense of humor, a mischievous smile, and an infectious, boisterous laugh that engaged everyone, including (despite himself) John Donovan's father. It was virtually impossible not to be charmed by Charlie's warmth and winsome appeal. In truth, he *was* just like John's mother, and John was pretty much convinced that somehow she had arranged this match, just the way he had asked her to.

So, for the second time that week, John Donovan journeyed to his mother's grave—this time to express his profound appreciation for her very efficient manner of granting his request. After praying at her gravesite for several minutes, he murmured his thanks for her rapid intercession and then began to talk out loud to her, as he always did, in the teasing, jocular manner he had adopted with her since he was a teenager. "So, gee Mom, I hope you have good company around here. . . . Any interesting neighbors?"

He didn't know where the impulse to ask came from. He had never given the neighboring tombstones even a passing glance. But this time his eyes involuntarily flickered to the gravestone immediately adjoining his mother's. His eyes widened. "Now, that's interesting," he muttered to himself. "Wonder if he's related? . . . Nah, what's the big deal?" he said dismissively. "It's a very common name, very common."

"Hey, Charlie," John said in conversation a few days later. "I know this is a long shot, but are you by any chance related to someone named Wayne Edwards?"

"Yes, I am, but Edwards is a common name, and we're probably not talking about the same guy anyway."

"Why do you say that?" pressed John.

"Because the Wayne Edwards I knew is long dead and buried."

"And is he by any chance currently residing in the All-Saints Cemetery?" asked John.

"How'd you know that?" asked Charlie with a puzzled frown.

"Wayne Edwards is buried right next to my mother. Charlie," exclaimed John with mounting excitement, "who *was* Wayne Edwards?"

Charlie turned to John, his complexion ashen but his eyes ablaze with wonder.

"John," he answered slowly, "Wayne Edwards was my *grandfather.*"

"Obviously," Charlie mused, "this was a match made in heaven!"

When Heather McCarty*
became engaged in 1971,
she was delighted with the beautiful diamond ring her fiancé presented
to her, and didn't anticipate that any more extravagant gifts or expensive
pieces of jewelry would be coming her way. After all, her prospective
groom was a struggling young man in his early twenties, and the diamond ring had been costly. So she was surprised and pleased when he
arrived at her home one evening proudly bearing aloft a jeweler's box
containing yet another gift.

"Oh, you shouldn't have!" she gurgled delightedly as she tore the gift
wrap off the box and opened it. Nestled inside was an heirloom antique
pin, a large gold cameo inlaid with emerald and cobalt stones, with a
second, smaller cameo dangling from it. The second cameo was an exact
replica of the first.

As soon as she saw the pin, Heather's heart sank and her delight turned
to chagrin, which she valiantly tried to conceal. She didn't want to hurt her
fiancé's feelings, but the pin was wrong for her, all wrong. First, she was a
small-boned, petite woman only five feet tall, and the pin was very large
and would engulf her. Second, her taste leaned towards the more modest
and conservative, and the pin was gaudy and ostentatious. What was the
point of accepting the gift if she was never going to wear it?

"You know," her fiancé told her proudly, "the jeweler I bought this
from says it's a one-of-a-kind piece. It was purchased as part of an estate
sale, and it was custom-made for the original owner. There's not a pin
like this anywhere else in the world!"

Gently, Heather told her fiancé that although she treasured his good
intentions and the sentiment that made him buy it, the piece wasn't for
her. "Do you mind if I go back with you to the jeweler and exchange the
pin for something else?" she asked.

He was disappointed but indulgent. The jeweler, however, was not as
accommodating. "You don't like this pin?" he asked, astonished. "It's a
magnificent piece—one of a kind! What don't you like about it exactly?"

Heather explained that the pin was simply "too much" for her small
frame and simple tastes—but the jeweler wouldn't hear of it. He per-
sisted tenaciously in his efforts to get her to keep the piece. He was a
strong and forceful person, and he tried his best to impose his will on
Heather, but she was no pushover either, and they remained locked in a
stalemate.

Finally, the jeweler shouted in elation: "Why didn't I think of this before? I have the perfect solution! Let me remove the second miniature 'baby' cameo pin that dangles from the larger 'mother' one. This will make the pin smaller and less flashy. What do you say?"

"Well . . ." said Heather dubiously.

"Look," said the jeweler quickly, "let me do it for you right now on the spot, and if you don't like the way it looks minus the second pin, I won't say another word." And deftly, he extracted a jeweler's tool from his pouch and the deed was done.

By itself, the "mother" pin was certainly less flamboyant and more in keeping with Heather's taste. It was still a little garish but definitely more discreet-looking with the replica removed.

"Okay," said Heather to the jeweler. "I can live with it now. I'll keep it. . . . So what are you going to do with the miniature cameo?" she asked as an afterthought as she prepared to leave.

"Oh, it's no problem," he answered. "It stands on its own. I can definitely sell it as a separate piece. Don't you worry about it; I'll sell it in a snap."

Over the years, Heather kept the pin in a bank vault, removing it only to wear on special occasions. She had never quite made peace with its flamboyant air, and only wore it at formal black-tie affairs. Whenever she did wear it, though, she could not help but think about the second cameo that had been separated from the larger piece. "It definitely looks as though something is missing from it," she would often muse, and she would wonder who owned the smaller piece now.

Twenty-one years later, Heather's daughter Micky became engaged. Her fiancé, a struggling young man in his early twenties, presented her with a diamond ring, and Micky expected nothing more.

But one evening, her fiancé came to her home, proudly bearing aloft a small jeweler's box.

Nestled inside was the second "baby" cameo pin. After two decades it had journeyed back to its source, thereby creating a true "mother and child" reunion.

"Millions of New Yorkers, millions of pieces of jewelry in the world," muses Heather. "My future son-in-law had never seen me wear the mother piece, didn't even know I owned it. How could this have happened? I'm still not sure what it meant, but for my daughter, the interpretation was clear. When she saw the pin nestled in the box, any qualms she might have had about the engagement vanished. For her, the pin's reappearance in our lives was a sign. It augured positive things, and a sense of destiny. In a word, it sealed the deal."

~⟨≈⟩~

Comment

Since everything in this universe contains a spark of divinity, everything plays a role in the divine plan.

$\mathcal{M}$*ichael* Yaeger* was driving his elderly father Morris to his summer cottage in a mountain resort, when the older man began speaking of the mysterious moments he had encountered during his life. One particular incident stood out in his memory, and he began to regale Michael with details of the event.

"In 1929," he reminisced, "I attended the funeral of my grandfather, Yeshaya Sholom Gross, known throughout Hungary as a very holy man. Thousands of people were in attendance at this funeral, which was held in the Jewish cemetery in Budapest. Just as the graveside ceremony was about to begin, a big, white, unusual-looking bird swooped down from the sky, alighted on the coffin, and squatted there, almost as if it had come to join in the proceedings. The people at the cemetery were riveted by the sight, not only because the bird was unusual-looking but also because it seemed rooted to its spot.

"Perched on the coffin, the bird didn't move from its position once, but sat there quiet and unblinking.

"Despite their grief, the people in the crowd couldn't help but glance at the bird as speaker after speaker rose to eulogize the great sage. They pointed and whispered. *Was it still there? It was. Still? Yes. How long had it been? Hours.*

"Was it conceivable that the bird had come to pay homage to the Holy Man? Who knew? Could the bird be a gilgul—*a reincarnation? Could be. Maybe the sage once helped a bird? Anything was possible.*

"The whispers got louder at the conclusion of the funeral. For at the precise moment that the ceremony came to an official end and the coffin was about to be lowered into the ground, the bird darted a quick look around the cemetery, flapped its wings, and flew onto a nearby tombstone. It continued to squat there until my grandfather was buried. It was only after the masses had filed out of the cemetery that the bird finally soared into the sky and disappeared from view.

"It had sat immobile during the entire funeral—three hours long.

"So, what do you make of this story?" Morris Yaeger demanded of his son as he finished the tale.

Michael Yaeger, a cerebral sort who embraced the rational and eschewed the mystical, laughed.

"That's a ridiculous story!" he scoffed. "It can't possibly be true. You're making it up. Or exaggerating. The bird probably sat on the coffin for a short period. In your grief, your sense of time became warped. No, I don't believe this story for a minute," he said dismissively.

Just then, a big, white, unusual-looking bird swooped down from the sky and perched on the hood of the car. Michael looked at the bird in disbelief, waiting for it to fly away as suddenly and abruptly as it had descended.

It didn't move.

Throughout the rest of the two-and-a-half-hour journey from New York City to upstate New York, the bird sat still and unblinking on its roost on the hood of the car. No matter how much Michael speeded up, and despite all the bumps and curves on the road, the bird steadfastly clung to its perch on the car, and it stayed there until their journey's end.

When the Yaegers reached their destination in the countryside, the bird darted a quick glance in their direction and then soared away.

Comment

Messengers do not always assume human shape. Validation may come in many forms; but only if we are open to the mysteries of the universe can we fully receive its blessings.

$\mathcal{S}$*heroll* Carby was a social worker at the Saint William's Center in Louisville, Kentucky. As part of her duties, Sheroll regularly made home visits, checking on her clients and tending to their needs.

On one of her weekly visits not long ago, Sheroll went to see one of her favorites, Joseph Wilson, a handsome elderly man with a delicate face framed by a full head of white hair. Sitting in his living room, she addressed his health concerns and discussed his poor eating habits. Suddenly, much to her surprise, she caught sight of a small pistol with a pearl handle lying on the couch beside him.

Trying to act nonchalant, she forced herself to interrupt their regular conversation. "Uh . . . Mr. Wilson," she stuttered, "what is that object beside your hip? Is it what I think it is? It can't be real." Sheroll was surprised—to put it mildly—that gentle old Mr. Wilson would possess such a weapon. Or any weapon.

"Yes, it's for real," said Mr. Wilson in a matter-of-fact manner. "I keep it for protection."

Sheroll was alarmed. She tried to understand his reasoning. She asked, "Is it necessary to keep it out in the open like that?"

"I hope it doesn't bother you. I don't remember why I left it out in plain sight," he replied. "Usually I hide it. I even sleep with it under my pillow."

Sheroll didn't know how to respond to this. She imagined the gun going off accidentally while he slept. After a brief silence she asked: "Is it loaded?"

"Well, honey," he said with some sarcasm, "it ain't much good if it ain't loaded."

Social workers, Sheroll realized, often encountered strange situations. Seeing Mr. Wilson's gun disturbed her. She managed to muster up the nerve to ask a question to which, she was sure, she would get a flat *no!*

"Can I have your bullets?" Sheroll asked.

To her complete surprise, he said, "I guess so." And with that, he handed her the gun. Sheroll tried to pry open the pistol. She had no idea what she was doing. She naively took a screwdriver to open the chamber and remove the bullets.

With the bullets dislodged, Sheroll felt somewhat better. She completed her unusual visit with Mr. Wilson and drove home. She was relieved to find her husband there, home early from the office. She told him about her bizarre visit with Mr. Wilson, and about how she had removed the bullets from the gun. He didn't seem the least bit concerned.

"He'll probably reload the gun anyway," he said. Sheroll felt annoyed at her husband's casual attitude.

"I don't have any right to take the gun away, do I?" she asked. That ended the conversation, but the thought did not leave her mind. The image of Mr. Wilson and his gun kept coming back to her. She dreamed about it all that night. The next day, while on her way to other clients, Sheroll could not stop thinking about Mr. Wilson and his pistol. Her next visit with him was scheduled for the end of the week. However, she felt compelled to go back and confront him again. She turned the car around and made an impromptu appearance, catching Mr. Wilson unawares.

She got directly to the point. "Mr. Wilson," Sheroll asked, "did you reload the gun after I left last night?"

"Why, of course I did," he replied openly.

"It really bothers me," said Sheroll. "Did it ever occur to you what might happen if someone stole your pistol? A crime could be committed with it."

"Well, I never thought about it in that light," he answered, stroking his chin.

All at once Sheroll found herself asking a question that sounded naive. "Can I keep the gun and put it somewhere for safekeeping?"

Again, to her complete surprise, he said, "Sure, you can *have* the gun."

Feeling uneasy about taking the pistol, she was nevertheless relieved that he relinquished it so easily. As soon as she left, Sheroll took the gun over to the nearest police station and had them put it in the property room.

Late the next afternoon, right before her office closed, Sheroll picked up the ringing phone. It was Mr. Wilson.

"You won't believe what happened!" he exclaimed. Sheroll heard the agitation in his voice and listened with bated breath. "Right after you left, a guy came to my door. Everyone in the neighborhood knows him as a junkie hooked on drugs. He crashed through my front door and started punching me. I fell to the floor on both knees. Then he ransacked my place and put a few things in his satchel. Nothing of real value, though. Suddenly he got really agitated and started to look under my pillow and mattress. I don't know what he expected to find, but I bet it was my gun."

Sheroll listened intently to every word. "You must be my guardian angel," continued Mr. Wilson, his voice calming down as he spoke. "I don't remember how long I've owned that pistol. But thank God you took it away from me when you did. There's no telling what he would have done if he'd found it. More than likely he would have shot me."

Comment

When we show care and concern for others, violence dissolves and love, peace, and harmony grow in its stead.

Finding a penny is supposed to bring good luck. Sharon Kovalsky found considerably more than a penny. Within two weeks, her discovery would pay her a very valuable dividend.

Sharon's good luck originated in the fast checkout line at the Super Duper Supermarket in Rochester, New York. While standing on line with her few purchases, she felt a lump under her right foot. She looked down. There on the floor was a wrinkled ten-dollar bill. She stooped down immediately to pick it up.

Her first impulse was to hand it over to the checkout clerk. On second thought, she quickly pulled back the money in her clutched hand. "He'll probably pocket it himself," she thought. Then another, more pragmatic option came to mind. "I think I'll keep it safe for awhile instead. I don't need it now. Who knows, maybe I'll get a chance to put it to good use later," she told herself. With that, she tucked the bill into a "safety" compartment in her wallet. She had never used that compartment before. She was pleased with her quick decision, which would let her forget the whole matter until the right time and place came along. With a smile on her face, she paid for her groceries and drove home.

Two weeks later Sharon found herself in the very same checkout line. Although she had only three items in her basket, she waited patiently behind an elderly woman, shabbily dressed. The temperature was frigid outside. Sharon felt compassion for this shivering woman whose face bore the telltale lines of many years of struggling to make ends meet. The cashier rang up her meager sale and was waiting impatiently to be paid. Sharon looked at the woman with complete sympathy. Then Sharon's chain of thought was interrupted when she heard the woman speak.

"Two weeks ago when I was here," she said to the clerk as her arthritic fingers rummaged through her empty purse, "I lost a ten-dollar bill. I don't have enough money now to pay for these few things."

What an extraordinary coincidence. "I can't believe my ears," Sharon said to herself. "This has to be the moment I've been waiting for." She immediately unzipped the safety compartment of the wallet she had in her hand.

To get the old woman's attention, Sharon tapped her on the shoulder. "Two weeks ago I was here, too, madam, and I found this ten-dollar bill on the floor." Without a moment's hesitation, Sharon pulled out her "lucky" find—the very bill the old woman had dropped.

John Evans* was in a foul mood. The grimy sink was overflowing with dirty dishes, toys were strewn around the kitchen floor, piles of musty newspapers were heaped on the dining room table, and stacks of laundry waiting to be sorted lay silently in rebuke on the living room couch. From the children's bedrooms came a cacophony of wild shrieks and loud music. "I can't cope with all of this!" John thought, frustrated and angry at himself for not being able to manage the chaos that had over-taken his home. "How did Heather handle the kids and the house so per-fectly?" he asked himself in awe. "She always seemed to be in total control."

Heather, his adored wife of seventeen years, had died three months before of breast cancer. John had been devastated by her death, but didn't have the time to mourn properly. He had been left with six chil-dren ranging in age from three to fifteen, and he could only afford a part-time housekeeper to come in a couple of times a week to give him a hand. He held a demanding job as an accountant in a big firm, and tax season was at hand. It was all he could do to maintain his workload and keep some semblance of order at home. He was beginning to feel as if he would break.

"Let's play hide and seek!" cried the two youngest children, three-year-old Todd and four-year-old Tracy, as they darted into the living room, oblivious of their father seated at his desk.

"You hide first!" commanded the older child. "I'll count . . . one, two, three, four . . . ready or not, here I come!"

"Dad . . ." Fifteen-year-old Jeff wandered into the room. "Have you seen my Meat Loaf CD?"

"Dad," Susie called from her room where she was working on a book report, "can you give me some help here?"

"Daddy . . ." Eight-year-old Jeff tugged at his arm. "I don't under-stand my math homework. Can you explain it to me?"

"Daddy!" shouted Tracy as she returned to the living room, scowling. "I can't find Todd anywhere. Have you seen him?"

"Aren't you guys playing hide and seek?" John said absently, rubbing his temples, where a vein was beginning to throb.

"Yeah, we are. But where could he be? I've looked everywhere."

"Just keep on looking, honey. He probably found a great place you didn't think of," answered John as he went to answer the doorbell.

A panhandler was standing on the steps.

"Yeah?" John grunted ungraciously.

"Good afternoon!" the man said brightly. "Mrs. Evans in?"

"Mrs. Evans is dead."

"Ohmygod!" the man clutched his heart in shock. "What happened? . . . I'm so sorry. . . . What a great lady. . . . What happened?"

"Breast cancer," John barked.

"Daddy! Daddy!" Tracy ran to the door, pulling at John's sleeve with urgency. "I *still* can't find Todd. I've looked everywhere!"

"Honey," John answered impatiently, "the front door was locked when I opened it now. He didn't leave the house. He's here somewhere. He's a tiny kid, he probably squeezed into a place you wouldn't think of yourself. You just have to look harder!"

"Listen," he said as he turned to the panhandler, "I'm really sorry, but I can't talk right now. . . . I've got tons of things to do; I'm up to my neck. Here!" And he thrust two dollars into the panhandler's palm.

"Uhh . . . Mr. Evans . . ." The panhandler shifted uncomfortably. "Sorry to bother you at a difficult time like this, but I wonder if I might have something to eat?"

"What do you think the two dollars is supposed to be for . . . booze?" John asked rudely.

"Mr. Evans," the panhandler said, looking at him chidingly. "Your wife was a very special woman. Whenever I came to the door, she never gave me less than ten dollars. *And* she always invited me in for a full, hot meal. I will never forget her kindness. I owe her a great debt."

"Well, I'm not my wife," John snapped.

"Mr. Evans," the panhandler entreated. "I haven't eaten in a day. Surely you have something in the fridge that you can spare?"

"All right, come in," John said grudgingly.

As he ushered the man into the living room, he caught sight of Tracy peering under the couch.

"Still can't find him, hon?" he asked.

"Dad . . . it's been so long . . . why hasn't Todd come out of his hiding place yet? . . . I'm worried."

"Please, Mr. Evans . . . I'm so hungry!" interjected the panhandler.

"Well, wherever Todd is, he definitely deserves a prize for outwitting you for so long, doesn't he?" John said distractedly to Tracy as he headed for the kitchen.

He opened the refrigerator and there, curled up inside, blue and unconscious, was Todd.

"You found him not a moment too soon," the hospital staff doctor told him later in the emergency room. "Probably just a few minutes more in the refrigerator and he would have been a goner for sure. What luck that you discovered him when you did! We've revived him and he'll be fine."

"Whoever was hungry at that particular moment," the doctor laughed over his shoulder as he walked away, "saved your son's life!"

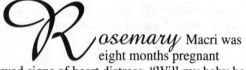 *osemary* Macri was
eight months pregnant
when the baby suddenly showed signs of heart distress. "Will my baby be
all right?" she asked, as she lay in New York Hospital's maternity ward,
hooked up to machines she could barely comprehend. "We'll do the best
we can," responded the doctor. "But I have to be honest with you—there
is only so much we can do."

A legion of doctors and nurses kept vigil over the fetus during the
next twenty-four hours. But despite their efforts, the baby's condition
worsened. The doctors made a decision to induce labor. Shortly thereafter, Rosemary gave birth to a baby boy.

For what seemed like an eternity, Rosemary lay waiting for her
child's prognosis. She watched the nurses come and go from their stations. She heard the sound of technology and television. She smelled
disinfectant. Finally, overcome with weariness and numb with shock,
she fell into a deep sleep.

As Rosemary slept, the staff was very concerned about the poor prognosis of Rosemary's newborn. They knew all too well the grave odds
against the baby's survival. They called in the priest. "The mother is fast
asleep," the priest said, "and it is my belief that given the circumstances,
the child should be baptized." Right there and then, the child was baptized.

All the while, Rosemary slumbered peacefully. In her dreams, a vision of her late Uncle Patrick appeared. "Don't worry," the calming
voice said, "your child will be well. Everything will be fine."

Just as the ad hoc baptism came to an end, Rosemary awoke from her
deep state of slumber. The dream about her uncle, and the soothing
words he had spoken, had made her feel comforted. But now her own
heart froze with terror when she saw the priest. He must have known, for
he spoke quickly. "My dear," he said, "hold on to hope because the situation has been so precarious, we baptized the baby. We named him
Patrick."

She was just opening her mouth to speak to the priest, to tell him
about her dream, when the doctors entered the room. The priest and
Rosemary looked at them pleadingly. "Your son will be just fine."

𝓙*erry* Simon* first met Yehuda Finerman* at a kibbutz in Israel. The young Simon had fled there after a brief stint in the U.S. Army, where he had encountered subtle and not-so-subtle forms of anti-Semitism. "Just a few short years after World War II," Jerry had thought in anguish, "and nobody seems to have learned any lessons. What kind of world do we live in?"

So he escaped to a different kind of world—a world that had captured the imagination of quixotic idealists and bold adventurers alike; a world that beckoned those who were disillusioned with the rat race and the dog-eat-dog existence of contemporary life: the seemingly idyllic world of the Israeli kibbutz.

In the early days of the Jewish state, Simon was one of thousands of foreigners who volunteered to work on a kibbutz, and it was there that he met Finerman, a European immigrant who had survived the Holocaust. Finerman was close-mouthed about the horrors he had endured, and Jerry discreetly avoided the subject.

But one hot summer day, when the two were toiling side by side in the kibbutz fields under the blazing sun and Finerman's shirtsleeves were rolled up high, Jerry could not help but notice the numbers tattooed on his friend's forearm. And when he had registered these numbers, he could not help but emit an audible gasp.

"What's the matter, Jerry?" Finerman asked.

"I—I'm sorry, Yehuda," Jerry stammered, "I'm not trying to be nosy or anything, but I couldn't help but notice the numbers on your forearm."

"Surely you've seen them on other survivors before," Finerman responded curtly.

"Of course I have. It's—it's just . . . well, what struck me as odd is that your concentration camp numbers—7416—just happen to be the last four digits of my American social security number!"

"That's what you're excited about?" Finerman scoffed. "It's just a meaningless coincidence!"

"Look, Yehuda," Jerry pleaded. "I know it's hard for you . . . but I care about you . . . deeply. Could you tell me how you got those numbers?"

Finerman looked at Jerry thoughtfully. "Maybe it *is* a mistake for survivors to hide their experiences from the rest of the world. Maybe we *were* meant to serve as witnesses. . . . All right, Jerry, I'll tell you exactly what happened."

And the two sat down in the fields under the blazing sun and Finerman recounted a story that was familiar and yet not familiar in its telling—a story that was his but not his alone.

". . . And then," an hour later Yehuda concluded, "we stood on line at selection . . . my brothers, my sisters, my parents, and I . . . and we were branded with these concentration camp numbers . . . in numerical order. . . . I was next to last, followed by my brother. Afterward, we were split up, and I never saw any of them again. I was the only one in my family who survived the war."

Jerry was silent when Yehuda's recital of the terrors he had suffered came to an abrupt end. In the face of such suffering, what could he possibly say? Now he understood why survivors were so loath to recount their stories. Their nightmare was truly unutterable, unspeakable—and words were impotent in imparting the full extent of the nightmare. But the story had to be told, didn't it?

Many years later, Jerry left the kibbutz and began working in the Jerusalem–Tel Aviv area as a tour guide for wealthy Americans who wanted to be personally chaperoned around Israel in a comfortable limousine. Most of his clients were kind and amiable, and Jerry generally enjoyed his job. But one day, he picked up a new client at the airport whose behavior was downright insufferable.

The man was domineering, rude, gruff, and harsh. He was a control freak, and continually shouted orders and commands at Jerry from the passenger seat in the back. Jerry clenched his teeth and made an almost superhuman effort to remain polite. Finally, just when he felt he couldn't take it anymore, the man inexplicably shouted: "Pull to the side of the road!"

"What?" Jerry asked, confused.

"I said pull to the side of the road! . . . Look," said the man to Jerry, who had turned around to face his tormentor, "you don't like me very much, do you?"

Jerry was silent.

"I know sometimes my behavior is obnoxious, offensive. Sometimes even I can't quite believe myself what I've become. I'm sorry; I apologize. It's just that . . . it's just that . . . I'm so alone in the world; I've endured so much . . . there are nights I think I just won't make it through . . ."

And then the man broke down and cried. "You think I'm an arrogant, wealthy American businessman," he said to Jerry. "What I really am," he sobbed, "is a Holocaust survivor."

He rolled up his shirt to show Jerry the numbers.

7 . . . 4 . . . 1 . . . 7.

The last four digits of Jerry's social security number was 7416. And the memory of a conversation, held long ago but still very fresh and poignant, sprang to his mind: ". . . We were branded in numerical order . . . my parents, my sisters, my brothers, and I. I was next to last . . ." he recalled Yehuda Finerman telling him that summer day years before in the kibbutz.

Jerry's reverie was broken by the American's tortured sobs.

"I lost my whole family in the concentration camp!" he cried. "Everyone was killed except for me! I have no one in the world!"

Jerry stared at the American in shock, and gently, very gently, he whispered, "My dear friend . . . you are wrong. Number 7416 is very much alive. And I happen to know exactly where he can be found."

Father O'Reilly* was a busy man. As a hospital chaplain who ministered at four local hospitals, he was on call twenty-four hours a day, and he had witnessed a lot of pain, heartache, and misery during the course of his ten-year career. To replenish himself and seek respite from the grinding schedule that occasionally wore him down, he often retreated to an abandoned theological seminary building where he had studied in his youth. Here he engaged in prayer, meditated, read, or simply allowed his mind to wander, his muscles to relax. He always felt renewed after a visit to this building. It was deserted, crumbling, and in a state of disrepair, but for him it had become a true sanctuary.

Late one afternoon, after a particularly taxing and difficult day, Father O'Reilly decided that a visit to the seminary building was in order. He yearned for its quiet and tranquil air, and his soul urgently needed to withdraw. He craved a place where he could breathe, think, and dream . . . alone.

He entered the old building, which had been forsaken long ago, but whose doors remained open to the few pilgrims who still sought its solace. He inhaled its musty odor of abandonment and smiled in rueful recollection as he envisioned the hundreds of hurrying students who had raced down its corridors with such life, such vitality. "Everything changes," he thought.

Just then, his hospital pager went off.

"Oh, no," he sighed. "Just when I was beginning to unwind."

He tried to retrieve his message, but for some reason it was strangely garbled.

"That's odd," he thought. "What's the matter with the pager?" Someone had paged him, but he couldn't figure out whom. Which hospital needed him?

The old seminary building had no operating telephones, so he had to leave its grounds to make his calls to the four hospital chaplaincy departments that had his beeper number.

No, said everyone he called. *We didn't call you. Try the other hospitals.* He tried them all, but the staff in each hospital was as perplexed as he was. No one who had his pager number had given him a call.

"The pager must be malfunctioning," he mused, as he returned to the old seminary building to continue his disrupted retreat. "I'll have to bring it into the company tomorrow to be repaired," he thought as he entered the seminary grounds.

Then he stopped and stared in disbelief.

During his absence, a wing of the old building had collapsed onto itself.

The very wing in which he had stood . . . only minutes before.

$\mathcal{I}n$ 1966, best-selling author and pilot Richard Bach was barnstorming in the Midwest in a rare biplane, a 1929 Detroit-Parks P-2A Speedster.

Stopping over in Palmyra, Wisconsin, Bach lent the plane to a friend, who upended the craft as he came in for a landing at the small airport. Working together, they were able to successfully repair the damaged plane, except for one part. A strut had been shattered and needed to be replaced. Bach and his friend felt discouraged by what they agreed were the very dim prospects for finding a replacement strut in Palmyra. There were only seven other biplanes in the world like his, and what were the chances of someone in a small town like Palmyra possessing that particular part?

As Bach and his friend stood near the plane, lamenting the hopeless situation, a man walked up to them and asked if he could be of any help. Bach replied sarcastically, "Sure. Do you just happen to have an interwing strut for a 1929 Detroit-Parks Speedster, model P-2A?"

The man walked over to a hangar and moments later returned with precisely the part that was required to fix the plane!

In his book *Nothing by Chance*, Bach reflects:

"The odds against our breaking the biplane in a little town that happened to be home to a man with the 40-year-old part to repair it; the odds that he would be on the scene when the event happened; the odds that we'd pushed the plane right next to his hangar, within ten feet of the part we needed—the odds were so high that 'coincidence' was a foolish answer."

Comment

Every once in a while we are reminded to take a step back, look up and simply acknowledge the hand that guides our life.

I thought my marriage was idyllic. I thought my husband was a respectable, upright, law-abiding citizen. I thought we had an open, honest relationship in which we knew everything there was to know about each other.

But when I discovered the cache of drugs hidden in his briefcase one day, I realized that everything I had assumed about my husband and about our marriage was a total sham.

Fifteen years of pretense came crashing down around me as I examined the small plastic bags of cocaine powder stashed in the pouch compartment. How had the truth eluded me all this time? How could I have been so naive? How could I have lived with a hard-core addict and not even known?

It wasn't the shock of discovering that he was an addict that pulled me away from him irrevocably. I could have lived with the knowledge that my husband had a serious problem; I am a loyal person and I would have given him my support. Together, we could have attempted to surmount the crisis. But the realization that all these years he had *lied* to me, perpetrated constant deceptions, engaged in endless subterfuge in order to maintain his habit and hide it from me: that realization I simply could not countenance.

For me, honesty between partners was the paramount thing; without it there could be no relationship.

So, there I was, a newly-divorced forty-year-old, with five children on my hands, and no marketable skills. All my life, I had devoted myself to home and hearth, eschewing the lure of the workplace in order to be a constant presence in my children's lives. When I had left my job to have my first baby, no office boasted a computer system. Now, they all did. How was I going to support my family?

"Displaced homemaker" was the term they used for me and tens of thousands of women like me.

I sat in agency after agency, scribbling applications for training courses and emergency relief. I was assured that help would soon be on its way. But in the meantime, there were bills to pay and five young and hungry mouths to feed. How was I going to get by?

I baby-sat a little; I tried telemarketing at night. But until I was accepted into a training program and acquired real skills, every month would prove a tremendous challenge.

One day, I couldn't take it anymore. The strain and burden were too great to bear. The next month's rent was due the following day and I was $240 short. The refrigerator and cupboards were bare; I didn't know what I would serve my children for supper that night. Each month I had somehow managed to pay the rent and feed the kids. But now, I seemed to be at the end of my rope. Everything was unraveling. Including me.

I began to weep. I felt utterly alone and helpless. To whom could I turn?

Pray! a voice inside me urged.

Pray? another voice scoffed.

Why not? I shrugged. It certainly couldn't hurt.

Out of the depths of my being, I prayed. From my torment and anguish and heartache and pain, I prayed. I prayed as I had never prayed before.

"Dear God," I prayed. "Please help me pay this month's rent and feed my children tonight. I'm not asking you to give me luxuries or extravagances; I'm begging you to allow me to *survive.*"

Just then, there was a knock at the door, and my aunt and uncle burst into the room, bearing bags of groceries. I stared at them in shock.

I was taken by surprise not merely because my aunt and uncle lived in a different part of town, but because for years they had been somewhat estranged from our family and had kept in touch only sporadically. I had not spoken to either of them in months.

Yet here they were, only seconds after I had completed my prayers— flesh-and-blood answers to my supplications!

So frightened was I by the juxtaposition of their sudden and unexpected arrival with my prayers, that I could only stammer my surprise and gratitude.

After they left, I pondered—with awe and fear—the mystery of their auspicious visit. I had not spoken to anyone recently who was in contact with them, and I had been too proud to tell my friends and relatives the extent of my troubles. No one had known that my cupboards were empty.

When I had attempted to ask my aunt and uncle what had brought them to my home, they had casually answered, "Oh, we were just in the neighborhood, and thought you could use some extra stuff."

An unsatisfactory answer, indeed.

I was overwhelmed with relief knowing that my children would eat heartily that night. But what would I do about the rent?

As I began to unpack the groceries, I noticed a white envelope discreetly tucked into one of the bags. It had my name on it.

I tore it open and found inside twelve crisp $20 bills. $240.

Two hundred forty dollars is a strange amount of money to give as a gift.

But it was precisely the amount I needed for the rent.

—*Chrissie Jenkins**

Comment

Set a prayer in motion and you've set a bird with a pointed beak soaring to the sky. Watch it, as it pierces the gates of heaven.

In 1977, Teri Baucum was swimming in a lake with her young brothers and her dog when she stepped on something sharp. She bent down to retrieve it and found herself clutching a mud-encased, mollusk-encrusted class ring. Inside the band of the heavy, aristocratic-looking ring was an inscription: *"K. Sprott, 1956."*

"Geez," she said, and emitted a low whistle. "This thing's been here a long time."

Perhaps, had she been older, she would have thought of pursuing inquiries that would have led her to the college that issued the ring and, ultimately, to its owner. Or she might have launched her own personal investigation of the lakeside area, in an attempt to ferret out the owner's name. But she was a mere slip of a girl, young and unsophisticated, and she was ignorant of the myriad ways one could track down an owner's identity.

Since class rings aren't particularly valuable, anyhow, it never even occurred to her to embark on an extensive search. Still, she didn't feel it was quite right to simply toss the ring back into the water. "I'll hold onto it," she thought. "You never know."

So she took the ring home, threw it in a drawer, and promptly forgot about its existence. But every time she moved, she retrieved the ring that was tucked into a corner of her dresser drawer and took it along with her to her new home. "Why do I keep holding on to this old ring?" she asked herself every now and then, perplexed by her own actions. "What's the point?"

Twenty years and four states later, Teri was happily married and living on a lakefront property. Early one Saturday morning, her husband was standing on the outdoor patio, admiring the view, when his attention was captured by an unusual sight. He ran into the bedroom shouting, oblivious to the deep slumber in which his wife was enwrapped. "Hey, Ter, wake up and come see this!"

Teri pulled the covers up over her head. She didn't work on Saturdays as her husband did, and she wanted to revel in the luxury of a late morning in bed. But her husband was insistent, and finally, to oblige him, she groggily pulled herself out of bed and stumbled outside to see the cause of his excitement.

A large hot-air balloon was floating serenely over the lake. "Very nice, honey," she said dutifully, and made a beeline back to bed. "Hope I can get back to sleep," she thought wearily, unimpressed by the spectacle that had so enthralled her spouse.

But fifteen minutes later, her husband rushed into the bedroom again, his enthusiasm now changed to alarm.

"You gotta look at this balloon *now,*" he yelled. "It seems like it's out of control. It's rushing over the lake and it's headed in our direction! This thing's gonna crash *right into our house!*

"Don't be ridiculous," Teri mumbled to her husband, pulling the covers up over her head once more.

But her sleep was interrupted a third time just a few minutes later by a furious pounding on the window. It was her husband, now gesticulating wildly. She dashed outside, galvanized by his frenzied behavior.

True to his dire prediction, the balloon had plummeted down from the sky onto their house!

The balloon was tangled up in the branches of the tree that shaded the house and in the wires from the television cable system, and the balloonist was hanging onto a rope for dear life. "Oh my God, he's going to die!" Teri thought in horror.

She watched helplessly as her husband carefully shimmied up the tree toward the balloon that was careening ominously over the side of their roof. Slowly, laboriously, he eased an older man and a young boy out of the basket in which they were trapped. Finally, after what seemed like an eternity, he had them successfully extricated and they were safe on the ground.

The older man brushed himself off and then gallantly extended his hand. "Thank you so much for saving our lives! My name is Kingswood Sprott Junior."

And without missing a beat, Teri replied:

"And I . . . I have your class ring!"

"**R**on, is that you?" came the frantic voice on the phone.

"Yes, what is it?" asked Ron, noting the concern in his sister's voice.

"It's Caron," came the reply. "She's sick, very sick, and she needs to go to the hospital! Meet us at Mount Sinai as soon as you can!"

Upset by the news, Ron turned to his secretary. "Carol, that was my sister. You remember my niece Caron Graham? Well, she needs to get to the hospital and I'm going to see if I can help in any way. Please cancel my afternoon appointments." Ron grabbed his coat from the closet and ran out.

When Carol got home from work she told her five-year-old son about Caron. He listened intently. He then went to his bedroom. A few minutes later he returned with a paper rose in his hand.

"Mom, could you get this rose to Caron?" he asked.

"Oh, honey," said Carol, obviously moved by her son's gesture. "I have such a busy day tomorrow. I'll try. Perhaps on my way to the office. Wherever did you find such a thing?"

"Last Sunday when we were at mass, Mom, I noticed this rose lying in the aisle beside our pew. When you went up for communion, I bent down to pick it up. That's when an old lady with a shawl wrapped around her, someone I had never seen before, came over to me and said that the rose was meant for someone who needed a miracle. And then she said, 'Be sure to put the rose into the person's hand so that it touches the skin.' I bet this rose was meant for Caron, Mom."

Carol looked adoringly at her son and took the rose. "I'll be sure to press it into Caron's hand. I promise. And, now, young man, how about some supper?"

The following morning Carol headed for Mount Sinai's intensive care unit, where she found several family members, including Ron, standing gravely around Caron's little bed. It was clear that Caron's condition was critical. The monitor perched on top of Caron's bed said it all. The reading was in the low sixties, perilously below the normal 100 mark.

Carol approached the bed. Gently she placed the paper rose in Caron's hand. Remembering her son's words, she made sure that the rose touched the frail girl's body.

She now waited. She had no illusions about any possible recovery. Nevertheless she closed her eyes and said her own silent prayer.

Almost at once she heard Caron's mother say excitedly: "Look, the number is rising!"

Carol immediately looked over at the monitor. Could her eyes be deceiving her?

Sure enough. The family members chimed in unison as the indicator started to climb: "64, 65, 66, 67, 68, 69."

The voices were now getting too loud for the intensive care unit. Alarmed, two nurses ran over to see what the commotion was about. The excitement around little Caron's bed was palpable. The figures continued to climb. They were now up to 95.

"Can you believe this!" Caron's mother cried.

"It's impossible," said Ron. The other family members shouted with joy the final five figures: "96, 97, 98, 99, 100!"

The rose had done its job. Color returned to Caron's face. No one seemed to understand what had happened. Carol, of course, did. Unobtrusively she released the little paper rose from Caron's grip and slipped it back into her purse.

All who were there in the intensive care unit—the staff, the doctors, the nurses, but most of all Caron's family—pause from time to time to remember what they saw that day. And to reflect with wonder and awe.

Comment

That which may seem to be mundane has the power to transform us in the most sublime way, for in truth, nothing in God's world is mundane.

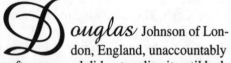

*D*ouglas Johnson of London, England, unaccountably took the wrong bus home one afternoon and did not realize it until he had traveled some distance. Instead of going back and getting his usual bus, Johnson decided to stay on the wrong bus and enjoy the scenery of a different ride.

The bus took him to an outlying district of London where he rarely went. The bus passed by the apartment building of a woman who had been a client two years before. Johnson impulsively decided to get off the bus and visit her, since he was in the area. He made his way to her apartment and knocked. There was no answer. Then he smelled gas. He knocked again and shouted. Still no answer. Johnson broke down the door and discovered the woman lying unconscious, her head in the oven, a suicide attempt.

Fortunately, Johnson was just in time to save her life.

—*Alan Vaughan*

Comment

To appear in the right place at the right time is to be a participant in a cosmic plan.

"I'm headed for the bar tonight. Do you want to come?" said Michelle Holder to her friend Dawn Montgomery. Rambunctious and restless, Michelle knew she could always count on her wild friend Dawn to party with her. This night was no exception.

"I'm waiting for you," came Dawn's eager reply. Moments later, Michelle pulled her car up in front of Dawn's building. She was dressed and ready to go. Dawn slipped into the passenger seat and beamed at her friend. Both their boyfriends, Shaun and Doug, were sailors away on duty. That meant they had plenty of time to themselves, and they felt the freedom.

"The night is ours!" laughed Michelle as she put the car into drive and stepped on the gas. Out of sheer habit, Dawn tried to pull down her safety belt, only to be reminded that, of course, it was no use. Over the entire three years she had known Michelle, the passenger safety belt in Michelle's car had been broken. Completely. Not only did it refuse to extend more than a few inches, but it had no buckle, just a strap. As usual, Dawn just shrugged and said, "Fine, hit the road."

Dawn never minded that the seat belt was broken. In fact, it was kind of fun. She lived recklessly, on the edge, and liked to court danger. If she saw a patrolman pull up alongside the car, she would pull the safety belt over her shoulder. Once they were out of sight, she could throw the broken belt back with impunity. "Ha! Tricked them again!" was her attitude.

That night Michelle and Dawn hit their favorite hot spot: the Beach Club Bar in Oceanside, California. The music throbbed and the liquor flowed. Dancing and flirting, both women drank a few too many cocktails. By the end of the evening, when they emerged from the bar, they were drunk—sloppy drunk. "Oh, my goodness," Dawn slurred, "I can't even see where the car is."

"Isn't it that one over there?" muttered Michelle, stumbling as she pointed to the far corner of the parking lot. The two could hardly walk, but they held on to each other, giggling, and eventually shuffled to the car. Their laughter subsided once they climbed in the car, however. Michelle had a momentary flash of lucidity and turned serious. "I think we should just sleep in the car," she said, "since neither one of us can make out the steering wheel."

"Great idea," agreed Dawn, slumping over. The two passed out cold.

It could have been minutes, it could have been hours, but sometime later Dawn woke up feeling wind in her face. For a fraction of a second she felt alarmed. "Oh, no!" she thought. "Is Michelle actually driving this thing? Could we be on the freeway?" But the effects of the alcohol had not yet worn off, and Dawn found she was unable to sit up. She dismissed her thoughts as being part of a crazy dream, and fell back into a deep sleep. But indeed, Michelle did decide to drive in her drunken stupor.

The next thing Dawn remembers is waking up to the bright white glare of fluorescent lights. Her body was covered with bandages, and a snarl of catheters connected her to all sorts of machines. She was struck with terror. "Where am I?" she screamed.

A policeman standing nearby came to her bedside. "This is an emergency room," he said. "I'm afraid you and your friend have been in a terrible accident."

From across the room Dawn could hear Michelle's screams. "How is my friend?" Dawn demanded.

"She's bad," the policeman replied gravely. "They're pulling glass out of her face. Your car hit a pole on the bridge, and she came flying out the window. Her face hit the ground with all the shattered pieces of glass."

Dawn leaned back and closed her eyes. Could this really be happening? Or was it merely a bad dream, an extension of her drunken slumber? To some extent, the alcohol was still in her system. On top of that, she had been given codeine to minimize the pain. Her feelings were somewhat dulled, but nevertheless, she felt welling up in her a sharp anger at God. "Why did you let me survive?" she cried. "Why didn't you just let me die?"

Just then, the urgent words of the policeman interrupted her thoughts. "You guys could've been dead," he said.

But Dawn was not in the mood to talk. "I know," she replied flatly, hoping to end the conversation.

But the officer would not be deterred. "If it wasn't for your good sense, we might have had to call your parents to identify you," he said.

"My good sense?" Dawn fired back. "What do you mean?"

"Wearing that seat belt!" the policeman replied.

"Seat belt?" Dawn was mystified. She shouted at the officer that the seat belt in the car didn't even work, that it didn't even have a buckle. But the officer would not be fooled, not this time. "Look," he said, pointing to the report of the paramedics. "Right here they wrote that they had to cut your sweater and seat belt to get you out of the car. They did it just in time, since the car was hovering over the side of the bridge. As soon as they got you out, the car tipped over and went plunging down into the water below. But I tell you—if not for your seat belt, you would have gone right through the windshield, and down in the water, too."

Dawn Montgomery could hardly believe what she was hearing; then she looked down at her body and was even more amazed by what she saw. There, across her chest and below her waist, was a black and blue mark, in an unmistakable outline. The bruise was in the exact shape of a seat belt.

During her several weeks of recuperation, Dawn was perplexed by the mystery.

Dawn left the hospital and Michelle stayed behind, still recovering from her wounds. So when the day came for her father to come pick her up from the hospital, she asked him for a favor. "Dad," she said, "on the way to the house, I'd like to stop at the junkyard. I hear the car was found, and I know where it is, and I just need to check something out." Once in the car, Dawn's father realized that the junkyard was out of the way, but he was so grateful to have his daughter alive and well that he agreed to her request. "Sure," he said, "just point the way." At the junkyard, Dawn scanned the heaps of twisted metal until she recognized Michelle's car. The passenger window was open, and she managed to peer inside at that old, familiar seat belt. What she saw made her shiver. Without any doubt, there was now a hard metal buckle where once there had been only a frayed strap.

Postscript: After the accident, which occurred on April 19, Dawn vowed to become sober. She made several false starts until July 22, when she finally entered the recovery program she has attended ever since. Dawn considers the day she became sober the first day she really began her life.

But what about the miracle that saved her life that fateful night? Maybe she had a kindred spirit watching over her. Dawn's grandmother, Irene Kohen, died long before she was born. Yet the family has always been amazed at how Dawn—with her vivacious personality, fiery red hair, and warm blue eyes—is the spitting image of Irene. Indeed, family members say the resemblance is so striking, they believe Dawn just might be Irene's reincarnation.

What's more, the two women's lives seem to have intersected on two key dates. The day of Dawn's accident, April 19, was the exact day that Irene Kohen passed away. And the day that Dawn started life anew and became sober, July 22, was—ironically— the day of Irene Kohen's birthday.

꒰ꇛꇛ꒱

Comment
When we are blessed with divine intervention, a life returned becomes a life joyfully reclaimed.

I love my work as television's "Frugal Gourmet," sharing my kitchen with viewers for half an hour each week. I'm glad I have been able to provide a comfortable life for my wife, Patty, and two sons, Channing and Jason. It's tempting sometimes to think that success is a by-product of my own hard work. But early in my career, when it seemed I had lost everything, I learned an important lesson about just who is really in charge.

Back when I was a young minister, I was the chaplain of the University of Puget Sound in Tacoma, Washington. I taught a course on first-century worship. One day a young woman gave a report on a book that discusses food and theology. This so caught the imagination of my students and me that we designed a new course called Food as Sacrament and Celebration, which also included daily lunch. The course was so popular it filled up every semester long before registration was officially opened.

I enjoyed working with food so much I soon opened a catering service with some of my students. It meant putting in long, hard hours, but I had always had workaholic tendencies. And since my wife and I had just bought our first house and wanted to start a family, it seemed to make sense to branch out. Finally, I left my job at the university to run a cooking school and open a cookware store. Since I'm an "in control" kind of guy, I had my hands in everything.

Then in 1973 a producer friend called and asked if I would do something for the local PBS station in Tacoma. I used to say the station was so small that it had a broadcast radius of six blocks. But this guy was a friend and he needed a favor, so once a week I brought all my own food, pots, pans and helpers over and we did a cooking show.

My students and I also printed our own cookbooks, which I stored in piles in my basement. With the school, the store and the shows, I believed God had given me a wonderful and unusual venue for ministry, reaching people I would never get to meet in a church setting. But often I felt frantic to keep up, to keep tabs on every detail of each project.

After several exhausting years the television program became so successful that the large PBS station in Chicago decided to produce a series for national syndication, with the promise of continuing it on a regular basis if all went well. I flew to Chicago to shoot several segments, and things went so smoothly we set a starting date for the next season. It was a good thing, because as far as my business was concerned, everything else was falling apart. Suddenly there seemed to be a cooking school and kitchen shop on every corner. We had been losing money for a while when I finally sold out in early 1982.

One day, after letting the business go, I sat down with a stack of bills and determinedly paid them in the order they came up. The money was soon gone, but there were still bills left to pay. Big ones. After all my hard work I was short $70,000.

Thank God for Chicago, I thought. In only two weeks I would have an income again. I would be back on the treadmill, rushing to keep up, to stay in control. . . .

All along my wife had been trying to get me to slow down. "Think of your heart, Jeff," she warned.

It was a prudent warning. When I was a kid, I had rheumatic fever and had appeared to have made a full recovery. It wasn't till I was 15 that I had my first real physical. My doctor asked, "How long have you had this heart murmur?"

He sent me to a specialist, who said I would have to have the damaged valve replaced one day. But valve replacement surgery was just being developed. Doctors advised me to wait. So I repressed the fact that I had a time bomb in my chest, and got on with daily life.

Then came the summer of 1982. For months I had been tiring easily, but I attributed it to stress. The week before I was to fly to Chicago, I woke up in the morning straining for breath. "Patty," I gasped to my wife. "I'd better get to the doctor."

When I walked into my doctor's office, he took one look at me and told his secretary to call Dr. Lester Sauvage, a well known Seattle heart surgeon. Dr. Sauvage ran tests and immediately scheduled open-heart surgery—for the day I was supposed to tape my first show in Chicago. Patty called the producers and told them I wouldn't be able to make it.

Dr. Sauvage was honest about the prognosis. There were three possible outcomes: The operation would be a success; it would fail and I would die; or the trauma would send me into a permanent vegetative state.

I'll never forget the night before the surgery. I lay alone in the room, pondering my life. I had tried so hard to control everything. I had worked around the clock. I had driven myself till I was miserable, and where had it gotten me?

I was 42 years old, with no job, a family to support and seventy thousand dollars in debt. Because of my faith, I wasn't afraid of dying, but the prospect of becoming a vegetable was horrifying to me.

And there wasn't a thing I could do about any of it.

It was then I remembered reading what theologian Rudolf Bultmann said about being pushed up against the wall: When you're so frightened you don't know what to do, you finally either know death or you know grace. And grace, to paraphrase Bultmann, is when you're up against the wall and you suddenly realize you're not in control of things—and that's okay.

My life was in God's hands; it had always been in God's hands. I had just acted as if it were in mine, as if everything were up to me. The word I got during that dark night was simply this: Trust the Holy One and relax.

"Lord," I said, "my life is yours. My health is yours. My debt is yours. Teach me to relax."

The next morning this message was again brought home to me. As I looked up at Dr. Sauvage in the operating room, I knew with absolute finality that control of my life was totally out of my hands.

When I woke up after surgery, my first thought was, *I can think!* This was the greatest joy I had known. I began a prayer of thanksgiving.

As I recuperated, I also felt a surge of spiritual energy. God had given me my life; I had given him my future. Every time I started to worry about my $70,000 debt, or my bleak job prospects, I wrested control from myself and gave it back to the Holy One.

The TV producers in Chicago called to find out how I was, and promised my wife they would keep in touch, but I didn't count on it. The old Jeff would have been in knots, but now I knew it was in God's hands, not mine. Then I got an unexpected invitation to be on Phil Donahue's show.

For luck, I took along copies of that old spiral-bound cookbook. "How much should we say they sell for?" Phil asked when I got there. Each book had cost me three dollars to produce, so I had been selling them for $4.75.

Three times, right before a commercial, Phil held up the cookbook, and a placard on the screen told people where to write. "This is the man! This is the book!" he shouted happily.

After the show, one of the producers said to me as I was leaving, "I hope you have a lot of books."

"And how," I said glumly. "I've got five thousand of them sitting in my basement."

I'll never forget the look of disbelief she gave me. "Five thousand?" she repeated. "You're in real trouble!"

It turned out I was. Orders started pouring in—and didn't stop! In those days, syndicated shows were shipped around the country from station to station. It took about nine weeks for a particular Phil Donahue show to air on all the stations, and I had to keep printing more and more books. At the end of those nine weeks, I had sold 40,000 cookbooks.

Not long after that, my phone rang in Tacoma, and it was Frank Lieberman from PBS in Chicago. "All right, Smith, quit fooling around," he roared in mock annoyance. "We know you've recovered. When are you coming to start a new TV series?"

I couldn't wait to get going again. Not because I was frantic to control every facet of my life, but because I wanted to work. I would work hard, but this time I would work hard out of devotion to God, not because I was driven to call all the shots.

For God in his mercy had truly shown me he could meet my needs. *You* do the math: Multiply those 40,000 books I sold times $1.75 profit, and how much do you get? *Seventy thousand dollars exactly.*

And a heaping serving of grace.

—*Jeff Smith*

When it came to love, Mary Margaret Dereu was blessed. For thirty-four wonderful years, she was married to her soul mate, Eugene. She had many pet names for him, but mostly she called him her "Prince."

Then, on October 24, 1995, Eugene unexpectedly passed away in his sleep. Mary was devastated. They were just three months shy of their thirty-fifth anniversary.

Days turned into weeks, which turned into months, and with the passing of time, a slow healing took place. But as Valentine's Day of the following year came around, Mary found herself inconsolable about Eugene's death. To distract herself, she took a drive downtown, ready to lose herself in the sights and sounds of the local market.

Once inside the market, Mary glanced at several booths, but nothing in particular caught her eye. Then, suddenly, she found herself beckoned by a row of camellia bushes in the corner of the marketplace. The flowers were majestic, in full bloom, pure white. They reminded her of the flowers at her wedding, and she purchased a bush without any hesitation.

At home, Mary chose a special place beside Eugene's favorite shade tree to plant her new shrub. While she covered the roots with earth, she kept repeating "Happy Valentine's Day, Eugene . . . Happy Valentine's Day, my Prince."

Then, just as she leaned on one hand to stand up, a small white tag attached to the base of the plant happened to catch her eye. She might easily have overlooked it.

"They must name these bushes just as they name rosebushes," Mary thought. She turned the tag in her muddy fingers. She read the name and felt the sting of a tear. There, in black ink, was the name of the pure white flower: Prince Eugene.

Perhaps it was his kiss, blown from beyond.

~~~

Comment

Flowers are often the messengers of our emotions, hopes, and dreams. Through them we send and receive, in this world and beyond.

*N*ineteen-year-old Chris Graham* and twenty-year-old Steve Ashton* were on their way from Manhattan to an upstate New York park that boasted superior recreational grounds and a large scenic lake. They had arranged to meet several friends at a specific site near the lake at exactly 1 P.M. and they looked forward to a day of boating, fishing, swimming, and more.

But all day long, as they traveled the New York State Thruway, they found themselves plagued by an unusual series of mishaps, crises, and problems, and it seemed to them as if they would never get there.

First, a flat tire. They pulled onto a shoulder of the highway and changed it quickly. "Not too bad," Chris muttered. "Only fifteen minutes gone. We'll still get there in time."

Then, after making a quick stop at a Thruway rest area, they turned the key in the ignition of the car and nothing happened. Several red signs began flashing a warning on the dashboard control panel, and Steve, who was driving, sighed. "I'm afraid the battery's dead. Gotta find someone with cables; I don't have any myself." It took about half an hour to find someone else who did.

When the battery was recharged, they sped down the highway to make up for lost time. "There are never any cops on the Thruway," Steve reassured Chris, who was nervous. "They all stalk Route 17 instead."

They were pulled over by a sheriff who didn't seem aware of this ironclad rule.

He took a *very* long time to write the ticket.

"We're an hour late already!" expostulated Chris. "The guys will never wait for us, and we'll never be able to find them. The park's huge."

"Relax," soothed Steve. "We're not so far away. I just gotta find the next exit and get off the highway here, according to the directions Johnny gave me. The rest of the way is small country roads. Maybe we'll have better luck on them than the Thruway."

But just as they pulled off at the exit, the car suddenly sputtered and died.

The two looked at each other.

"Now what?" cried Chris.

"Is this for real?" Steve shook his head in disbelief.

It took an hour for the tow truck to arrive.

"Remind me to call the customer relations department of AAA tomorrow and give them a piece of my mind," Steve said crossly.

"It's the fan belt," the mechanic at the shop said. "It'll take at least two hours."

"I give up!" shrieked Chris. "Can you believe our bad luck? When the car's fixed, let's head back home."

"I'm not a quitter," Steve said stubbornly. "The park's only about twenty minutes away from here. I don't want to turn around at this point. We're almost there. Let's go to the park and see if we can find the guys. We still have a couple of hours of sunlight left. I bet we'll find the guys after all; you'll see," Steve promised Chris in an optimistic voice.

But when they finally arrived four hours late at the appointed meeting site near the lake, the place was deserted.

"I just can't believe our day," Chris grumbled to Steve. "We came all this way for nothing!"

"Help!" they suddenly heard a young voice shout.

"Help us, please!" a second voice cried.

For a frozen moment, Chris and Steve were motionless, their gaze riveted on the sight of two little boys flailing in the lake. Then the two—certified lifeguards both—raced to the water's edge and dove in. They pulled out the kids, administered CPR, and saved their lives.

Afterwards, a shaken Steve turned to Chris and asked in a trembling voice, "Do you understand what went down here, Chris?"

"I do, Steve," Chris answered somberly. "I most certainly do."

"If we hadn't gotten to the park at precisely the time we did, surely those kids would be dead."

Comment

It's a mistake to believe that "coincidences" happen only for *our* sakes. Sometimes, they happen *to* us, but they may not be happening *because* of us or *for* us. What seems to be happening to us is actually occurring for the sake of another. It's not really *our* script, even though we may be major players. When a coincidence occurs that makes no sense in how it impacted our lives, we must also ask: But did it impact someone else's?

I rarely allow myself the luxury of a taxi, but on this particular day in September 1997 I found myself suddenly caught in a torrential downpour in midtown Manhattan, lacking an umbrella or a raincoat and on my way to an important job interview. It wouldn't impress anyone, I thought glumly, if I arrived in a rain-splattered suit and had a sopping mass of tangled curls. "Drenched" does not translate into "dresses well," a definite requisite for any job candidate these days. So I hailed a cab and hopped in.

I saw the bracelet immediately. Its gold veneer glinted at me and I lifted it from the corner of the passenger seat where it rested. It was studded with diamonds, and although I am neither a connoisseur nor an expert, I knew they were real. This was an expensive piece of jewelry, I thought, the kind of jewelry I myself longed for but could probably never hope to own. Out of my league completely, or at least for the next decade, I sighed, envisioning the lean years that lay ahead until my young husband and I established ourselves financially.

I examined the bracelet closely and saw that its clasp was broken. "The woman passenger before me must have lost it just as she left the taxi," I thought. "She probably didn't even realize it was gone."

"Hey, look at this! . . ." I began to shout excitedly to the taxi driver, then suddenly reconsidered, mid-sentence.

"Whaddja say?" he asked, turning around to stare at me through the bulletproof partition.

"Look at this . . . rain!" I dissembled. "Isn't it unbelievable!"

"If I show him the bracelet, he'll just pocket it himself," I thought. "Why does he deserve it more than me? I'm the one who found it! Besides, Judy's brother's engagement party is coming up Saturday night. Her mother's always dripping with jewels and looking so classy. For once, I'd like her to see me looking classy, too. This bracelet would really impress her."

So I pocketed the bracelet and didn't breathe a word to the cabbie.

In truth, I had absolutely no qualms about what I had done. There are over seven million people living in the metropolitan New York area, and at least 20,000 cabs. Even if I tried to find the owner, given the odds, the chances were slim.

But back in Brooklyn my mother's equanimity was shaken, shaken badly, when I recounted to her the tale of my triumphant find.

"I'm shocked," she said, her voice cold. "Shocked and very disappointed. I thought I imbued my children with a sense of honesty and integrity. How could you have taken it?"

"If I had given it to the cabbie, he would just have taken it for himself," I argued. "What should I have done?"

"You *should* have brought it to the taxi company that owns the fleet of cabs. Or the Taxi and Limousine Commission. I'm sure they have a lost and found department. Not only *should* you have done this, you *will* do this," said my mother, her voice now steel. *"Today!"*

"Geez, Mom," I expostulated, "I really wanted to wear the bracelet to Judy's brother's engagement party Saturday night. It wouldn't do any harm if I keep it until then."

"Today," my mother commanded.

Saturday night, I entered the catering hall in Queens with trepidation. "Everyone in Judy's family dresses so fancy," I thought crossly. "If only I had that gold and diamond bracelet, I would feel more chic."

I latched onto the line of well-wishers filing past the family, and when I reached Judy, her brother, and his fiancée Sandy, I gave them each a hug and a kiss. I felt more distant toward Judy's mother, though, and, refraining from my usual more effusive displays of affection, reached to shake her hand. Regal and aristocratic, she extended her hand to me graciously, and I clasped it firmly.

It was then that I saw it. The bracelet. Her tiny-boned wrist was encircled by the same gold and diamond bracelet I had found in the cab earlier that week in Manhattan. Could it be? Was it possible? Maybe it was a replica? Maybe the designer had made dozens? It couldn't be the *same* bracelet I had found, could it? It was just a coincidence, right?

But when I later took Judy aside and gushed convincingly about the "gorgeous bracelet your mother is wearing," Judy told me proudly: "It's a one-of-a-kind creation. My mother's friend, a famous jewelry designer, designed it especially for her. It's my mother's favorite piece. She lost it earlier this week, in a cab, and was utterly devastated. She thought she would never get it back. Thank God, an honest citizen found it and brought it into the Taxi and Limousine Commission. She was so relieved. She would have felt terrible if she had not been able to wear it tonight."

—Sally Larson*

Comment

Attempts to hide the truth are futile, for truth, like oil in water, will always rise to the surface.

*W*hen the phone rang, Debby picked it up, not expecting anything out of the ordinary. But when she heard the voice on the other end of the line, she froze in shock. It was the hospital, with the kind of news that is every mother's worst nightmare.

"Your son's been in a car accident—get here as soon as you can," said the official on the other end of the line, before elaborating on the grisly specifics.

Though Debby could hardly speak, she did manage to say, "I'll be there in fifteen minutes."

"Hurry," came the ominous response. "Come sooner if you can."

Debby hung up the phone and ran to her car. All the way to the hospital, she fretted and tried not to imagine the worst. But when she got there, she found her dear son of sixteen, Dan, in critical condition and near death. In fact, he registered 6 on the trauma scale, which is the point at which the hospital calls a coroner.

She wanted to throw her arms around him, but she could not, because there were tubes everywhere. Bending down to her son, she choked out, "Dan, Dan, can you hear me?"

The doctor came to her side. "Your son is in a coma," he gently told her. "He cannot hear you."

Debby was beside herself. The full reality of the situation came crashing down on her, and she broke into sobs. Not long ago, Debby's husband had passed away, and the thought that she might now lose her only son was unbearable. "This can't be happening," she cried.

But it was happening, and it only got worse. For the next few hours, Dan lay perfectly still, eyes shut, a far cry from the laughter-filled kid that he had been. To make matters worse, the doctors had no prognosis with which to quell Debby's fears. "It's still too early to tell" was the only medical report they could give her.

And thus the horrible hours went by. The hours turned into days and the days turned into weeks, but Dan remained in a coma. Seven weeks later, when he was deemed medically stable, he was transferred to a rehab hospital.

Meanwhile, Debby herself lived her life as if in a trance. When she wasn't working, she came to the hospital to sit by her son. Often she read to him, hoping that the sound of her voice would reach him somewhere, somehow. She kept a constant vigil for any signs of life, but his only response continued to be a slow, steady breathing.

And then, one Thursday night just before nine o'clock as she sat at

Dan's bedside, Debby was struck with an idea. She was closing her book when she realized it was time for *Seinfeld* on television. For years, the *Seinfeld* show had provided Debby's family with laughter and an occasion to gather in the den. The memory of these evenings made Debby feel warm for the first time in weeks. The dog needed feeding, and she needed sleep, but this night, instead of heading for home, Debby decided to tune in. "It will do me good to watch the show," she thought. "And it will be good for Dan too—after all, *Seinfeld* is his favorite show."

As the opening credits rolled, Debby settled into her chair. The familiar music drew her in, and the plot began to unfold. Then, as she turned to make herself more comfortable, she glanced at Dan and caught sight of his expression. His eyes had flown wide open. "Oh, my goodness!" she cried. In her amazement, she lurched from her seat, thinking the volume might be too loud. But his eyes remained open wide, confounding the nurse who came in to change his IV. Still, the show ended, and he didn't speak. It came time to leave. "Honey," she said, leaning over to say her good-byes for the night, "I'm going home. I've got to feed the dog. She's been in all day." She was in the process of straightening up when suddenly Dan's eyes began to flutter. "Where am I?" he managed to say. He was coming out of his coma.

Then it hit Debby in a flash. He had been watching his favorite show, and the familiar music and voices had reached him.

And yet, there is an ironic twist to this story. The *Seinfeld* show that night was actually about comas. Much to Debby's disbelief, the episode had centered on Kramer, who rented a video about a young woman in a coma—the result of an accident. Who could have known that tuning in that evening would reach Dan's slumbering mind and, in the end, help guide him back to life and laughter?

*S*ince I had invited two couples for dinner, I made yeast rolls in the morning and set them aside to rise. After I dusted, I kneaded the rolls down again and left them to rise once more.

The rolls were no sooner in the oven when two delivery men arrived with my new bookcase. They patiently moved the heavy bookcase to another wall space when it didn't look right in my first choice.

Following the men to the front door to thank them, I remembered my rolls.

"Wait a minute," I told them. "You worked so hard, I want to give you something." I covered the rolls with waxed paper and handed them over. "You can have these with your lunch."

I made another batch. When I kneaded them for their second rising, they looked every bit as good as the first batch. The doorbell rang again. It was my decorator, who had come to put up my needlepoint cornice board. When he finished, it looked so pretty with the new bookcase.

The decorator asked, "Do I smell homemade bread?" Handing over the waxed paper bundle with a smile, I thought, "Well, I still have plenty of time to make a third batch.

At about four that afternoon, a car pulled into my driveway. A friend dashed into the kitchen.

"I found these tomatoes on sale and thought you'd like some for your company tonight," she said.

Then she smelled the rolls I had just taken from the oven. "Oh, my husband thinks your rolls are better than anything in the world!"

Reaching for the waxed paper once again, I said, "Take these to him."

"But don't you need the rolls for your guests?" she asked.

"Don't worry," I reassured her.

After she left, I reasoned, "I guess tomatoes are healthier then rolls." It was too late to make more anyway.

When my guests arrived, Marge, first in the doorway, said: "I have a surprise for you!"

She handed me a fragrant loaf of bread, still warm from her oven.

One day I'll learn. You just can't outgive the Lord.

—*Faye Field*

abbinical students at one of the most demanding and renowned theological seminaries in Israel lead an austere and Spartan life. They rise at 6 A.M. for morning prayers followed by a rigorous eighteen-hour day of exacting Talmudic studies. Except for mealtimes, their only real break comes in the late afternoon when they are allotted time off for the chores that typically consume young men living on their own for the first time in their lives.

During one such break, a throng of students had seized the opportunity to convene outside the seminary walls to enjoy the crisp autumn day. The air was brisk and invigorating, and after a muggy summer of steaming sidewalks and torpid temperatures, they welcomed the bracing chill in the air. They stood relaxed, chatting amiably, discussing the day's studies (some complex Talmudic passages that had confounded many), a few surreptitiously smoking cigarettes. The atmosphere was calm and pleasant. Absorbed by conversation and camaraderie, few paid heed to the action unfolding on the street.

The interest of one sharp-eyed young man, however, was piqued by a speck growing in the distance, and, stiffening, he motioned to his friends.

"Look at that!" he said, jabbing his finger at the spot rapidly advancing towards their street.

"How sad!" murmured several of his comrades, transfixed, as they absorbed the scene and assimilated its implications.

One lone Jewish hearse, unaccompanied by the customary long procession of mourners, with no entourage whatsoever and without a single escort in attendance, was moving slowly down their street.

The young men were riveted by the solitariness of that single hearse; it evoked a profound sense of pathos within them. How could someone go to his death so completely alone? Where were the family, the neighbors, the friends? Was it possible that the deceased had lived a life so detached and apart from the community that no one even knew—or cared—that he or she was dead?

They huddled together in silence, overcome by the dismal and melancholy scene. Their experience of the Jewish community was one of friendship, solidarity, unity, and support. They had never before witnessed such a stark demonstration of the lonely life that could be lived within it.

"This is just heartbreaking," one young man whispered.

"To be buried this way is a terrible thing," said a second.

"We've got to do something," urged another.

"Let's do what clearly has to be done," said a fourth. "Let's follow the hearse to the cemetery and participate in the burial."

"But not just *us*," exhorted another. "Let's run into the building quick and get *all* the guys to come!"

And they did.

Soon the hearse was escorted by a long and impressive cortege of hundreds of students, who followed it to the Jewish cemetery on the outskirts of town. It was only when they reached the gravesite and a rabbi—the sole occupant—emerged from the hearse, that they learned the identity of the deceased.

"Well, this is very fitting!" the rabbi exclaimed, when he asked who they were and from what yeshiva (seminary) they had come. "How did you learn about her death? No one even knew she existed anymore! She was such an eccentric, and she lived the life of a hermit for the last fifty years, rebuffing everyone's efforts to reach out to her. I'm shocked that anyone was even aware that she had died . . ."

The young men looked at him strangely, puzzled by his assumption. "Excuse me, rabbi," one said quietly. "We don't know the deceased. We don't know whom you're talking about."

Now it was the rabbi's turn to look discomfited. "You don't know whose funeral you're attending?" he asked in shock. "Then how and why are you here?"

The young men explained how affected they had been by the sight of the solitary hearse and how they had been moved to escort the deceased. How they had wanted to perform—purely and for its own sake—a *mitzvah,* a good deed.

After listening to the young men's earnest explanations, the rabbi began to cry.

"My dear friends," he said softly, "your presence here was clearly ordained. Seventy years ago, a wealthy Jewish businessman donated an expensive piece of real estate to the Jewish community for the purpose of building a rabbinical seminary. *Your* rabbinical seminary.

"Beyond the initial donation of the land and the building, during his lifetime the businessman continued to support the fledgling seminary with large sums of money that helped it flourish and become one of the premier institutions of its day.

"As he got older, the yeshiva, in recognition of his outstanding philanthropy, wished to bestow special honors and awards on him, but he was a humble man and he shunned them all.

"He had only one child—a daughter—whom he loved excessively.

When rabbis would approach him and ask, 'How can we repay you for your unbelievable charity?' he would smile good-naturedly and say, 'Thank God, I am a rich and happy man; I don't need anything. But maybe one day, you can be of service to my beloved daughter. Maybe one day, she'll need your help.'

"The rabbis gave the philanthropist their solemn oath that the yeshiva would not forsake his daughter.

"After a long and productive life, he died, and sad to say, his daughter abandoned the religious traditions of her youth. She disconnected herself from the Jewish community, and was in and out of psychiatric institutions all her life.

"The rabbis who remembered their promise to her father tried repeatedly to keep in contact with her and lend her their support. But she rebuffed their overtures and lived a hermitlike, eccentric existence. Soon, the original group of rabbis who had made that pledge to her father died, and the pledge was forgotten. The daughter was abandoned and lived the sad and misbegotten life of a recluse.

"But, my friends, it is to *her* funeral that you've coincidentally come today, the funeral of the daughter of the benefactor of your very own yeshiva. With your presence here today, you have both fulfilled your rabbis' pledge and repaid the benefactor's largesse, once and for all."

Later, the rabbinical students learned that the hearse was not supposed to drive down their small, obscure street, blocks away from the main thoroughfare.

The driver had gotten lost, and had driven down their street by mistake.

hroughout her forty-year marriage, Kelly O'Brien* had been a long-suffering, forbearing wife. Her husband, Chris, was the quintessential "Type A" personality—an aggressive, driven man and a veritable workaholic, whose ambition and energy had propelled him to the top of his field. Kelly, a mild-mannered, gentle woman with modest dreams, had stood discreetly on the sidelines while Chris determinedly pursued and fulfilled his goals.

She had been so patient. It seemed as if she was always waiting for Chris: She had waited up for him countless late nights keeping his dinner warm, long past the hour when he had originally been due home. She had waited in front of Broadway theaters and elegant restaurants, glancing ruefully at her wristwatch as appointed meeting times with Chris came and went with impunity. And she had waited for scheduled vacations, which she planned eagerly, to materialize, but they never did. At the last moment, Chris would invariably beg off, citing a "crisis at work," a "last-minute snafu," or an "unbelievable opportunity" that had to be "seized immediately."

"When are we finally going to live?" Kelly would gently chide.

"When I retire, honey," Chris vowed solemnly. "And I *will* ask for early retirement, I promise."

So Kelly waited patiently for her life with Chris to finally begin. "Just another six months," she whispered to herself, "before he turns sixty-two and retires. Then . . . we'll really start to live!" And she began to call travel agencies, avidly collecting brochures and travel guides and letting her imagination wander down paths she had avoided before.

But the free and idyllic existence Kelly yearned for was not meant to be.

Chris came home one day with a guilty look on his face mixed with ill-concealed excitement. "The company is starting up a new branch in Houston," he announced, "and they want me to head it. They'll pay for all the relocation expenses and double my salary. What do you say?" He looked pleadingly at his wife.

"Chris . . . you promised early retirement!" she said, astonished by the sudden turn of events.

"Ohgawd, Kelly, I can't retire! I love what I'm doing. I can't see myself playing golf or bridge, or even playing tourist. It was unrealistic of me to promise early retirement. I'll go nuts!"

Kelly saw her dreams dissolve into the vortex of her husband's dynamism, a dynamism so strong that once it was unleashed it carried her along on its powerful current. She could be unwilling with Chris but never unyielding. Once again, her own needs would have to be sacrificed on the altar of his ambitions.

"But . . . Houston," she objected feebly. "All my friends are *here*. The only person I know in Houston is your third cousin Katherine, whom I haven't talked to in ages. I'm too old to start over."

"Honey, look at it as an adventure!" he wheedled. "And I'll try my best to get us an apartment right near Katherine so you won't be lonely."

But the apartment he ultimately found proved to be on the other side of town.

"So sorry, hon," he apologized, embarrassed by his inability to make good on at least one promise. "But apparently, all the apartment complexes are clustered together in a newer section. Where Katherine lives there are only big houses, no rentals. I know you don't want to undertake all the work and headache that a house entails.

"Anyway," he continued more confidently, "you'll love the apartment complex. It has a pool and a spa and all kinds of classes. I'm sure you'll meet lots of new people right away!"

But she didn't. Most of the residents of the apartment complex were yuppies in their thirties and forties, away all day at work. Kelly felt lonely and isolated. She had called Chris's cousin Katherine a couple of times, but they hadn't been able to get together. "Soon," Katherine promised vaguely, underscoring Kelly's anxiety. It seemed that the promises made to her lately had all been insincere and had all been broken.

"When," she thought sadly, "will Chris finally keep one single promise he's made to me? Will he ever consider *my* needs?"

She brooded over these questions constantly, much as she tried to banish them from her mind.

"I'm turning into a cranky old hag!" she scolded herself. "Better do something constructive, keep my mind off my problems. I know what I'll do!" she thought, brightening a little. "I'll whip up a homemade cake for his birthday tonight and we'll celebrate. I haven't baked in years. Won't he be surprised!"

All day long, Kelly puttered happily in her kitchen, blending, stirring, whisking ingredients until she had produced a lovely cake that satisfied her own impeccable standards and made her proud. "Chris will love this," she thought. "He'll be so surprised to receive a cake."

She had planned the surprise with such girlish excitement, she couldn't help but be disappointed when Chris came home from work that night, carrying a big box containing . . . a birthday cake!

"Who gave it to you?" she asked, downcast that someone else had stolen her surprise.

"Oh, the guys at work thought I'd feel lonely having a birthday in a new place, so they chipped in and bought me this. Wasn't that nice?"

"Well, guess what?" she said cheerfully, trying to hide her chagrin. "Now you have *two!*" And she held aloft her famous Hawaiian Delight cake that had been his favorite years ago, and placed it in front of him.

"Mmm!" he murmured in delicious anticipation. "My all-time favorite! I remember how complicated this particular cake is to produce. It must have taken you hours. This is really a treat! Who can compare a bakery cake to a homemade one, especially one made by you! And, honey," he added, darting her a thoughtful look, "I promise that when *your birthday* comes up in a few months, you will also have *two* birthday cakes!"

The two laughed and giggled and chattered together like a pair of teenagers. "Maybe it's not the start of the new life I envisioned," Kelly mused to herself, "but maybe it won't be so bad, after all. It's not so hard to be in a strange town when the man you love is right there with you."

That night, Chris woke up with severe chest pains and called out to Kelly. Before she could reach for the phone to call the police, she heard a strangulated choking sound from his throat, and he was gone. Chris was dead.

"Come back to New York!" her friends and relatives urged Kelly after the funeral. "There's nothing there for you." But she was too depressed, too paralyzed by shock, to move. She had no energy, no will, to make the calls and take the necessary steps to facilitate her return. Just the thought of calling the utility companies to close her accounts made her weak. "I will come back," she promised, "but I can't right now. Too many things to do."

But Kelly couldn't muster enough strength to do even one chore. "Tomorrow I'll get out of bed . . ." she promised herself. "It's too hot outside to go anywhere, anyway."

"Tomorrow" stretched into an interminable expanse of yesterdays, and Kelly's depression deepened. She felt forsaken and desolate, her loneliness heightened by the knowledge that it was in fact her sixtieth birthday and she was marking it . . . alone.

Kelly was sitting at her kitchen table in her terry-cloth robe, sipping a cup of coffee, when the doorbell rang. Standing at the threshold was Chris's cousin Katherine, holding aloft a large box.

"Open it," she urged.

Inside was a homemade birthday cake.

"B-but how did you know?" Kelly asked in astonishment.

"Kelly, I swear to God, I had the strangest dream last night. Chris came to me in the dream and said: 'Tomorrow is Kelly's birthday. I want you to make her a cake.' Who am I to argue with Chris?" Katherine joked. "So . . . happy birthday!"

A few minutes later, the doorbell rang again and a stranger was standing outside, also bearing a cake box.

"Mrs. O'Brien?" the elderly woman inquired sweetly. "I'm your next-door neighbor, Mrs. Thomas. May I come in? I feel so badly that all this time has passed and I never came round to introduce myself to you. Please excuse my terrible manners, but just at about the time that you first moved in, I was having some surgery and not feeling quite well. Then I heard your husband died—I'm so sorry—and I didn't want to impose upon your privacy or your grief. . . . Well, just today, I was in the bakery and was drawn to a cake in the showcase that said 'Happy Birthday!' Well, I know this sounds downright fanciful, but it seemed to be beckoning to me. And beyond any reason or logic, an inner voice deep inside of me said, 'Bring this cake to Mrs. O'Brien.' Well, I've lived long enough to know to obey my inner voice, so I hope you won't mind a foolish old woman's actions. . . . Now, it isn't by any chance your birthday today, is it?"

Comment
A patient heart is a fertile field for life's sweetest miracles.

*W*hen my first child was born, I was living in Newton, Massachusetts, and I knew very few people there. I did not own a car; and the few married friends I had made in the neighborhood did not yet have babies. They were not involved in domestic life the way I became as soon as my baby was born.

Prior to my marriage, I had worked first as a teacher and later as a journalist for the *Boston Traveler.* But the year was 1947, and at that time it was customary, virtually the rule, for women to stay home with their children. So I found myself confined to my home practically all day long, and feeling very lonely. Truthfully, I was also very bored. My baby was my only companion and I felt my isolation keenly.

When my second child was born three years later, I vowed to make a different kind of life for myself. I was desperate to add a new and different dimension to my painfully solitary existence. So I hired a young woman to come in every day, and I taught her how to take care of the baby and my older son in my absence. She was very competent and I felt satisfied that I had prepared the way for my own separate life in addition to my life as a wife and a mother. There was only one minor problem: I didn't know what that "separate life" looked like or was going to be. Now that all the pieces were in place, I had absolutely no idea what to do next! I was ready for activity and involvement, but I didn't know what kind. Nonetheless, I was filled with yearning and hope. I waited with growing excitement for my destiny to unfold.

One day the telephone rang, and I heard a young woman's voice say: "Hello, I'm calling to invite you to join Hadassah."

I had been reading about the attempts to form the Zionist State, which was not yet the State of Israel, and I was very sympathetic to the cause. So, without pause or hesitation, I immediately said: "I would like to!"

The young woman on the other end of the line must have been quite surprised by my enthusiasm because she quickly responded: "And would you like to participate in our Membership Committee?" (I guess she wanted to make certain that I would become involved!) Again, I said "Yes!" without a moment's reservation.

Joining Hadassah was really ideal for me; it was a way for me to meet people and, at the same time, do something helpful for what I hoped would become the Zionist State. "It's the answer to my prayers," I thought jubilantly.

I agreed to join and the woman on the other end of the telephone was delighted. Then she said: "Now let me see whether I have your name spelled correctly and your address," and she started to spell a name, but it was not *my* name at all; it wasn't even remotely similar. It was a completely different name.

Then it dawned on us both. The woman had gotten a wrong number when she called. She had called me by mistake!

After we laughed about the mix-up, she asked if I still wanted to join, and I said I certainly did, telling her that I was very happy the mistake had occurred. I gave her the necessary information, and she promised to call me when the next meeting was scheduled.

I attended and met lovely women my age who were very warm and welcoming. At this first meeting, which was held at Temple Emanuel in Newton Center, I sat beside a pretty, young, blonde woman named Gilda and I couldn't help but notice her. She was extremely friendly, and began to engage me in conversation. We began to talk, and we started a friendship that has lasted now for forty-seven years. She is my very best friend, and closer than a sister. There is a deep love that runs between us and will last as long as we live.

Beyond this extraordinary friendship, my membership in Hadassah brought me into the community. I hate to think what would have become of my life had the woman not dialed my number by mistake. But, who knows?

Maybe it wasn't a mistake at all.

—*Sybil Gladstone*

Comment

The more open we are to taking chances, the more apt we are to receive blessings.

It was Labor Day and Mother's Day all rolled into one when sisters Mary Luca, Catherine Naughton, and Toni Higgins at Methodist Hospital, Brooklyn amazingly gave birth to three beautiful babies just hours apart.

The multiple birth is believed to be the first time in the United States three sisters delivered on the same day.

And keeping the family theme: The obstreticians who delivered all three babies are brothers—Drs. Santo and Gary Fiasconaro.

The first of the three cousins was 7-pound, 4-ounce Daniel Vincent, born Friday morning by Caesarean section at New York Methodist to Mary Luca, 32, and her carpenter husband, Erik.

Mary's sister, Catherine Naughton, 31, gave birth later that morning to 6-pound, 2-ounce Kevin Patrick, also by C-section.

"The baby is tremendous. It's a terrific feeling to see a little baby born," said father Kevin. "And the fact that there are three of them at the same time, that's quite a coincidence."

The third sister, Toni Higgins, delivered 6-pound, 13-ounce girl Tyler, Friday night, completing the trifecta.

All three sisters say they conceived naturally nine months before.

"I don't quite know how it happened," Mrs. Naughton said. "I don't think anyone could have planned something like this."

The sisters had all been together May 4, 1996 for a niece's first Communion.

"We were all at Mary's daughter's Communion . . . and then three weeks later we were pregnant. So we must have eaten something . . . or drank something!" said Mrs. Higgins.

For Mrs. Luca, this is her third child—and one that was unplanned.

"I was speechless. I was not expecting it in a million years."

So how is the family holding up?

"We're all tired, and the doctors look like they're a little beat," said Kevin Naughton. "And my mother-in-law really has her hands full, what with three daughters in the hospital and three babies heading home soon."

A computer search showed the previous record for same-day births by siblings was held by two sisters in Chicago in 1995.

—Roger Field

Comment

Sometimes the ordinary is exalted to the extraordinary only because of its placement in time.

$\mathcal{M}ay$ 30, 1983, was a glorious day and Sherry Vyverberg's spirits were high. She had just completed her exams, and her first year at Monroe Community College was finally over. Tall, with blue eyes and long blonde hair, Sherry had risen early and gotten out on the highway to pick up her boyfriend Keith Gandy, along with friends Greg Grant and Mike Jerocki. Together, they were looking forward to spending their Memorial Day weekend at Niagara Falls, an hour's drive from their hometown of Rochester, New York.

After stopping on the Canadian side of the falls for breakfast, the four young friends drove along the Niagara Parkway, winding along the bank of the Niagara River. Dazzled by the view, they parked their car beside the Toronto Power Station, an abandoned generating plant. Both Greg and Mike kept Keith company as he leaned against the old stone powerhouse. Recently he had broken his ankle; his leg was in a knee-high cast and he was on crutches.

Dressed in a new pink tracksuit, Sherry went alone to explore. She was drawn to the fine mist and the roar of the water, which cascaded over a wide crest to a boiling spume below. The churning water had a hypnotic effect on her and she wanted to get as close as she could.

A few feet from where she stood, a concrete observation platform beckoned. To get there, Sherry stepped around a metal railing and then walked across a short stretch of grassy bank onto the narrow observation ledge that hung twenty feet over the water. Standing just feet from the crest of the falls, Sherry stood mesmerized by the furious turbulence below that roared like muffled thunder and threw up a perpetual cloud of spray. Sherry marveled at the sense of exhilaration the falls gave her; she knew that she was peering over the rim of one of the seven wonders of the world. What she did not know was that below were some of the most dangerous rapids in the world, where 700,000 gallons of water fell every second from the 2,100-foot-wide crest.

Sherry's attention was drawn to the water that spilled from a sluiceway of the old powerhouse, just six meters below her. Carefully she leaned over to look at it. In that instant, she lost her balance and plunged headfirst into the forty-degree rapids.

"She's in the water!" screamed Mike, who had seen Sherry topple over the edge. Greg scrambled down the bank. "Where is she?" he shouted. "I can't find her!"

Sherry felt the shock of hitting the cold water, which pulled at her with enormous force. Somehow she was able to hold her breath under water and suddenly she was shot back to the surface. Keith spotted her just before she was sucked down again. "She's downstream!" he yelled. Gasping for air, Sherry made a frantic effort to reach the shore as the current pulled her into calmer waters. But she was thirty feet farther from shore and moving rapidly toward the crest of the falls.

Greg scaled the cliff and raced along the bank. When he caught up with Sherry, he dove into the frigid waters. He managed to swim out five meters before the torrential rapids overwhelmed him and forced him to make his way back to shore.

Meanwhile the water continued to slap at Sherry's face and shoulders. She felt the relentless pull of the river grow fiercer. In an attempt to stay afloat and to stop swallowing water, she quickly rolled over onto her back.

From a distance, the young men were shouting, "Hang on! We'll get you!" but Sherry couldn't hear their voices over the pounding waters. What she heard instead was her own loud voice praying to God. "I'm young," she pleaded, "please don't take me now!" Sherry remembered the beautifully wrapped gifts that she had placed in the deep recesses of her closet, each awaiting an appropriate occasion. Mugs for Dad and Gramps for Father's Day; a bank as a graduation gift for Wesley, her brother; and an Anniversary Waltz music box for her parents. "How sad those gifts would make them now," she thought.

Morbid thoughts rushed through Sherry's mind and paralyzed her body with fear. But in a monumental act of determination, Sherry realized she could not give in. Instead she drew on her inner reserves to calm down. "I've just got to trust in God," she said, and then she continued to pray that her friends would somehow manage to save her.

Meanwhile Keith threw down his crutches and hobbled to the parkway. There he tried valiantly to flag down someone who might be able to help. The first vehicle just drove on by, but the second one stopped.

Pete Quinlan, Joe Camisa, and John Marsh were ironworkers who had been driving from their nearby work site. Their normal route had been changed to one-way, so they took a detour. They had forgotten their hard hats at the site and were on their way back to retrieve them when John noticed a man hopping up and down on one foot. Thinking there had been some accident, John rolled down his window and called out, "What's wrong?"

"There's a girl in the water! A girl in the water!" shouted Keith. John jumped out of his truck and ran down to the riverbank. At first, he saw only rushing water. Then he spotted Sherry's head, which looked like a beach ball some 300 feet out.

"She's way out!" yelled John. "We're never going to get out there."

As a native of the area, he knew what Sherry was up against, and he even thought she might be done for. But as he witnessed her being swept downstream he thought, "I'd rather jump in than watch her go over the falls and spend the rest of my life second-guessing myself."

"I do a lot of fishing here," said John to his co-workers. John had grown up alongside Niagara Falls. Being an expert fisherman, he had rope in the back of the truck and he knew the patterns of the rapids. "Out where she is," he said, "the current is going to the falls. But if I cast out there, nine times out of ten my line drifts inside the weir, down by our powerhouse. If she doesn't go over the wall, she'll come drifting in to the powerhouse."

But he had to act quickly. Sherry was now only 245 meters from the brink of the falls. If she got carried through the intake gates to the turbines, she would be cut to ribbons. Once the current swept her over the weir, it would indeed be hopeless.

John Marsh and his co-worker Pete Quinlan were in the habit of working together. Immediately they went into gear as a team, grabbing rope from the back of the truck and knotting it together. John tied one end of the rope around his waist as Pete and Joe secured the other end to the steel railing of the bridge. John looked at the 175-foot drop below him, then yelled "Now!" and in a flash he jumped into the rapids.

The violent appetite of the current sucked John under, until he managed to thrust himself upward and stay afloat. The chill of the water slowed his movements, but he used all the energy and stamina he was able to muster and swam forward. Feeling the pull of the eighty-foot rope now fully extended, John called desperately to Sherry, who was now trying to reach him.

"Don't let me miss her," he begged. Sherry was still on her back, her long blonde hair floating behind her. John stretched every part of his body as he made a desperate lunge with his hand. Sherry was moving quickly as the current pulled her away from the weir. There was now just an inch between the two of them, one tied to a rope, the other boundless, floating rapidly downstream. "Don't let me miss her," John prayed again, then with one last attempt he stuck out his hand. This time, instead of coming up with only air, he caught the tips of Sherry's long hair and clutched it in his hand. "Thank God," gasped Sherry through her exhaustion. With her teeth chattering and her lips numb and blue, she looked at John, who had wrapped her in his arms and was pulling her in. She managed to say, "Thank you, too."

It was a feat getting both John and Sherry back to shore. Ambulances waited to treat Sherry for shock and hypothermia. She was released within two hours but in that time, the news media had gotten word of the miraculous rescue. Once John Marsh saw that Sherry was safe in the ambulance, he got into his vehicle with his buddies, ready to drive off. Canadian police officer Constable Caddis hailed him down and got his name. Now all those who wanted to bestow accolades had a name attached to the heroic deed. John Marsh did in fact receive tributes from Canadian and American politicians. He received a letter from President Ronald Reagan, who commended him for his heroism. Marsh went on to be awarded ten medals and plaques, including the Carnegie Medal, the ITT American Character Award, and the Royal Canadian Humane Association bronze medal, along with the Star of Courage from the governor general. "Why all the fuss?" John Marsh asks.

"So much of my rescue hinged on coincidence," Sherry is quoted as saying. "If John hadn't gone back for his crew's hard hats, if his normal route hadn't been changed to one-way, if he hadn't known the area so well or had a rope in his truck, I wouldn't be here today."

Comment
The distance between life and death is always one inch. We need the hand of God to bridge the gulf and pull us through.

In 1947, I was riding the New York subway late one night, on my way home to Brooklyn from the evening session at Hunter College in Manhattan. I had gotten on the BMT line at Thirty-fourth Street, and noted with just a little chagrin that the subway was practically empty, with just a handful of people scattered throughout the car. I wasn't too concerned, though—this was the 1940s and subway incidents were uncommon. Still, I felt a little uncomfortable being one of the few passengers in the car.

One stop later, at Twenty-third Street, a gentleman got on the train, and I felt relieved that there would be another presence in the subway car. My relief, however, turned to uneasiness when he chose to sit in the seat immediately adjoining mine.

"Now why did he do that?" I wondered, distressed. "The entire subway car is practically empty, and yet he decides on a seat so close to mine. How strange!"

I peered into his face anxiously, and was reassured to see a mild-mannered man, with a pleasant countenance and an amiable manner. Rather than appear threatening, he seemed almost meek and timid.

"Ah! That's it! He's scared of the empty subway car himself! He's huddling close to *me* for comfort!"

I almost laughed.

In truth, he did not look like the average brash, aggressive American I often encountered on the subways.

"Maybe he's a foreigner," I mused.

My suspicions were confirmed seconds later when he withdrew a foreign-language newspaper and spread it out on his lap.

"That's it, then!" I reassured myself. "No need to worry, he's harmless." I settled back into my seat and returned to my book.

At the next stop—Fourteenth Street—a middle-aged woman boarded the train. Her head swiveled back and forth as she examined the nearly empty subway car. Then she, too, began to wend her way in the general direction of where I and the man were sitting.

She's going to sit nearby, too, I decided.

But to my surprise, she didn't even select an adjoining seat. Instead, she eased herself into the same seat as the foreign gentleman.

"Now that's peculiar," I thought. "The whole car is practically empty and she has to sit right next to a strange man, and real close at that."

I began to watch the woman with interest.

She peered over the man's shoulder to see what he was reading. And then she began to address him in a language in which I was not fluent, but which I could certainly identify.

She was speaking to him in Yiddish.

I didn't know Yiddish, but I did have an excellent command of German, which is quite similar. So I was able to follow the dialogue with very little difficulty.

"Where are you from . . . originally?" she inquired.

The man named a country in Eastern Europe.

"What city?" she asked.

He answered again, noncommittally, but beginning to look confused by the interrogation.

"What did you do . . . before the war?"

He named his profession.

"Look at me. Look *at* me!" she commanded. "Don't you recognize me anymore?"

They were husband and wife.

They had been separated in 1938 at the outset of World War II. Each had endured the horrors of different concentration camps and, at the war's end, each had assumed that the other was dead.

Each had made his way alone to New York City to begin a new life.

And they had found each other, nine years later, on a subway car on the BMT line.

As the reunion (which caused a sensation in New York and was reported widely in all the local newspapers) unfolded before my disbelieving, tear-filled eyes, I understood what force had compelled the woman to take the seat immediately adjoining the man's.

But what about *me?* I wondered, as my subway stop came around the bend and it was time, regretfully, for me to disembark.

Why had both chosen to sit next to *me?* What was my role supposed to be in this drama and what was my purpose?

As a very young woman, I didn't know. Today, some fifty years later, I think I do.

Perhaps I was placed there to serve as a witness. And perhaps I needed at a tender young age to learn a thing or two. To be imbued, from an early age on, with the sense of mystery and excitement and awe that such a tableau inspires.

And, having witnessed such an incredible "coincidence" unfold before my very eyes, to stand at the threshold of life knowing clearly that with God . . . all things are possible.

—*Ruth Fisher*

Comment

To be witness to a miracle is a miracle, too.

*T**om** Stone* first met the blonde at a mechanic's shop in Las Vegas where their respective cars were being fixed. He chatted her up with animation, hoping that she was as attracted to him as he was to her.

She wasn't.

When he asked her out, she brusquely said no.

Tom shrugged his shoulders in disappointment, but took the rejection well. At least he had tried, and it wasn't as if the two traveled in the same social circles. He would probably never see her again.

He was wrong.

One month later, Tom noticed a car parked on the shoulder of a road, its hood up, signifying trouble. He stopped to offer his help.

It was the blonde.

Once again, he felt the strong pull of attraction towards her. Once again, he asked her out. Once again, despite his obvious virtues (and mechanical aptitude, for he had indeed been able to locate the source of the car's trouble and rapidly repair it), she brusquely refused. Once again, Tom took her rejection well, and they parted ways.

But not for long.

One year later, on a different highway in a different part of town, Tom was riveted by the sight of a car on fire. He pulled up quickly behind the one that was ablaze, and discovered that it belonged to none other than . . . the blonde!

The scenarios of previous times were replicated faithfully. Tom successfully doused the fire, and then asked her out. Once again, the blonde said no.

Three years later on a bridge in San Francisco, Tom stopped to help victims of a multiple car accident. Surprise! One of them was . . . the blonde.

This time, even *she* was impressed by the coincidences that kept bringing them together, and—finally!—agreed to a date.

They arranged to meet at a restaurant in town, and Tom was elated.

His elation was short-lived.

The blonde never put in an appearance. After waiting for more than two hours at the appointed place and time, Tom concluded that she was a "no-show" and had rejected him again.

After that, Tom quit stopping at the scenes of car accidents. And he hasn't encountered the blonde since.

Comment

When I first read this story (which originally appeared in the *San Francisco Chronicle*), I was bitterly disappointed. I had had visions of the two sailing off into the sunset in sheer bliss. What was the point, after all, of this unusual series of coincidences, if not to bring the two together in matrimony? I was very annoyed at the unsatisfactory resolution of this tale. I never thought of transcribing the story, because it had no real conclusion, I thought, and therefore lacked inherent value. But the story kept nibbling away at my consciousness, and troubled me greatly. So I began to ask others what they thought of this tale. And one wise woman said, "Maybe the story isn't over yet." Hmm . . .

Another soul offered, "Maybe this story demonstrates what can happen if you are *not attuned* to coincidences. The blonde didn't heed their message. The script would have been different had she opened her heart to them. But we are, after all, given free will, and she made her choice."

he late afternoon sun was quickly descending on Linda Carlisle's hometown in central Ohio. It was December, and snow was falling lightly on the mile-and-a-half stretch to the high school. Mountainous snowbanks lined both sides of the road. Such a scene, where time almost seems to stand still, might have been painted by Grandma Moses. That was certainly the look of Linda's town thirty years ago.

Linda, with her flute tucked tightly under her arm, was late for band practice. To make matters worse, she had forgotten her mittens. She hustled as fast as the slippery terrain underfoot would permit her. And it was the time of year when it gets dark early.

Linda walked at a fast clip. Although she was tall for her seventeen years, she was beginning to run out of energy—the frigid air was sapping her strength. She could see her own breath coming out in short puffs. She had to slow down. Suddenly she saw that she had company. It came in the form of an enormous dog that bounded over the snowbank. The dog was so big its back came up to Linda's waist. He placed himself between Linda and the snowbanks. With the side of his husky body, the dog kept pushing Linda toward the street.

Linda was a little frightened. "Move away," she kept repeating to the dog in a firm voice. She didn't dare antagonize him because of his size. In the quiet street her words reverberated through the cold air. But the dog paid no attention to her stern commands. Refusing to obey, he continued to press his body against hers, pushing her away from the snowbanks and the rows of houses behind them.

Just as Linda quickened her pace to get away from the dog, a man with bright red hair and a demonic look in his eyes leaped from behind a snowbank. He lunged for Linda. The dog, who stood between the stranger and Linda, jumped on the man and pinned him to the ground. This action gave Linda the necessary seconds to escape.

The terrifying stranger was no match for the huge dog that was now gripping his leg in its jaws. Kicking himself free, the man scrambled over the snowbank and disappeared.

Linda was now ahead on the road, panting for breath. She still had a half mile to go when the dog reappeared, seemingly from nowhere. Once again, the dog pressed himself against Linda—this time on her left side so that he was protecting her from passing cars. She did not try to push the dog away this time. Overcome with gratitude, she patted the dog on its head. "Thank you," she said with heartfelt appreciation. And she meant it. "Thank you," she repeated.

Together they walked side by side until they reached the school. It was now so late that the door to the main entrance was locked. But she could hear the band practicing inside. Linda went around to the band door in the rear. She pounded loudly while the dog sat faithfully in the snow by her side. Eventually, one of the girls in the band opened the door.

"My goodness, Linda!" the girl exclaimed. "You look like you've just seen a ghost! Is there anything wrong?" It was difficult for Linda to speak. When she did, she described her harrowing encounter with the man on the road. "And this dog saved me," she said, as she turned to where the dog was sitting.

But the dog was no longer there. Nor was it anywhere in sight.

Linda knew, somehow, that she would never meet her four-legged savior again. For several months she kept perusing books about dogs in the school and town libraries. She wanted to know if there was a type of dog that protects people from harm. Or was it, as she suspected, one of a kind?

Linda is now forty-five and no longer lives in that small Ohio town. Despite all the research and the dozens of inquiries she has made over the years, she has never found a dog comparable to the one she encountered on that lonely cold night in the snow almost three decades ago.

Comment
One never knows the form in which a miracle will appear; therefore, we would do well to regard all that is around us with a degree of awe and wonder.

Rabbi Shlomo Carlebach, one of the most original and inspired leaders in the Jewish community, was known throughout the world as "The Singing Rabbi." A great spiritual master in the mid-to-late twentieth century, he reached out to people of all persuasions. There were many beneficiaries of his fabled warmth and magnanimous heart. The stories told about him after his death in 1994 reflected a humanitarian who performed benevolent deeds of epic proportions.

Wherever he went—and he was a true globetrotter—he would always hug and kiss strangers and ask them for their names and phone numbers.

"Oh, holy brother!" (or holy sister, depending, of course, on the gender of his new friend), "it's awesome to meet you! I want to know all about you! Give me your name and phone number and I'll give you a call real soon."

Scraps of paper, slivers of napkins, ribbons of old menus, and tattered business cards were stuffed into his overflowing pants and coat pockets. Some people wondered, half cynically, if there was any point in giving their number to Rabbi Carlebach, or "Shlomo" as he was more affectionately known. "Probably throws the number out as soon as he gets home," some jaded souls would laugh.

It wasn't so. After his death, one family member estimated that at least *half a million names and numbers* had been accumulated—and saved—by Rabbi Carlebach during his lifetime.

Sometimes, his calls would come immediately on the heels of the initial meeting—just minutes or hours later. Sometimes they would come years later, long after the stranger had given up hope of ever hearing from the famous personality. But when they came, they always seemed to come at precisely the time when they were needed most.

In November 1997, at a weekend meeting of JACs (Jewish Alcoholics and Chemically Addicted), a man stood up and told this story about Shlomo Carlebach's famous phone calls:

"I had given him my phone number at a concert ten years before. He hadn't called, and I was sorely disappointed. But I was philosophical, not bitter. I figured he was a very famous, very busy guy, and how could he possibly call all those tens of thousands of strangers he met each year at the concerts and classes he gave throughout the world?

"I was wistful, but shy. I would have liked to have had the courage to call him up myself, but I didn't. My heart longed for a connection with this saintly man, but even though he seemed warm and unassuming, I was too timid to take the initiative myself.

"Ten years passed. I never saw him again. And then, one morning, the phone rang.

"I didn't want to answer it. I was in a very despondent state and didn't want to talk to *anyone.* But it rang repeatedly, insistently. The caller refused to give up. It must have rung twenty times. Reluctantly, I went to answer the phone.

"Hey, holy brother, what's happening?" the caller asked in a jovial, familiar voice.

It was Rabbi Shlomo Carlebach.

I was stunned. It had been ten years since he had first scribbled down my name.

"Shlomo," I asked, in total shock. "What made you call just now?"

"Well, I was looking for an old Bible which I haven't used for some time, and when I found it and opened it, a little piece of paper with your name and number fell out. I figured it was a sign from God I should give you a call!"

An electric jolt coursed through my body and into my very soul. "Shlomo," I said, staring at the noose that was dangling from the ceiling and at the chair underneath it which I had just prepared.

"You called just in time."

❦

Comment

Even in the darkest moments of our soul there may very well be someone, somewhere holding the torch that can guide us back to life.

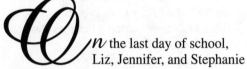*On* the last day of school, Liz, Jennifer, and Stephanie went out to dinner to celebrate. They ordered drinks, but there was no atmosphere of merriment. Like many public schoolteachers in inner-city Tampa, they were feeling the sobering effects of burn-out after yet another tough year.

Though normally a very sentimental bunch, they talked about how demoralized they felt at the end of this particular school session. "I haven't made a difference to anyone this year," said Stephanie.

"Oh, I'm sure you have," said Liz.

"Of course you have," said Jennifer.

Yet nobody seemed convinced. The three teachers paid their checks and with weak smiles they wished each other a good summer.

Stephanie Osborne headed home, feeling dejected and down. She feared bitterness; she feared that the daily realities of her job in the school system would eventually whittle away the idealism that fed her soul. As she drove she tried to boost her spirits with positive thoughts. "I am a seventh-grade language arts teacher in the inner city," she said to herself. "My strength is that I can relate to the students no one else gets along with. Just look at the work I've done with the 'at-risk' kids in the after-school mentoring program."

It was true—she *had* made a difference, at least in the life of Steve, the first student she had mentored. At first disruptive and belligerent, with her help he became thoughtful and caring. He had only been acting out because of a rough time at home. Stephanie knew that every child had a positive core that needed only to be revealed and allowed to grow. How good it had made her feel when Steve's grades improved and things began looking up for him.

But that had been two years ago. This time, nobody had hugged her to say good-bye on the last day of school, as Steve had. Somehow, the past two years had brought not only successes, but some failures as well—kids who slipped through the cracks.

Was she losing her touch? Was it really worth it after all? Was it just youthful idealism to believe that every being on earth has something unique and positive to offer?

She was ashamed by her thoughts, and as she drove she asked for a sign from above. And then, as she pulled into her driveway, she heard the telephone ringing. Who could it be at this hour? Quickly she parked and fumbled for her house keys as she tried to catch the phone before it was too late. She opened the door, ran inside, and picked up the receiver.

"Hello," she said, out of breath.

"Mrs. Osborne?" came a familiar though tentative voice on the other end. "It's Steve!"

Stephanie could not believe her ears. Her heart swelled as her former student went on to tell her that he was out of trouble, doing well in school, and employed. He said he had been thinking about her.

Steve could not have known how much that phone call meant to her. Stephanie went to bed that night with her spirits lifted, wondering if, just maybe, the next few years might bring a similar call from someone else.

Comment
A gift of gratitude often rekindles inspiration gone dim.

The blue-green sea spread out before me like a blanket as I waded into the warm water of Lydgate Lagoon on the Hawaiian island of Kauai. Could a month in paradise help me heal?

I wasn't sure anything could.

Only a month before, I'd been lying in the hospital back home in New England, admitted for heart problems and exhausted from multiple sclerosis. "My daughter and I are supposed to be on a plane to Kauai at this very moment!" I had told the doctor.

"Don't worry," my twenty-three-year-old daughter Dorene had reassured me. "We'll just postpone the trip. It's not the end of the world."

But it felt like it.

At forty-nine, with my divorce behind me, I wanted to believe I still had a lot of living to do. But instead, my heart was racing, my left side was weak—and I felt that I was falling apart.

Seventeen long days had passed in the hospital as I lay in bed wondering if I'd ever feel strong again. But this trip would do more for me than I could ever have imagined.

The sun was on my face as I fed the tropical fish that swam below the surface. I wanted to dive into the glassy blue, but my doctor's words echoed in my mind. "Take it easy," he had warned.

I'm not much of a swimmer anyway. Once, as a young girl, I went swimming in a lake and got a cramp in my leg. Before I knew it, I was under. I panicked, feeling that my lungs were ready to burst. Finally, someone pulled me out. But ever since that time, I couldn't put my head underwater. I'd just paddle and float.

So I paddled and floated out, and when I could no longer feel the sandy floor, I just let the water support my body.

I watched a man swim to shore to look after his three children while his wife went in, scuba gear in hand. Then I kept floating out—about 100 feet—to the deepest part of the lagoon.

There may have been ten other swimmers, or rather, snorkelers, their breathing straws skimming and bobbing in the water. But my vision was drawn farther out to a figure whose jerking movements had suddenly caught my eye.

"Hey," I thought. "That's the mother of those children!"

Without making a sound, the woman threw up her arm, which twisted like a corkscrew. And she was gasping as she tried to yank off her diving mask.

Instantly, I knew I was witnessing an epileptic seizure. I had seen one years ago. And now, there was only still water where the young mom had been.

My mind went blank as my body took over. I paddled over as fast as I could, my heart pounding. And then, without thinking, I dove beneath the water.

I don't even remember pulling the woman to the surface. But suddenly, there I was, floating, holding onto her with my stronger right arm to keep her afloat. And then I found my voice and screamed, "Help!"

None of the snorkelers heard me. So I kept screaming, trying to keep the woman—convulsing and clutching me—from pulling us both under.

On the shore, I saw Dorene jump at the sound of my voice, and she started shouting, too. And then the woman's husband suddenly realized what was happening.

"Ellen," he cried. "Ellen!" The sound of his plaintive cries made my heart break.

"I can't wait for help," I thought. "We have to get to shore." So with my weak left arm, I swam with all my might. Will we make it? I panicked. But then I saw a man swimming quickly toward us.

Panting, he reached us. "She's having a seizure!" I cried.

"Take her legs," he shouted, and together we towed her to shore.

When my feet finally touched bottom, I called to the crowd: "Get a doctor!" As it turned out, there was one on the beach, who performed CPR and emptied her lungs of water. Within minutes, she and her family had disappeared in an ambulance.

Standing in the water, I realized for the first time what had happened, and I started to sob. My fellow rescuer came toward me. "You saved her life," he said.

"*We* did," I replied.

"You know," he said, "strangest thing. . . . I'd postponed this vacation because I was ill. I was just wading in the water when . . ."

Then I told him my own story.

For a moment, we just stared at each other, knowing we had shared something incredible.

Maybe it wasn't just a coincidence that we were both there to save that woman, I thought. Maybe, just maybe, God wanted to give us something: the feeling of strength when we felt weak. To show us something: that we could do something wonderful for another person even when we weren't sure what we could do for ourselves.

We called the hospital and learned that Ellen had been released. She never knew that the stranger who reached out to her that day was me.

I think about Ellen a lot. Whenever I feel tired or weak, I remember the feeling of my legs and arms moving furiously and the sensation of power taking hold.

If I could pull a woman out of the ocean, I can do anything!

If you asked Ellen, she'd probably tell you that I was her guardian angel.

But if you ask me, I'd have to say *she* was *mine*.

—*Arlene Nunes*

Comment

When we reach beyond ourselves to care for another, we are often led past our own fears and limitations.

"*Who* the heck keeps on doing this?"

Wayne Morgan* bellowed at his wife as he stomped into the kitchen early one fall morning, laden with groceries, shaking the rain from his overcoat.

"What're you talking about, honey?" his wife Linda asked absently, concentrating on the pancakes she was skillfully flipping.

"Some idiot keeps tampering with the garbage cans. For the last few days, somebody keeps moving one of the garbage cans from the front yard into the alleyway right under the bedroom windows. Is this some crazy kind of joke? I keep moving the garbage can back into the front yard, and the next day it's in the alley again!"

"Listen, honey," his wife soothed, "I know it must be annoying to have to keep on moving the garbage can back to the front, but really it's no big deal."

"Yeah," he grumbled, "it's no big deal, you're right, but still I find it extremely aggravating! And it just seems so senseless, so stupid!"

"Well, did the same thing happen again just now? What's the fate of the wandering garbage can today?" Linda teased.

"Yeah, well that's what got me going. Last night, I moved the garbage can into the front yard, and this morning when I left for the supermarket it was back in the alley. So I returned the can to the front, and when I got home from shopping, there it was in the alley again!"

"Well, at least you're finally getting some exercise!" his wife tried to joke.

"Well, I didn't move it back this time because I was carrying the groceries," Wayne said. "I'll go do it in a minute after I have my coffee."

"Listen, when you get a chance," Linda asked, casually changing the subject, "can you please fix the guardrail on the baby's window? It's very loose and now that she's crawling around and standing, I'm afraid she can hoist herself up to the window seat and who knows what could happen?"

"Oh my god," Tom shrieked. "You didn't tell me the guardrail was broken! I opened the window this morning and I took the baby out of the crib before I left for the market."

The two exchanged a frantic look and raced to the bedroom.

The guardrail was gone from the window, the baby missing from the room.

Linda screamed and slumped into a chair. His heart palpitating with fear, Tom willed himself to look out the open window, expecting the worst.

A choking sob escaped from his lips—half-gasp, half-benediction, as his eyes widened in amazement at the scene below.

Two stories beneath the open bedroom window, a familiar cooing sound came from the baby, whose little arms were flailing energetically as she tried to extricate herself from the cushion that had buffered her fall.

She was nestled in the garbage can filled with the soft leaves that her father had raked and collected the week before.

Comment

Sometimes the cure arrives before the curse, but blinded as we mere mortals often tend to be, we fail to recognize either one for what they truly are.

In the winter of 1977, Miriam Altschul* moved with her husband and baby to Brooklyn from the Bronx neighborhood where she had grown up as a child.

The move was not an easy one. Every street, every signpost, every store in the old Bronx neighborhood had been familiar and known to Miriam. Most were replete with special memories and nostalgic moments. She knew all the local people and considered many of them to be her close friends.

In Brooklyn, she didn't know a soul.

Still, as her practical husband had convincingly persuaded her, the old Bronx neighborhood was deteriorating, and it was no longer an ideal place to raise a child. Flatbush, on the other hand, was a flourishing section bursting at the seams with young families like theirs, pulsating with energy and vitality. It boasted fine schools and excellent shopping and would provide them with the quality of life they sought.

But without friends, life felt hollow indeed.

As winter wore on, Miriam grew melancholy and despondent. "Perhaps it was a mistake to move to an apartment building where the living is so anonymous," she thought. "Everyone is holed up in their own individual cave. Maybe a private house would have been a better idea," she conjectured.

"And a move smack dead in the middle of winter! What were we thinking?" she berated herself.

The frigid temperatures, icy conditions, and perpetual snowfalls of what was a particularly hard winter that year kept her prisoner indoors with the baby much of the time. "At least if we had moved during the fall or waited for springtime, I could have gone out to the park and met other young mothers there," she thought with rue.

Miriam was a warm, sociable, gregarious type who liked and required company. Without it, she withered. She felt increasingly depressed, imprisoned in a cocoon of intense isolation. "I need a friend," she thought in desperation.

One morning, when the temperatures had climbed a bit and the sun shone brightly, Miriam decided to venture outdoors with her child. Impulsively, she did something that was not characteristic of her. She lived on the second floor of the apartment building and, young and nimble, she normally took the stairs down to the lobby. It was faster than waiting for the elevator, which was slow and ominously creaky. But on this particular morning, some inner voice told her to choose the elevator instead, and she waited patiently for it to arrive. When she opened the door, she saw a young woman with rosy cheeks and flashing eyes, cuddling a child her son's age.

She had found her friend.

The vivacious young woman smiled at Miriam invitingly and introduced herself, bubbling: "You must be the new tenant! I heard you moved in, and I wanted to drop by and say hello, but I'm so sorry, I just didn't get the chance. Hi, my name's Toby Green.* What's yours? Where are you from? How do you like it here so far? Do you have friends or relatives living here? No? Oh, my, that's terrible! Are you stuck inside all winter just like me? Well, the kids look like they're around the same age—let's get together then!"

Toby not only befriended Miriam, she took her under her wing. She shepherded her around the neighborhood, acquainting her with its different shopping districts and other facilities, introducing her to various people, escorting her to meetings of women's volunteer groups, and in general making sure that Miriam's presence was known to the community at large. The two became inseparable and went everywhere together—doing errands, going on outings with the boys, exercising, eating out, and more.

Toby proved to be a veritable blessing in Miriam's life, banishing the loneliness that had hung over her like a dark cloud. Miriam was soon able to successfully integrate herself into the new neighborhood and create the social life she longed to have. "I owe so much to Toby," Miriam often thought with gratitude. "She's helped me a lot. What would I have done without her?"

One year later, Toby moved to Toronto, Canada, and Miriam never saw her again.

In 1994, Pinchos Altschul, Miriam's seventeen-year-old son, graduated from high school and decided to pursue additional studies at a prestigious institution in Israel. It would be the first time in his life that he was away from his family for any significant period, and the first time he would be on his own in a country frequently besieged by bomb scares and terrorist attacks.

It was also the first time in his life that he would be heading for a new school without any friends in tow. And for a young boy of seventeen, it was that scenario that produced the greatest anxiety of all.

Pinchos, a friendly, outgoing boy, had always had a large circle of friends and an active social life. But although several of his high school classmates in New York had chosen to study in Israel, they had struck out in separate directions, and each had selected a different institution. None had opted for his school. Although no one in his family was worried about Pinchos, knowing his capacity to make friends easily, he himself was filled with misgivings. A foreign country . . . a new school . . . no family . . . all alone. "I hope I find a good friend soon," he thought wistfully.

The boy had rosy cheeks and sparkling eyes, a warm smile, and a sunny personality. Pinchos bumped into him one morning in the corridor of the dormitory, and the boy flashed him an impish grin. "Hey, are you the new kid down the hall?" he bubbled. "I heard about you and wanted to come say hi but I just didn't get around to it. My name is Sholom. I'm also new here and I bet you're feeling a little down and lonely and of course that's natural but I'm also new here so how about we combine forces and do stuff together OK?"

Sholom took Pinchos under his wing, introduced him to the other guys in the dorm, taught him the ropes, shepherded him around Jerusalem, and in many different ways helped him adapt to the new and different rhythms of dormitory life. Because of his friendship with Sholom, Pinchos adjusted easily, thrived in school, and had a valuable growth experience that would heavily influence the course of his future academic career. Most important of all, he was happy.

"I owe so much to Sholom," Pinchos often thought. "How can I ever repay him for all that he's given me? Maybe, when school's over, I can invite him to New York for the summer . . ."

"Hey, Mom," Sholom asked his mother a few days after his return home to Toronto in June. "Would it be OK if I vacationed in New York this summer?"

"What would you do there? Where would you stay?" his mother asked.

"I was invited by this kid from school. We were very close friends in Israel."

"Really? What's his name?" his mother asked.

"Pinchos Altschul."

"Altschul . . . that's an unusual name . . . could he possibly be related to Miriam Altschul?"

"That's his mother's name. Do you happen to know her?"

Silently, his mother walked to the closet where she stored old photographs and withdrew an ancient-looking album whose pages were yellowing. She motioned Sholom to her side and pointed to a faded photograph of two young women in outdated shirtdresses, arms linked around each other warmly, with a pair of cherubic toddlers sitting side by side on their laps.

Sholom recognized the spirited-looking woman with the flashing eyes; it was his mother, of course. And the child enfolded in her embrace was him.

But who was the other pretty woman she was hugging so affection-ately, and what was the name of the little boy on *her* lap?

"Pinchos Altschul," Toby Green of Toronto said softly, wiping away a tear. "His mother, Miriam, was my best friend in New York in 1977. Without knowing it, Sholom, it seems as if you and your childhood play-mate have reenacted a script that was written almost two decades ago."

∼⚬∼

Comment
Whether they be blood feuds or love stories, certain forces that are set into motion in one generation are often repeated in the next, and seeds sown in the distant past bear fruit in a future we can never envi-sion.

Throughout her childhood, Sara Ain Flascher had sustained her fair share of bumps, bruises, scrapes, and cuts, but she had never endured the painful sting of a bee. Thus, she was completely unaware of the fact, and had never had cause to suspect, that she was allergic—extremely allergic—to bee venom.

When she was subjected to her very first bee sting, she was already an adult, oblivious to the danger that awaited her and completely unprepared for it.

She felt the sudden stab early one fall afternoon, as she chatted animatedly with friends whom she was visiting at their home in Newburgh, New York.

"Ouch!" she yelped in distress as the stinger penetrated her skin. Her finger immediately began to throb, and she felt it grow tender.

"Kurt!" she called out to her husband. "Come quick! I think I've been stung by a bee."

Kurt ran to her side to reassure her and downplay the effects of bee stings. He, too, was unaware of the grave peril his wife faced, a peril that would grow more serious by the minute.

"Don't worry; it's nothing," he soothed. "I know people who've had dozens of bee stings and it's really nothing to get upset about. The pain will subside soon."

But the pain increased rather than diminished, and the finger began to swell to ominous proportions. Then Sara's arm began to throb.

"Kurt," Sara asked in alarm, "you know I get weekly allergy shots for all the things I'm allergic to; could I possibly be allergic to bee venom as well?"

No physician had ever warned Sara of the possibility, so neither of them realized that this was indeed what they were dealing with—a serious allergic reaction to a bee bite.

Just then, the doorbell rang. The friend they were visiting, who had been anxiously hovering over Sara, reluctantly turned to answer the door. "Be right back," she promised.

A middle-aged woman was standing on the threshold with a worried look on her face.

"I'm so sorry to disturb you," she apologized in a soft voice, "but I live down the block and my mother has Alzheimer's disease and she wandered away from home and we're looking for her everywhere and wondering if perhaps one of the neighbors has seen her or taken her in and I feel so guilty because I should have been watching her more care-fully but I was distracted by an emergency phone call from a patient of mine and . . ."

Sara's friend interrupted the woman in mid-sentence. *"Patient?"* she exclaimed with excitement. "Are you a doctor, by any chance?"

The woman nodded a puzzled yes.

Sara's friend pulled her into the house. "Please take a look at my guest. She was just bitten by a bee and seems to be having an unusual reaction . . ."

The doctor rushed in.

Sara's arm was now swollen and the finger had ballooned.

The doctor rapidly pulled out the stinger, then rushed around the kitchen using household supplies like baking soda and ice to pack Sara's hand. Then she took a second look at her and hustled her into a car, speeding to her office—a minute away—where she administered an in-jection, which, she explained, was an antidote to the bee venom.

Later, after the excitement had died down, the swelling had begun to re-cede, and the Flaschers had expressed their thanks and appreciation effu-sively, the doctor said thoughtfully, "You know, Mr. Flascher, the rapid intervention I was able to administer saved your wife from serious conse-quences. If I hadn't rung the doorbell when I did, who knows what might have happened?"

Many years after the incident, the Flaschers still retell the story with awe and gratitude. It's a "small miracle," they say, one they'll surely re-member for the rest of their lives.

Comment
Those seeking help from you may very well come to be the source of your salvation.

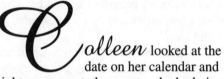 **C**olleen looked at the
date on her calendar and
sighed. A lifetime before—eighteen years, to be exact—she had given
birth to a baby girl and given her up for adoption.

Throughout the years, the thought of this child had haunted her: was
she smart, was she pretty, was she healthy, was she happy? Now, it was
getting close to the child's eighteenth birthday. By law in Canada she
was finally free to conduct a search to discover her daughter's destiny.
Did she dare?

She decided to make a move, albeit a small one. Though she had
since moved to a town hundreds of miles away, Colleen called the newspaper in the town of Alberta, Canada, the baby's birthplace.

"Let me speak to your classified section," she asked the operator at the
Alberta *Times*. "I'd like to place an ad."

"Sure," said the operator, "what's your message?"

It was such a long shot, Colleen considered hanging up. But timing
was critical; the ad needed to appear on the exact date of her daughter's
birth.

"Happy birthday," she began. Then she provided the name she had
given her daughter when she gave her up for adoption eighteen years before, along with a simple message announcing her search and her phone
number in the remote town where she lived.

That might have been the end of the story, if it hadn't been for an editor toiling late in the newsroom who noticed Colleen's ad. "There's
something going on here," he said to himself.

That very same day, a woman named Jodi Mitchell had called the Alberta *Times*. Although she did not live in Alberta, the woman was hoping
to find somebody who might. Eighteen years ago, Jodi had been
adopted. The only information she had about her adoption proceeding
was that she was born in Alberta. With the hope that her biological
mother still lived in Alberta, the young woman had placed an ad announcing her search.

Immediately, the editor picked up the phone and called Colleen. It
was almost 11 P.M. Colleen became concerned when she learned who it
was. "Is there a problem?" she asked.

"No!" replied the editor, "it's just that there's a coincidence here
that's too big to ignore. There's another ad in here that sounds, you
know . . . similar to yours." Colleen got goose bumps when he told her

about the other ad. With a shaking hand, she wrote the number down and called the young woman.

Indeed, Jodi Mitchell turned out to be Colleen's daughter. Who would have guessed they would place identical ads, in the same distant paper, on the same day? Like mother, like daughter.

~⌘~

Comment

Know that there is a master weaver bringing together those who are meant to be with one another.

ayne grabbed his swimsuit and loped towards the door. "Bye, Mom, I'm going to my friend's house," he said.

"Hold on just one minute!" Pat said, jumping in front of her teenage son. She looked for his eyes under his baseball cap. "Now, when will you be coming home?"

Wayne rolled his eyes. This was a familiar routine. He told her he would be back the following night and kissed her on the cheek.

But Mom wasn't so easily put off. With a shake of her finger and a smile, Pat said, "I want you to call me by noon tomorrow." She handed him a scrap of paper so he could write down the friend's number. When he was gone, she placed the number on her headboard with the intention of taking it to work in the morning. How well she knew her Wayne.

The following day at work, Pat anticipated a call from her son. But noon turned into 1:00, which rolled into 2:00, and still he hadn't called. Pat shook her head knowingly. She worried in spite of herself. She fished through her wallet to retrieve the friend's number and then slapped her knee as she realized she had left it at home. "Now what do I do?" Pat fretted.

She was in a fix. She couldn't leave the office, but the thought of waiting to hear from her son on his teenage time clock was unsettling. She would be preoccupied with thoughts of Wayne and his well-being all day. Closing her eyes and willing herself to be calm, Pat tried to recall the numbers scribbled on the white piece of paper. As a shot in the dark she phoned the number she was best able to recall.

After two rings, a man answered.

"Hello," Pat said, timidly. "Is Wayne Brown there, by any chance?"

"Let's see, Wayne Brown, Wayne Brown . . ." the man repeated slowly, as if he was thinking. Pat debated hanging up.

"I don't seem to recall any Wayne Brown having come by today," he said.

Pat thanked the man quickly, explained that she had the wrong number, and was about to hang up when the man said, "How old is Wayne?" Pat looked at the phone quizzically. What a strange question! "How old?" she said. "Sixteen." She wished she hadn't answered, but something impelled her. Nevertheless, the man said he could not help her, and hung up. Pat decided dialing any more numbers was a bad idea, and tried to keep her mind on work.

Four hours later, a coworker answered the telephone and handed it to

Pat. "Hello?" Pat said as she placed the receiver to her ear. Much to her relief, it was Wayne. His voice sounded incredulous. "Mom!" he cried, "how did you know to call me at the dentist's office?"

Pat stood up from her seat. "What are you talking about?" she laughed. With characteristic animation, Wayne explained the story. "My friend needed to have his braces removed, and asked me to go along with him. I said, 'Why not?'

"I walk into the dentist's office," Wayne continued, "and my friend introduces me to this dentist I've never seen before. 'This is Wayne Brown,' my friend says, and the dentist says, 'Your mother is waiting for your call.'

"I thought the dentist was joking—I mean, how could he possibly know that? Then he tells me you had called his office. Now Mom, I didn't even know I'd be coming here, *so how in the world did you know?*"

It turns out that Pat had indeed dialed a "wrong number." The dentist was on a lunch break; he was in his little house behind the office. Ordinarily he would not be answering a phone, but this number rang on his private line so he picked it up.

This took place in Anchorage, Alaska, where there is a population of a quarter of a million people with an untold number of telephone lines crossing through. For Pat, though, she needed just one call, from her son, and by God, she got it.

~⚬≈⚬~

Comment

Although the umbilical cord is severed within the first few moments of life, its spiritual counterpart continues to pulsate forever, transmitting a stream of unspoken messages between mother and child.

He was the runt of the litter—small, puny and sickly-looking, almost too feeble to stand on his weak legs, cowering in a dark corner of the barn.

"You don't want him," said Bill, the puppies' owner, brusquely, motioning toward the four robust ones tumbling in the hay. "Any one of those would be a better choice."

But my gaze remained fastened on the pitiful looking pup, who returned my glance with entreating eyes, and a soft, sweet expression that could melt the coldest of hearts.

"Does he have a name?" I asked.

"Listen, Johnny," Bill sighed, "I'm a good friend of your father's and I don't want to steer you wrong. I'm not even sure that pup is gonna make it."

Like me, I thought. They weren't sure that I was going to make it, either.

The previous year, at the age of thirteen, I had been diagnosed with leukemia, and I was now in remission. But I had been as fragile as the eight-week-old pup that now bounded over to me from across the room, licking my hand enthusiastically.

"Well, I'll be doggoned." Bill scratched his head. "He never did that before. He's such a shy, scared pup, 'fraid of everything and everybody. 'Fraid of his own shadow. Seems like he really likes you, though."

"We have something in common," I said wryly, more to myself than to Bill.

As I bent down and stroked the pup, I felt the strong connection surge through me.

"Does he have a name?" I asked again.

"Miracle," said Bill grimly. "Cause it sure is one that he's still alive; he was so sick the first few weeks."

"I'll take him."

Bill touched my shoulder in a gesture of compassion. "I don't want to see you getting hurt, Johnny. What if the pup dies on you? You've gone through a lot this year. I don't want you to suffer the pain of losing him. Take my advice; choose another pup, please!"

But I left the barn with Miracle cuddled in my arms. I wasn't called stubborn for nothing.

Over the years, Miracle proved that first appearances can be deceiving. He learned to be as feisty as me. His spirit turned into an indomitable one, and we taught each other how to fight: death, disease, other peoples' bad insights and poor judgments. There were precarious times in both of our lives, but we endured them together and triumphed over adversity. We survived.

Was ever a boy and his dog so connected like Miracle and me? He walked me to school along the rural roads of Maine where I lived, and then raced himself home; he was promptly outside the school building at 3 P.M. to escort me back. He slept at the foot of my bed, and his sleeping patterns matched mine exactly. He was keenly sensitive of my moods, inundating me with wet sloppy kisses when I was especially blue, fiercely protective when my siblings teased or taunted me.

"We are bonded forever, and we will be together always," I often fancifully thought.

"Forever" came to a crashing halt four years later. I had been accepted to a prestigious university in Boston and had received a scholarship I had tenaciously pursued and sorely needed. My dream had finally been achieved: I had been admitted into one of the most elite academic institutions in the world.

"What am I going to do about Miracle?" I wondered aloud to my mother one day, when I learned that students were required to live in the school's dormitory, where no pets were permitted.

"You have no choice," my mother said. "You'll have to leave him behind. I know it's hard for you to be parted from him, but you'll see him on Christmas vacation and at Easter."

My heart was heavy with grief as I said my final farewell to Miracle the day I left home. "I wish I could explain to you why I'm leaving," I told him sadly. "And I wish I could find a way to let you know I'm coming back. When I call, I'll have Mom put your ear to the receiver so you can hear my voice."

But I never got the chance, because the day after I left, Miracle was gone.

My mother broke the news to me gently, with a tremor in her voice.

Miracle had disappeared. He had gone out in the morning to roam the neighborhood in pursuit of canine adventures, but he had not faithfully returned in the evening, as he always had before.

An accident? I asked, throat tightening, body stiff with fear.

All the animal hospitals, shelters, and veterinarians in town had been called. Ditto for police stations, fire departments, and emergency medical services.

No one had seen Miracle.

A dognapping? I proposed.

My mother was dubious. It was true that Miracle was a beagle—a pure breed—but he was male and five years old. And besides, our sleepy little town was not exactly the kind of place where dognappers skulked and snatched prey.

So what could have happened to Miracle?

Everyone was mystified, my mother said.

But I . . . I was heartbroken.

"Hey, pal," I whispered, "we were a team, remember? Forever is supposed to be a long time."

I called my parents daily for several weeks to hear if Miracle had been found. But the news was never good, and "Not yet, Johnny" soon turned into "I don't think that he's alive, son."

I stopped calling.

When I came home for Christmas, Easter, and the summer holidays, I went looking for Miracle. All the favorite retreats we had haunted together—a favored fishing hole, a choice site in the woods, a verdant pasture where Miracle always romped joyously—all held no signs of him and yielded no clues. I walked the streets of my little town, anxiously asking everyone I encountered: "Have you seen my dog Miracle?"

But no one had seen him. "Not for months," they said.

"I think it's time that we accept that Miracle's really gone," my mother said.

"I can't accept that," I said. "Because it's not the truth."

One year later, I was in my dorm room at the university thinking about Miracle, when my roommate turned to me with a puzzled look.

"What's that noise?" he demanded, scowling.

"What noise?" I asked absently, engrossed in my thoughts and not hearing anything irregular.

"Like . . . a peculiar scratching sound. . . . Listen, don't you hear it, now?"

I raced to the door and flung it open wide.

He rushed into my arms with little whimpering cries, and I hugged him tight. There was no flesh on his skeletal frame, and his fur was matted with grime. His eyes looked dull and feverish, and his stance was unsteady. Despite the changes that a year on the road had wrought in his appearance, it was undeniably my beloved dog.

"This is your dog that disappeared a year ago in *Maine?*" demanded my roommate with incredulity. "How could that be? How could the dog travel so many hundreds of miles in all kinds of weather and survive? . . . But more important . . . how did he find his way to you in *Boston?* How is that possible?"

"Anything is possible," I whispered.

"*My God,*" my roommate shouted, "it's a miracle."

"No," I corrected gently, "it *is* Miracle!"

Charlene Wheatley was a cosmetics salesgirl at Bloomingdale's. For nine years she had worked at the Prescriptives counter, seeing thousands of faces and handling all sorts of customers from countries across the globe.

One day a tourist appeared at her counter. Since Charlene's sister-in-law is Japanese, she immediately detected the woman's Japanese accent, and understood how to put the woman at ease by speaking slowly and politely.

"May I help you?" she said with a smile, a bow, and a soft tone.

"I . . . would . . . like . . . skin . . . care," said the timid woman in halting English.

With patience and care, Charlene showed the woman the full line of Prescriptives products, explaining the benefits of each. Although it was not easy, the two women managed to communicate through nods, gestures, smiles, and a few words.

Charlene's courtesy obviously made a big impression on the woman, for she bought several products and then thanked Charlene repeatedly. "Thank you . . . thank you . . . for this time you spent with me," said the woman. She paid, bowed once more in gratitude, and left the counter.

Charlene was still smiling about the encounter when the woman appeared again, half an hour later. She had decided to stock up on all her items before returning to Japan. "Happy to oblige," smiled Charlene. As she went about collecting the items, Charlene felt friendly enough with the woman to mention her Japanese sister-in-law. It was rare that Charlene actually shared anything of her personal life with her customers; her conversations almost always focused on the products.

"Oh yes?" responded the woman with surprise, looking up from her selections. "Oh yes!" Charlene said, giggling, emboldened by the woman's response. "I even know a few words of Japanese—like *Musashi*—that means samurai warrior." The woman giggled back. It was funny to hear such a familiar word spoken by an American.

"As a matter of fact," continued Charlene, "that's the name of my nephew." But Charlene had forgotten herself—she had forgotten to speak slowly. The woman looked confused. "Nephew," Charlene repeated. Then she had an idea—she pulled a picture of her beaming eight-year-old nephew out of her bag.

"See? Musashi, my nephew," said Charlene, and she handed the picture to the woman, expecting her to smile. But when the woman's eyes settled on the picture of the boy, her expression froze in shock. Her hand flew to her mouth and she shrieked.

"What is it?" cried Charlene.

Customers and salespeople alike all turned around at the sound of the loud voices as the woman continued to exclaim—"Can not be! Can not be! . . ."

"But you must tell me! What is it?" insisted Charlene. The woman finally seemed to catch her breath, and then spoke. "This boy," she said, pointing to the picture in her hand, *"he my godson!"*

In the best words she could muster, she tried to explain to Charlene that the boy's mother, Charlene's sister-in-law, had been her best friend back in Japan. The family had moved years ago and the two had lost contact over the years. In fact, she was now in New York trying desperately to find them.

"Thank you!" she said with a more radiant smile than any lipstick could ever give her. "Thank you!"

Within a matter of hours, best friends, godmother, and godchild were reunited.

⟿

Comment

From one nation to another runs a line that connects one heart to another.

*T*ommy Hoyt* heard the screams before he actually saw the scuffle. Then he realized that the flurry of movement his brain had barely registered a second ago wasn't an animated discussion, as he had assumed, but a furious struggle. On the other side of the subway car, a man was ripping a gold pendant from the neck of a young woman with an angelic face and startled sapphire eyes.

Everyone in the car seemed to freeze. Later, Tommy would reflect that what some people mistakenly attribute to apathy is actually a form of collective shell shock. Everyone seemed chilled, hardened into a kind of slow-motion freeze-frame. It wasn't that the passengers didn't care, it was that they simply couldn't move.

Tommy was the first to regain his wits. He shook himself out of his paralysis and moved toward the girl. She was still locked in battle with the mugger, feistily (or foolishly) refusing to surrender her necklace. "If only I can reach her before the guy gets it," he thought, pushing through the hordes of subway riders blocking his passage. But only a few feet away, he watched helplessly as the mugger gave a savage yank and succeeded in tearing the pendant off her neck. The train had just reached the station and the mugger ran out the open door onto the subway platform.

"Help!" the victim cried feebly.

Tommy dashed out the door in pursuit of the thief. He caught up with him at the end of the platform and tackled him. He grabbed the pendant out of his hand, as the mugger slipped out of his grasp. "At least I got the necklace back," Tommy thought with satisfaction, "even if the mugger did get away."

Tommy wondered what the angelic blonde would say when he made his victorious return to the subway car, proudly bearing the necklace he had recovered.

But he would never know, because as he headed towards the subway, he realized with a start that the train had already left the station and was gone.

"Didn't somebody stop the train while I chased the mugger?" he wondered, confused. "Didn't people see what I was up to? Is it possible the girl doesn't even know I tried to get the necklace for her?"

Tommy was disheartened. Here he had gone to all this trouble, even put his life in danger, and it seemed as if amidst all the tumult, nobody had even realized what he had set out to do.

"Now what?" he wondered.

He decided he would stick around the subway platform in case the girl *had* noticed his heroic efforts, after all, and returned to the station to thank him and find out what happened.

He waited futilely for a full hour, and then concluded that the girl must never even have been aware of his gallant attempts.

"Was all this trouble for nothing?" he wondered, disheartened. "And what do I do with the necklace? The police?" He shook his head. "She doesn't even know someone retrieved it; why would she go to the police? Nah, that's not a good idea . . ."

For some reason that he couldn't quite explain, Tommy decided to hold onto the necklace himself, and keep it with him in his jacket pocket.

And whenever he happened to finger it, as he did from time to time, the vivid recollection of an angelic face with startled sapphire eyes came swimming back to mind.

Three years later, Tommy walked into a bar in midtown Manhattan and there she was. The angelic face and sapphire eyes were unmistakable; he recognized her in an instant. She was perched on a stool near the bar, stirring her drink bemusedly, looking like she was waiting for someone.

"Maybe she's waiting for me," he thought inanely, as his heart lurched.

"This is not a pick-up," he said quickly, as he eased into the stool next to hers. "This is a pick-*me*-up, instead."

"A pick-me-up?" she asked, wrinkling her freckled nose in bewilderment. "Whatever is that supposed to mean?"

"That means," he said, triumphantly pulling out the gold pendant from his pocket where he had kept it all these years, "that when you see this, your spirits will surely be picked up!" And with a theatrical flourish he smugly handed her the necklace, as she stared at him aghast.

As he had correctly discerned in the subway station three years before, amidst the chaos and commotion of the mugging no one—including the girl—had actually seen him dart out the subway door in hot pursuit of the mugger. No one—including the girl—knew that the necklace had been retrieved. And no one could have been more grateful or surprised than she.

"It was my grandmother's," she explained. "Beyond anything else, it has great sentimental value. . . . Tell me," she asked softly, "what can I give you as a reward?"

"How about a date?" Tommy asked.

They've been married for five years now, and Tommy told their story last year on the Valentine's Day program broadcast on a local New York radio station.

In recounting the coincidence that brought them together, Tommy said: "She may have gotten back her necklace, but it was surely *I* who acquired the gem!"

∼⤙❦⤚∼

Comment
Little acts are the seeds from which mighty miracles grow.

lga Whittaker and John Kane, strangers until Tuesday, May 6, 1997, were brought together in a Miami jewelry shop—by fate, coincidence, or was it something else?

Kane, 45, of Fort Lauderdale, was trying to sell a Rolex watch. Whittaker, 36, of West Palm Beach, took a look at the man. She let out a shriek and grabbed him. The jeweler locked the door.

"I prayed to my God that He would kill you, but instead He delivered you into my hands!" Whittaker cried.

The Rolex, she declared, was stolen Sunday from her husband, John K. Whittaker. While running a jewelry booth at an antique show in West Palm Beach, he took the watch off and put it down where he thought it was safe. It was not.

Gone forever, the Whittakers figured, until whatever mysterious wonders were performed Tuesday.

Olga, in Miami for a medical test, went browsing in the Seybold Building, a tall downtown edifice devoted to the jewelry trade.

When the police got there, they found Whittaker, the shopkeeper and a few other people guarding Kane. There was a switchblade knife in his pocket and some open arrest warrants for grand theft on his record, police spokesman Delrish Moss said.

How did Olga Whittaker get him? A miracle, she swears, but she has a police officer's eye for a suspicious character.

"He was at the antique show," she said. "He came to our booth three different times, asking the price of this, the price of that. He looked very pale and nervous then, and the same today."

She also recognized the watch, but needed proof. Her husband brought West Palm Beach Police the papers, which were faxed to Miami, proving that his wife bought that very Rolex for $3,200 in 1990.

Olga Whittaker said she had been praying for a sign that God is real. "This is a big sign," she told Moss.

Kane also spoke to Moss: "Do you know why I was arrested?"

"You tell me," the officer said, hoping for something profound, and the suspect replied, "Bad luck, I guess."

—Arnold Markowitz

Comment

Coincidences are not the result of bad luck, but rather an invitation to look inside and see what might be "bad" that is creating the "luck"!

Jamey Martinez and Leslie Duncan were best friends. Even when Leslie switched schools in tenth grade, the two girls stayed close through lots of letters filled with heartfelt confessions and outrageous gossip. Jamey's day always brightened when she saw the familiar blue of Leslie's stationery in her mailbox.

But one crisp fall day, Jamey learned that she would no longer get to share stories with Leslie. A mutual friend broke the incomprehensible news at school: "Jamey, did you hear about Leslie?" Brenda Shwartz, a classmate, asked in a most concerned tone.

"Heard what?" responded Jamey.

Brenda, who had grown up with the two, seemed surprised that Jamey had been in the dark. She stuttered and seemed to falter over her words but then finally she came out with it: "Leslie died last night," she managed to say.

"OK, sure," responded Jamey in a sarcastic tone, "ha, ha, ha."

"No, I'm serious!" Brenda said solemnly.

Jamey knew her friend Brenda very well, and she detected an earnestness in Brenda's voice that told her that she might not be joking after all. Brenda's words were now sinking in.

"No!" screamed Jamey. "No way!" Finding no other words to say, Brenda simply nodded.

Jamey ran back home and got on the phone with Leslie's mother. "Is it true?" she said, trying to choke back emotion. "Is Leslie gone?" There was a long pause as Jamey heard Leslie's mother sobbing on the other end of the line. "Yes," came the choked reply, "Leslie complained that she wasn't feeling good when she came home. She went to sleep and never got up."

Jamey felt that she was swimming in a sea of confusion. The day took on a surreal quality. She wanted to know more; she was unwilling to accept that her friend was gone. Sometime during those hours, Jamey noticed a stack of letters that had come in the mail. There among her parents' bills and correspondence was a familiar blue envelope. A letter from Leslie.

Jamey ripped the letter open with a trembling hand. She hoped it would contain a clue, any information that would shed light on Leslie's mysterious death. But there was no such evidence. It was the usual kind of news. Lots to tell about different classes, things that happened with friends, and places that she had visited.

And, of course, boys. "I want you to meet this guy," the last part of the letter said. "We've been out a couple of . . ." But Jamey stopped reading before the end of the letter. All that seemed trivial now. She folded the letter and placed it with all the other letters from Leslie that she had lovingly saved. The following day she attended her friend's funeral.

Over the next few months, Jamey found solace in making a scrapbook of pictures, letters, and a variety of mementos that helped keep the memory of her deceased friend alive. As the days turned into years and Jamey grew into a woman, she looked at the scrapbook less and less, but she always knew it was there. She had an ache in her heart that was hard to fill. When, in her early twenties, she met a man who filled her with the same kind of joy she had known with her lost friend, she counted her blessings. They got married and moved into a new home.

During the move Jamey came across the scrapbook. Rather than simply putting it away, she opened it. She allowed the contents to take her back in time, smiling at the pictures and reading through some of the letters.

Jamey picked up the last letter she had ever received from Leslie and held it lovingly in her hand. The paper was crumbling a bit, and creased. This time, she read it slowly, to savor the words. And, for the first time, she read the end of the letter that she had skipped ten years ago.

"I want you to meet this guy. We've been out a couple of times," it said. "He's really nice, and you'll like him, I know. I want us all to be friends. His name is Eric Knorr."

As she read the name, her hand flew to her mouth and she let out an audible gasp. The man who filled her heart, the man who shared her home, the man she had married . . . was Eric Knorr.

Leslie's grave is less than a mile from Jamey and Eric's home. The couple visit regularly and lay down a wreath in memory and gratitude, for they believe that their friend's wish played a part in bringing them together.

Comment

Love is the connecting line that links the past, the present, and the future into one everlasting bond that stands the test of time.

$\mathcal{O}$*n* preparation for the onslaught of the Gulf War, when the menacing threat of chemical and biological warfare from Saddam Hussein's factories of death hung over the country of Israel like a dense and sinister fog, Israeli citizens were instructed to create a "sealed" room in their homes to which they could retreat when the Scuds fell.

Almost everyone in Israel understood the grave peril that they faced and the nightmare world into which they had been plunged. They took both Hussein's threats and the worst-case scenario seriously, and in their "sealed" room most Israelis stockpiled abundant supplies of food, medicine, clothing, furniture, books, toys for the children, and additional essentials. Others, however, were more sanguine and consequently didn't equip their room quite as completely as they should have.

The Ben Simone* family belonged to this very small minority. Their sealed room lacked many basics, including furniture. When the first siren went off in Tel Aviv, indicating the beginning of the initial assault, the large family rushed into the sealed room in a state of dazed disbelief. The only piece of furniture in the room was a lone armchair, and practically everyone headed for the floor. Two people remained standing: an elderly grandfather and his young, nine-months-pregnant granddaughter. They both looked at the single armchair and then at each other.

"Grandfather," the young woman urged, "please . . . sit down."

"No, heaven forbid, my sweet, precious grandchild," the elderly man replied. "*You* sit down."

"Not in a million years! I wouldn't think of it! Please, *you* sit down!"

"*I* should sit down while my nine-months-pregnant granddaughter, almost in labor, stands? Never!"

"Well, Grandfather, you might as well sit down, because I absolutely refuse to take *your* chair!"

And so it went, for minutes, a veritable stalemate, both arguing stubbornly, both refusing to yield, the chair remaining empty, unoccupied.

And wasn't it fortunate? Because as they argued, something hit their roof with a loud thud, and a large piece of an unexploded Scud burst through their ceiling and into the armchair where neither of them sat.

Comment

When we interact with others with love, respect, and consideration, we are enfolded by a protective light.

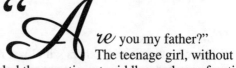**"A**re you my father?"

The teenage girl, without preamble or explanation, hurled the question at middle-aged men frantically, as she raced around the cemetery, seemingly possessed.

It was Father's Day, and droves of people were meandering down the labyrinthine burial grounds searching for the graves where they would pay their respects. The atmosphere had been serene and peaceful until the girl had made her frenzied appearance, moments before. Her distraught cries and bizarre behavior unnerved many, and they gazed after her with troubled eyes.

As soon as she had entered the cemetery, the girl had begun waylaying strangers one by one, demanding of each, in breathless tones, if he was her father. As soon as each man shook his head "no"—some pensively, a few annoyed—she would hurry on to accost another.

"Are *you* my father?" she asked, sprinting in a frenzied state from man to man.

"How weird," one woman whispered to her husband.

"Must be on drugs, poor soul," he murmured back.

"Weirdo!" another woman declared, in emphatic tones.

Despite the assured pronouncements of the bystanders, the girl was neither drugged nor crazy.

She had been adopted at birth, and the identity of her biological parents had been kept shrouded in secrecy. But when both of her adoptive parents had died the year before in a tragic car crash, she had launched a desperate search to find her natural mother and father. All that she had learned from the adoption agency was that her natural mother had also died recently and that her biological father's whereabouts were unknown.

But somewhere in the cemetery, a man was waiting. He was leaning up against an old oak tree, eyes scanning the crowd. He was waiting for a teenage girl to approach him and ask, "Are *you* my father?"

He didn't put much stock in dreams, but he had been searching for his daughter for many years without success. And the previous night, a holy man with a luminous face, a long white beard, and piercing eyes had appeared to him in his sleep, with news.

He instructed him to travel to this particular cemetery.

And wait.

A young girl rushed down the path, accosting strangers. His body stiffened. Was it she?

"Are *you* my father?" she asked, desperation tingeing her voice. She had scoured the entire cemetery and was beginning to feel the hopelessness of defeat.

"Are *you* my daughter?" he responded with a tender smile.

"It *is* you, then." She faltered for a moment, gazing with rapt interest into his smoky hazel eyes, replicas of her own.

Later, much later, he asked what had brought her to the cemetery and why she had thought of searching for him there.

"I don't really believe in this kinda stuff," she answered slowly, "but last night a man appeared in my sleep and told me to come to this cemetery today. He said I would find you here for sure. I've been so desperate to locate you, I was ready to try anything. So I did."

"Tell me . . ." the father asked urgently. "What did this man look like?"

"Well, he—umm—kinda had this radiant aura about him, very shiny face, you know? And he had burning eyes. And . . . uh . . . yeah . . . he also wore a long white beard," the daughter said.

"And did he come to you at about two o'clock in the morning?"

"Why, yes," the girl replied, astonished. "I woke up right after the dream—it kinda freaked me out—and looked at the clock on the night table. But . . . how did you know?"

"Honey," the father said softly, "this same man appeared to me last night, too. At the exact same time. Because I also woke up after the dream and looked at my watch. And it was . . . same as you . . . two o'clock.

—*Norman Kelbalkan*

"**D**o you have experience in telecommunications?"

Joie Giese inquired of the prospective employee.

"Yes, most certainly," said Merrilee Woeber, trying to put her best foot forward.

"Could you tell me about the places where you have worked and the sorts of jobs you have had?" asked Joie.

Merrilee described her work history, and Joie listened carefully. As supervisor at Network MCI Conferencing, Joie prided herself on creating a dynamic and friendly workforce. In charge of several company projects, she sought to hire men and women of the highest caliber who would add to the positive work ethic that she tried to foster.

So it was without hesitation that Joie decided to hire Merrilee. Intelligent and hard-working, Merrilee fit the job description to a T. Plus, she had a very positive attitude, and Joie found herself extending the interview just because she enjoyed the chat and the pleasant company.

Joie ended the interview with the exact words that Merrilee hoped to hear: "Welcome aboard!"

Merrilee began working for the company almost immediately. The two women became good friends as well as colleagues. They discovered that they had an uncanny similarity in tastes. "I love your outfit," said Joie as she passed Merrilee in the hall one day. "Thanks," came the reply. Several days later it was Merrilee's turn to offer the compliment. "Now, that's a gorgeous dress," she exclaimed. "Well, thank you," replied Joie. The two found themselves having this sort of exchange repeatedly.

"Look at that," said Merrilee as she placed her ring next to Joie's. Joie was amazed; they both broke into laughter. From the infinite variety of diamond rings available, both women had chosen rings of yellow gold, with identical channel diamonds around the band and a diamond in the center.

One year after being hired, Merrilee was promoted to supervisor. Her desk was now within earshot of Joie's office. Shortly thereafter, Merrilee was working at her desk one afternoon when she overheard Joie chatting with a few coworkers on break. They talked with no particular topic or focus. One woman made a reference to having an Italian complexion. Joie, with her fair skin, made a sarcastic remark. "Yeah, me too," she joked.

Then Joie mentioned in passing something that Merrilee had not known: she had been adopted. Joie said she knew little about her biological parents. Those who knew Joie knew this about her: that she loved her adoptive parents for the abundant love they had given her.

"Do you know your nationality?" the Italian woman asked. "I believe

I'm Irish," replied Joie. "The only thing I know about my biological mother is her name. It was Dunne, which is Irish."

It was then that Merrilee stopped typing. Her curiosity got the better of her. She got up and walked right into Joie's office. "I assumed my husband's name when I got married, but my maiden name is Dunne," she said, and then added with a spark of hope, "maybe we're cousins. Where were you born?"

"Here in Davenport," replied Joie.

"That's where I'm from," said Merrilee, eyebrows raised. "When were you born?"

"In 1946," replied Joie.

"I was born in 1945!"

Merrilee and Joie both felt a mounting sense of excitement. They sensed that they were on to something.

"Do you know your biological mother's full name?" asked Merrilee.

"Lenore Dunne," said Joie.

"NO!" Merrilee was incredulous. "Are you sure you didn't perhaps just pick up that name from my files?"

"Of course not!" Joie assured her. "That's the name on my adoption papers."

At this point, everyone in the room sensed that something eerie was afoot. One by one, out of courtesy and respect, they filed out. Merrilee and Joie were facing each other alone.

That afternoon, Joie made a dash to her safety deposit box in the bank to retrieve the adoption papers she had received when she turned eighteen. Merrilee, at the same time, looked for a signature from her mother, now deceased. The two women caught up with each other, placed the two signatures side by side, and then simultaneously let out a thrilling cry.

It was unmistakable. No wonder they had so much in common, no wonder they felt an instant connection. They were not only related, they were sisters.

Sisters, born of the same woman—Lenore Dunne. She had had two daughters: one she placed for adoption and one she raised. Each had no knowledge of the other, until now, over half a century later, when they discovered one another while working side by side.

❧

Comment

To find the greatest of all treasures, you may not need to search the world over.

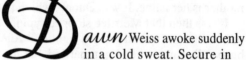

awn Weiss awoke suddenly in a cold sweat. Secure in her job, safe in her apartment, and surrounded by family and friends, she had no reason to be frightened. Nevertheless, in that early January morning of 1994 the secure world Dawn knew was literally crumbling around her. At first she had a flashback to the days when she was an active alcoholic. Her bed shook and the walls started to crack open. But she was sober now, this was not a hangover, and she knew it. The noise was deafening. What Dawn could not know was that Northridge, California, and its environs were being rocked by an enormous earthquake.

Dawn shot up in bed. Her immediate thoughts were for her beloved Harley, a gray angora cat. "Harley!" she screamed. But the floor was literally swaying beneath her. She had no time to waste as she sprang from her bed. "The whole place is coming down!" she yelled as plaster fell in large chunks from the ceiling. Her natural instincts told her she had no time to save Harley and only seconds to save her own life. She could not even spare a moment to change out of her nightclothes.

She suddenly realized that her second-floor apartment afforded an easy, possibly a simple escape. She ran immediately to the open window. Well within her reach was a large tree branch, which she immediately grabbed.

As the building continued to shake, she lurched for the branch with both hands. Cautiously yet with great trepidation, she groped her way down through the branches to the firm ground below.

The earthquake was relentless as it roared through the area in those dark early-morning hours. It appeared to engulf the terrain around her. As she ran to her car, her apartment building came crashing to the ground like a pile of toy blocks. The parking lot split into a vast crater, swallowing up the cars parked there. The neighbors who had managed to escape stood huddled together, comforting one another yet in shock themselves. Amidst the pandemonium, Dawn spotted Harley the cat. She ran to hug him and held him tight.

In the darkness—through rubble and fallen power lines—holding Harley, Dawn walked for more than a mile to a friend's apartment. Desperately the two of them searched the immediate area for loved ones. Their efforts were not in vain. Within two days Dawn had accounted for all her friends, parents, and other relatives—all, incredibly, alive and uninjured.

For the next two weeks the earthquake's aftershocks made it difficult to trust the earth underfoot. Dawn wanted to believe that the worst was over and that it would never happen again. But then another shock would make the ground tremble. Would it ever cease? After the first week Dawn's nerves were worn thin, leaving her uneasy, uncertain, and anxious about each forthcoming tremor.

"I've got to get out of here, Dad," she told her father. "I can't live like this anymore."

"But, Dawn," pleaded her parents, "everyone you know lives here. We're happy to have you stay with us until you can pull your life together again. Where will you go? What will you do?"

All choked up with many conflicting emotions, Dawn looked at her parents and said simply, "I've got to go. I've just got to get out of this maddening place."

Dawn and her parents paused to reflect. Then gently her father asked again, "Where will you go?"

"I've decided to go to Nashville."

"Tennessee?" asked her father incredulously. "I don't understand that. Do you know anyone there? Why would you choose Nashville?"

Dawn thought for a moment. "I'm not sure, Dad—this whole experience has undone me. I don't feel safe here. I only know that I want to go somewhere—anywhere I'll feel secure. So that's where I'm headed."

Her father was visibly upset. "Dawn," he implored, "you sound just like you did when you were drinking. You don't know anyone in Nashville! Seems to me that this is an irrational choice. You have your network of Alcoholics Anonymous buddies here in California. Dawn, are you relapsing into old behavior? Is this self sabotage?"

"I am not relapsing, Dad," said Dawn. "I've just got to get out of this maddening place and I've chosen Nashville." Her father saw that Dawn would not be dissuaded. He said nothing further about the subject and quietly hoped she would return one day.

Dawn soon learned that her closest friends had also decided to move away from California. Each had found a different place to relocate. With a mixture of sorrow and excitement, Dawn said good-bye to her family and friends, took Harley, and embarked on her tentative journey.

Starting her new life in Nashville, Dawn feared that she would quickly run out of money. She grabbed the first job that was offered to her, as a waitress in a country-style restaurant and bar called Long Horn Steaks. She worked the evening shift so that she could enroll in Middle Tennessee State University. For a number of years she had wanted to earn a degree in mass communications. She now could find the time.

And then, after the third week in Nashville, her past—like the earthquake—came crashing in on her.

The initial excitement of starting her new life had worn off. All of a sudden Dawn looked at her life and was struck by the awesomeness of all that had just transpired. "I can't believe this!" she cried out loud to herself. "The earthquake! All my friends moved away! I'm in a strange new place with new people! All that I have known—everything that's comfortable and familiar—is gone!" She found no solace in her new life. Dawn was struck by a tremendous sense of loss.

In painful self-recognition she turned to God. "I have been sober for three years! I have been so good. Haven't touched a drink all that time. Is this the reward for all my hard work? Must my life spin out of control?" Dawn felt that old familiar urge to drink. She hated it. She was overcome with grief coupled with enormous pain. Having been a member of Alcoholics Anonymous for several years, she knew what she was supposed to do. All she had to do was pick up the phone and call someone for help. She also knew that if she reached out to the Alcoholics Anonymous community, she would find someone with a compassionate ear—someone who would understand and lend as much support as was needed.

Dawn knew all that, but at this moment all she wanted was a bottle to drown her feelings. She longed to submerge herself in some dark haze of oblivion.

Every night, when she should have been focusing on her job, Dawn's thoughts turned more and more to drinking. Alcohol, she felt, would help her blot out a life that was too hard to bear. She watched, almost with envy, the chattering, happy patrons at the bar. It only intensified her desire for a drink.

"That's it," she declared one Friday night on the way to work. "I'm going to have a drink." Dawn figured that there would be more customers than usual at the bar that evening. She could easily blend in unnoticed by others. She entered the restaurant through the back door and proceeded directly to the ladies' room. There she broke down and cried. She was tired of reaching out to new people. She resisted anyone who might understand her plight. Instead she turned once again to God.

"How can you do this?" she found herself repeating. "I sponsored three people who themselves had sponsored others. I volunteered in a women's prison, reaching out to pregnant women and their babies. I came into the program with so much—not like others who come to be sober because they had nowhere else to turn. I was an upstanding, cultured girl. I traveled. I went to the best schools, had loving parents. I had a good job and a car. I'm not supposed to be afflicted with this disease! And this awful life in Nashville is my reward? I'm not even left with a photo album! I have nothing! I feel so abandoned! How much do you think I can endure? I want a drink and now!"

As the door to the ladies' room opened, Dawn quickly wiped away her tears and made sure to muffle her sniffles. Being new at her job, she didn't want to expose herself to anyone. Kim, one of the waitresses, had entered.

"Dawn," she inquired, "who's Bill W.?" Dawn's heart stopped. She was thrown completely off guard by the question. It was the first time she had heard that name since coming to Nashville.

"Bill W.?" Dawn repeated. "He was the founder of Alcoholics Anonymous. Now why would you be asking me that?"

"Haven't you noticed?" Kim replied with some exasperation. "Everyone out there in the restaurant is wearing a pin saying "I AM A FRIEND OF BILL W."

"What?" Dawn blurted in total astonishment. She opened the door and surveyed the fifty tables, each filled with an average of five to six people—there must have been close to three hundred people in the restaurant. Sure enough, everyone was wearing a pin declaring his or her allegiance to Alcoholics Anonymous. Then Dawn looked over at Long Horn's popular bar, where she had been planning to have her first drink in three years. It was now completely dark, shut down for the night.

"Oh, my God!" Dawn declared. She approached the first table. "Uh . . . what's going on?"

"Why?" came a voice from the table.

Dawn guessed that no one wanted to break the anonymity of an alcoholic in recovery. "I, too, am a friend of Bill W.," she stated, her voice quivering.

They all sensed her despair. They knew her immediate need. Together they applauded. Then one person spoke up. "We're all here to attend the Alcoholics Anonymous convention. It's our biggest convention ever. Thousands of people from around the world have come to this."

Dawn could hardly believe her ears. Another patron caught her glance. "Yes, we rented out the restaurant for the night, and as for the bartender, we told him that he might as well go home. He was sure to be bored with us."

Dawn sat down at the table. Her fellow A.A. members intuitively understood it all. Intently they listened to her painful story and showered her with love. When she was through, another member spoke up: "What time do you finish work?" she inquired.

"Midnight," answered Dawn.

"What are you doing after work?" the woman asked.

"Well, I was going to drink," said Dawn, "but now . . ." Her words were interrupted. "All six of us were going to the movies after dinner," spoke up another member at the table. "But instead we'll all sit right here until midnight. When you complete your shift we'll all go over to the convention together. There will be twelve step meetings through the night."

"Imagine this," said Dawn with complete gratitude and awe. "Here I was praying for just one person to talk to . . . but God must have thought I was in really rough shape, so he sent me three hundred."

Comment

It is possible to be standing on one side of a door and perceive the world as a dark and lonely place, while on the other side of that very same door are countless people just waiting to lend support and cheer you on. All that is required is that you turn the knob.

*T*he call for fire crews came late in the day after dark storm clouds had pitched lightning into the dry grasses, sagebrush and juniper trees covering the deserts of northern Nevada, southern Idaho and Utah. From the Salt Lake Interagency Fire Center frantic calls were made to assemble crews to fight the many fires that had erupted throughout the region.

As I sat on my fire gear in Salt Lake City, waiting for the rest of my crew to arrive, I looked at my hands, callused and swollen from a summer of digging fire lines. It was late July 1994. I was a junior-high-school teacher who spent summers working for the Forest Service. Now, in the hopes of becoming a school social worker, I was scheduled to begin graduate school in the fall. If I were younger, I would have felt more confident. But I wasn't sure I could keep up with the studying. Was I on the right career path?

"Hey, Wright, we're ready to go!" My crew boss, Mike, waved me toward a white bus.

The cargo area in back was already half-filled with shovels, rakes and Pulaskis—tools with an ax on one side and a hoe on the other. As I boarded I put my career concerns aside. The fourteen men and five women on our crew were talking about the fire we were assigned to fight. It was located about 250 miles away in Elko County, Nevada, and had started the day before but had gone unnoticed until that afternoon when winds fanned the flames and enlarged the burned area to thousands of acres.

Just outside of Elko I could see smoke in the distance. We drove up to an old trailer and the bus's air brakes hissed. "A helitack crew has already been flown in and is at work on the mountain about ten miles north of here," the incident commander told us. *Helitack* is a blended word meaning "helicopter attack," when a helicopter crew is flown in to fight a fire. "You're to join them," the commander continued. "Here's the map."

Our bus rumbled on. Pink flags marked our turns, then we pulled up to a makeshift landing pad. As Mike went to get instructions, I sat in the dirt with my back to the hot wind. Soon a faded white helicopter came beating out of the sky toward us. I ducked my head between my knees to keep sagebrush and sand out of my eyes as the copter came down.

"Listen," Mike shouted. "With this wind, the fire is getting bigger fast. They're going to fly us in so we can get right to work. We'll join the helitack crew on top.

"Tim, you're with the first group." By the time I got to the copter, four others were in the back, so I climbed in the seat next to the pilot. As I put on my seat belt harness, I felt the engines gain power and the copter lift. In a few moments we were climbing above the valley and toward the fire.

I watched the skyline apprehensively. A band of ominous dark clouds was getting closer and closer. Along with the drifting smoke, strong winds were kicking up dust below.

Through the haze I saw something moving. Who or what could be down there? Straining my eyes, I saw a pickup truck on the road below, heading for the mountain, following the switchbacks that wound up and around the burning hill. Probably a rancher hoping to save his cattle.

"Ground control—this is Alfa Charlie Seven," the pilot radioed. "Be advised the winds are picking up. The fire's spreading fast." There was a crackling of communication, then another tense exchange. "We've got another problem," the pilot said. "There's a rancher driving up the mountain. Contact him if you can and get him to turn back. With these winds and the way the fire's spreading, he's heading for trouble."

The copter swung high. As the crest of the mountain appeared, the pilot circled, trying to find a place to land. By now we were close enough to see the earlier helitack crew, four people spread out in a line in front of the fire about a mile away from a nearby road. We knew their plan: They would set fire to the area in front of the road, burning it out and creating what is known as a "black." Then, as the main fire roared up to the burnt-out strips, it would run out of fuel and be extinguished.

As the copter dipped toward earth, I fastened my thick, flame-resistant shirt tighter. After many seasons with the Forest Service, I knew what I was in for. In the blazing heat, sticky smoke surges into your face, poisoning the air and stinging your eyes. Green aspens turn to billowing whiteness as leaves, bark and wood dry, then burn with a slow intensity. Goggles and wet bandannas help little. Rocky ground and twisted sagebrush resist blows from the Pulaski, and caulked steel-toed boots grow heavy with sweat. No, I didn't envy those guys on the ground one bit.

I was as ready as I'd ever be. But just as we were about to touch down, the wind gusted and blew the helicopter sideways. The pilot reacted by quickly climbing. The blast continued, swirling black ash into the air.

We rose rapidly to get out of danger. Fed by the sudden winds, the flames had suddenly multiplied, igniting most of the hillside. We watched in horror as the helitack crew, unable to find a way into the "black," began to run from the fury of the fire approaching them.

If the winds diminished and the four firefighters made it through a barbed-wire fence and onto the road, they might have a chance. But where would they go from there? The gap between the firefighters and the flames narrowed. *Run, run!* I thought. The four of them ran for their lives.

I had seen many training films about this sort of situation. We had been instructed to dig an area free of grass and branches and deploy a fire shelter when flames approached and there was no escape. Fire shelters are like small pup tents made of thick fire-resistant cloth with an aluminum coating intended to reflect heat away from the person inside. But there was no time to dig. If the four stopped to take out their fire shelters, they would be incinerated. They continued their desperate run as we watched helplessly from above.

I watched in aching frustration as the four sprinted frantically to reach the dirt road. But with the flames roaring 50 yards behind them and a barbed-wire fence to climb, it seemed impossible.

"Come on, come on," our crew was yelling from the back of the copter. There was no chance of our setting down to help; our pilot was doing all he could to keep the helicopter under control in the fierce gusts. We could only pray, and I did—hard. *I can't see how this is going to work out, God, but maybe you do. Maybe you see something we don't.*

Suddenly out of the swirling blackness it came—the rancher's truck we had seen climbing the other side of the mountain minutes before. He must have seen the running ground crew! Swerving off the dirt road, the truck barreled toward the barbed-wire fence and jerked to a stop alongside it. The rancher jumped out, a pair of wire cutters in his hand. We watched in astonishment as he cut the fence and yanked back the wire.

The rancher leapt back into his truck, waving and yelling at the four to keep running. The flames were almost at their heels as the first firefighter jumped into the back of the truck, then pulled the others in after him. The flames were around the truck as the last one climbed in. The rancher gunned the engine and took off.

"They made it!" I screamed as the pickup sped down the mountain road. We all cheered with relief while the pilot relayed the news to ground control, then pulled away to land at another site. In a half hour we were on the ground establishing a fire line.

It took more than a week to put out that fire, but I never ran into those guys on the ground and never found out how that rancher happened on those trapped firefighters.

Yet as we watched overhead, two seemingly unrelated scenarios unfolded and came together in a lifesaving rescue. I thought of that dramatic rescue in graduate school as I struggled with my courses and set out to find a new job. Today when I find myself caught with worries about family and work, I remember being high in the sky over Nevada. I think of a fire crew on one side of a mountain frantically trying to outrun a raging firestorm, and a rancher on the other side driving toward what could have been disaster—but what turned out to be a hidden plan.

—*Timothy S. Wright*

Comment

Even in the perilous moments of life when all seems to be engulfed in flames, salvation can be but a heartbeat away.

*M*y wife and I were living in Long Beach, California, in the early seventies and I had just gotten a job in the San Francisco Bay area. I was driving my little Volkswagen (we called her Twinky Wilma) up Highway 5, all alone, when it broke down in a desolate and empty expanse of concrete, an isolated and bleak stretch of the freeway. As well as I knew, the nearest gas station or town was more than fifty miles away. My prospects of securing help seemed bleak. I tinkered with the car valiantly, but nothing I tried could get it going again. I finally gave up.

I had been sitting by the side of the road for about an hour, feeling very helpless and forlorn, when I looked at my watch and noted that it was 6:15. Nervously, I wondered if I would get to San Jose in time for my first day of work, 8 A.M. the next morning.

Suddenly, without thinking about it, I automatically reached for the keys and tried to start the engine again. I don't know what prompted me to do that; some inner urge which I could not explain just compelled me to make another attempt. To my stunned surprise, the engine sprang to life as if nothing had ever been wrong with it. What a shock! I got my stuff together, shifted the car into gear and drove the rest of the way without mishap.

That night, I called my wife Kathie to tell her that I had arrived safely in San Jose and that everything was OK.

"Oh," she said, "I wasn't worried. The kids and I prayed for you at dinner tonight. We did a special prayer for Twinky Wilma."

"Do you know what time that was?" I asked.

"Absolutely. I was watching the clock on the stove so dinner wouldn't burn."

"So, what time was it?"

"Six-fifteen exactly."

—*Brad Fregger*

Comment

When we pray, we are speaking to God. When a miracle happens, God is speaking to us.

$\mathscr{I}t$ was late June and I was living in Philadelphia, where I had lived for nearly a decade, when my employer of six years informed me that after a new corporate structure was put in place on September First my services would no longer be required.

I'm sure this is a scenario familiar to many people and I considered myself more fortunate than most. I was single; I had two months in which to begin my job search while still being employed; and I would be given a six-month severance package. Regardless of this, losing one's job is a very disquieting and distressing event. The initial shock of being laid off soon gave way to emotions wavering somewhere between anger and despair, and although I had the support of my friends and family, I was still left each day with a feeling of isolation.

Over the next two months my job search progressed well. I had already been on several promising interviews and had strong leads on positions in a number of cities: Chicago, Cleveland, New York City, and Washington, D.C. A recruiter based in New York City had even mentioned an opportunity with Hallmark Cards in Kansas City. I had only been in touch with them once or twice, however, and was not considering it as a serious option. Instead my primary focus was on Cleveland, a city within an hour's drive of my family in Youngstown, Ohio. Over the past five years both my brother and sister had moved back to Ohio and I believed, as my parents did, that this job search was the event that would guide my path back home as well.

When you're in the midst of a job search one of the most discouraging times can be the onset of the weekend. For the next two days you hear nothing in response to past inquiries; nothing progresses in the corporate decision making process; and nothing tangible occurs to bring you closer to your goal. For me this was especially disconcerting. I was used to feeling with certainty that I was where I belonged. Even when difficulties arose I always took solace in the notion that this was the right direction, this was my path, and if I stuck with it long enough, things would be resolved. I had come to rely on the strength that assurance gave me, but now that inner support was gone. I was adrift with no clear direction.

One Friday evening in late August, feeling especially disheartened by the events in my life, I walked to a local pizzeria to order a sandwich. It was a shop I was familiar with, and after placing my order, I walked to the front window to watch the last of the daily commuters file from the train station to make their way home for the weekend. I felt melancholy.

What depressed me was not the work involved in my job search—I enjoyed the challenge and things continued to progress well—rather it was the uncertainty of where my life was headed.

Although I would not consider myself a religious person (not having attended church on a regular basis since childhood), I have always considered myself to be very spiritual. The nature of my relationship with God is more a dialogue than ritualistic reverence. That night, standing by the window, I asked God for a sign, anything that would give me an idea of what my future held and where my path would lead.

I turned from the window telling myself there was nothing to be done, it was the weekend and I should try to relax. At the same time I became aware of the television that the owners had installed on a shelf in the corner above the window to watch, among other things, the game show *Jeopardy*. As my anxiety began to abate, my mind became attuned to the show, and the first question I clearly recall the host asking dealt with naming the company that began marketing a small line of Collectible Ornaments in 1973. While one contestant answered incorrectly, another responded, "What is *Hallmark?*" to which the host replied, *"Hallmark is the correct answer."*

At first I couldn't believe what I had just heard. I turned toward the television and was even more surprised to find that the contestant who had answered the question correctly was named Matt. That's my name, I thought. How strange.

My job search would take many twists and turns over the following two months, and regardless of the sign I had been given that night at the pizza shop, I had resigned myself to believe that I would either stay in Philadelphia or move back closer to my family in Ohio. Neither was meant to be. Offers that I felt confident were forthcoming never materialized, while others were clearly not the right choice. All the while I could feel a gentle but firm hand pushing me in a new direction, toward Kansas City, where I now live, and Hallmark Cards, where I've been gainfully employed since early last December.

—*Matt Eichmann*

*L*ife's *a little thing!*
Robert Browning once wrote.
But a little thing can mean a life. Even two lives. How well I remember. Two years ago in downtown Denver my friend, Scott Reasoner, and I saw something tiny and insignificant change the world, but no one else even seemed to notice.

It was one of those beautiful Denver days. Crystal clear, no humidity, not a cloud in the sky. We decided to walk the ten blocks to an outdoor restaurant rather than take the shuttle bus that runs up and down the Sixteenth Street Mall. The restaurant, in the shape of a baseball diamond, was called The Blake Street Baseball Club. The tables were set appropriately on the grass infield. Many colorful pennants and flags hung limply overhead.

As we sat outside, the sun continued to beat down on us, and it became increasingly hot. There wasn't a hint of a breeze, and heat radiated up from the tabletop. Nothing moved, except the waiters, of course. And they didn't move very fast, either.

After lunch Scott and I started to walk back up the mall. We both noticed a mother and her young daughter walking out of a card shop toward the street. She was holding her daughter by the hand while reading a greeting card. It was immediately apparent to us that she was so engrossed in the card that she did not notice a shuttle bus moving toward her at a good clip. She and her daughter were one step away from disaster when Scott started to yell. He hadn't even gotten a word out when a breeze blew the card out of her hand and over her shoulder. She spun around and grabbed at the card, nearly knocking her daughter over. By the time she picked up the card from the ground and turned back around to cross the street, the shuttle bus had whizzed by her. She never even knew what almost happened.

To this day two things continue to perplex me about this event. Where did that one spurt of wind come from to blow the card out of that young mother's hand? There had not been a whisper of wind at lunch or during our long walk back up the mall. Secondly, if Scott had been able to get his words out, the young mother might have looked up at us as they continued to walk into the bus. It was the wind that made her turn back to the card—in the one direction that saved her life and that of her daughter. The passing bus did not create the wind. On the contrary, the wind came from the opposite direction.

I have no doubt it was a breath from God protecting them both. But the awesomeness of this miracle is that she never knew. As we continued back to work, I wondered how God often acts in our lives without our being aware. The difference between life and death can very well be a little thing.

Comment
Miracles often blow unseen through our lives.

*E**ditor* Arnold Fine of the *Jewish Press* once received an unusual letter from an elderly reader. "I faithfully read and enjoy your column 'I Remember When,' and am often struck by the warmth and sensitivity of your writing. You seem like a person who really cares, which is why I am turning to you for help.

"Although I am now eighty years old and a widow, I cannot forget my first love, Harry. I was seventeen and quite sure—at my tender age—that I had already found my soul mate. Harry, a mature twenty-three, was also convinced that we were fated for each other and that his quest for his life's partner was also over. We were madly, passionately, unrestrainedly in love.

"But my parents didn't share my enthusiasm for Harry. They were bitterly opposed to the relationship not so much because of our youth—although it was a factor—but because Harry was from the 'wrong side of the tracks.' My parents were wealthy, influential, fourth-generation American-Germans; Harry's were indigent and newly arrived Eastern European immigrants. Consequently, my parents did everything in their power to sabotage the match.

"They were so alarmed about the possibility of my marrying Harry, in fact, that they took me to Europe for a year. When I returned, Harry seemed to have disappeared from the face of this earth. He had moved, and had left no forwarding address. No one seemed to know his whereabouts. I tried desperately to find him, but never succeeded. I was heartbroken. I would never love anyone again the way I had loved Harry.

"A few years later, I married a wonderful man with whom I lived happily for almost sixty years and we did have a very good life together. He died last year.

"I guess I have a lot of time on my hands now, but lately I just can't seem to get Harry out of my mind. I constantly wonder what happened to him, and if he's still alive. I know it's a long shot, but I thought if anyone could help me, it would be you, Mr. Fine. I know you are a busy man, but if you could possibly help me try to trace Harry, I would be eternally grateful.

"The only clue I can provide is this ancient envelope with Harry's old address which I am enclosing. I now live in the Crown Manor Nursing Home* in Long Beach, where I await with faith and yearning, your answer."

The letter was signed Ida Brown.*

Arnold Fine was indeed a busy man. In addition to his editorial duties at the *Jewish Press,* he worked during the day as a special education teacher in the New York City public school system.

But the letter had moved him, and he vowed to help Ida. Using all the investigative expertise that he had acquired from years working as a newspaper reporter, he set out to find Harry. He embarked on the project with both hope and trepidation. He would be deeply gratified if he could indeed locate Harry and reunite the two. But what of the other possibility? What if he had to report to Ida that Harry was long dead?

Several weeks later, Arnold Fine journeyed to the Crown Manor Nursing Home for a very special occasion. First, he went to the sixth floor, where he shook hands with an elderly but chivalrous-looking gentleman, alert and vital, eyes snapping with wit and energy despite the cane at his side. Arnold draped his arm gently around his shoulders and carefully guided him into the elevator, which they took to the third floor where Ida was waiting.

"Harry?" trembled Ida as she stood looking at him from across the hall.

"My God . . . Ida!" he stammered.

Unbeknownst to one another, the two had been living in the same nursing home for five months, three floors apart.

Several weeks later, Arnold Fine traveled to the Crown Manor Nursing Home a second time. This time, he had come to attend Ida and Harry's wedding, some sixty years in the making.

Comment

The heart that loves does not forget. Its passion is like a burning flame that is kept alive by memory.

arly one morning, Pat was rudely awakened out of a deep slumber by the shrill ringing of the telephone. Groggily, she raised her eyes to the digital clock on the night table and was astonished to see that it was only 5 A.M.

"This better be good," she thought.

It was an obscene phone call.

She slammed down the phone angrily and tried pulling the covers over her head, willing herself back to sleep.

But she couldn't exorcise the man's foul language or lewd suggestions from her head.

"Maybe it's not such a good idea for me to live alone," she thought.

She tossed and turned in bed, but it was useless, really. She couldn't get back to sleep. Her nerves were jangled from the call. Under her breath, she cursed the caller over and over again.

"Better get up and make yourself a strong cup of coffee," she advised herself.

She stumbled into the kitchen, still cursing the caller, God, life, the universe, fate, and anyone else she could think of for disrupting her sound night's sleep.

But her perspective changed the moment she turned on the overhead light. Her kitchen window, which she had firmly closed the night before, was now wide open. And a wicked-looking butcher's knife that she did not own lay on the kitchen table, together with a ski mask and a rope.

When Pat absorbed the significance of the open window and the malevolence of the items on her kitchen table, she gasped.

What had happened or was about to happen to her was clear.

An intruder had slipped into her apartment, preparing an attack.

And at that precise moment, the telephone must have rung.

Scaring her out of her mind.

And scaring the attacker out of her apartment.

"Thank you, God," she murmured. "And thank you, Mr. Obscene Phone Caller," she added. "I was disgusted by your call, but apparently it saved my life."

Comment

One can never be sure when to laugh or when to cry. When to curse or when to bless. For life often speaks to us in cryptic signs and we can't be sure of the final picture until all the pieces of the puzzle fall into place.

$\mathcal{I}t$ was in the middle of a blizzard, and my brother was trying to get home from work. After waiting an hour for a bus, he decided to try to walk home. The snow was very high and walking was very difficult, but he kept at it. After what seemed like a lifetime he was nearly home. It was a good thing too, because he was freezing and didn't think he could last much longer.

Just then his foot hit something and to his horror, he realized that a woman was lying in the snow. At first he wasn't sure that the woman was alive, but as he knelt down he heard her moan. She said that she too had been trying to walk home but she fell and wasn't able to get up. My brother didn't know what to do. He could hardly drag himself along, but he made a tremendous effort and picked her up.

Somehow he got her into a building next door where she sat and warmed up. They exchanged names and addresses and when he was sure that she would be able to make it home, my brother left her and walked the remaining three blocks to his apartment.

My brother didn't make too much of this incident. He thought he had just done what anyone else would have done, but to us he was a real hero.

Imagine his surprise when the following week in the same envelope as his paycheck, there was a check for $5,000 and a note from his boss thanking him for *saving his sister's life!*

"Chronic renal failure," doctors told my cousin Larry, hooked up to dialysis machines for more than four years but deteriorating rapidly. "Your only hope is a kidney transplant." I, among several other relatives, was asked to give samples to see if a compatible donor could be found. I readily agreed, without contemplating the consequences. It came as a shock to learn that I was the perfect match.

The call came from the hospital in the middle of my four-year-old daughter's birthday party. My wife, eight months pregnant with our second child, threw me a wary look when I hung up the phone. She had caught the nuances of the muted conversation, my careful responses. I hadn't wanted to spoil the party, for her sake or my daughter's. "What is it?" she asked. "Not now," I said, looking pointedly at our child and the birthday cake.

"This is really *big*, Ronnie," she said, distressed, when our daughter fell asleep later that evening and we withdrew to the kitchen to talk. "Can we think about this for a while?"

"He doesn't have much time, Debra. I told the doctors I would give them an answer tomorrow."

"Tomorrow?" she shrieked, furious. "What do you think . . . the kidney is an extra tire? What happens when you need a spare? Will someone be around to give *you* one?"

"Debra," I said, "this isn't easy for me, either. Believe me, I'm absolutely terrified! And I'm torn and ambivalent. If I'm really honest with myself, I have to admit I would have been vastly relieved to find out I *wasn't* a match. But the fact is that I am."

"Ronnie," Debra said firmly, "this is a *major* surgery, with serious risks involved. I forbid you to go through with it!"

"Larry is like a brother to me, Deb. It's not something I *want* to do; it's something I *have* to do. What's my life going to be worth if I deny Larry the right to live?"

"This is a *major* decision, Ronnie, one that involves *all* of us. You have a family now, and a responsibility to this family, too!"

"Debra," I said weakly, "I have to sleep on this."

"I don't want you to do this . . . Ronnie, I just can't allow you to take the risk!" And she stormed out of the room, her eyes ice cold, her chin set in determination.

Part of me longed to cave in to her demands and accede. I could blame it on her . . . "So, sorry, Larry, but as you know Debra's about to give birth and she just won't allow me to . . ." I envisioned myself saying. But another part of me repudiated that scenario, ashamed.

That night, I tossed and turned in bed in a restless slumber, agonizing over what to do. And then I had a dream.

In the dream, I was visiting Larry at the hospital.

I walked in, arranging a cheerful face prior to my entry, and called out in an insincere, hearty manner: "Hey, buddy, how's life?"

"*This* is *not* life," Larry answered bitterly. "Can't eat food . . . barely allowed to drink . . . hooked up to the machine for hours, and when the hellish procedure is over, I feel worse than ever."

"But Lar," I interjected, still attempting false cheer. "At least, this procedure lets you move and you're free!"

"Yeah, free!" he replied sourly. "Free to go *to* dialysis and *from* dialysis." He motioned toward the wires hooking him up to the machine. "I'm twenty-eight years old and I've got an umbilical cord that's like a ball and chain!"

"Larry," I said helplessly, "what can I do?"

"I can't go on like this anymore. Help me, please!" he cried.

I woke up in a cold sweat.

And I resolved—despite my wife's anger and my own misgivings—to give him my kidney.

As I was wheeled into the operating room, the doctor at my side murmured encouragement. "You're in good hands, Ronnie," he said. "You've made a decision you can live with."

The next morning, I woke up groggy and saw a doctor hovering near my side. "Good morning, Ronnie!" he said cheerfully. "How are you feeling . . . aside from the normal postoperative discomfort?" he asked.

"Doc," I groaned, "I don't know what normal is, but I sure am in a lot of pain."

"Yes . . . well . . ." He hesitated for a fraction of a second. "I must tell you that something we were not prepared for occurred during the operation . . ."

"What's happened to Larry?" I asked, alarmed.

"He's still on dialysis, but don't worry, we have another match all lined up for him."

I stared at the doctor, confused.

"Ronnie," he began gently, "I doubt that you have ever heard of *renal cell carcinoma?*" I shook my head no. "It's an incurable form of cancer," he continued, "virtually always fatal."

"Are you saying that Larry has . . ." I asked tremulously, my heart palpitating, even as the doctor interrupted me in mid-sentence.

"No, Ronnie, he was spared. . . . And so were you. Your ultrasound indicated two healthy kidneys, Ronnie. Either one of them would have saved your cousin. And it was arbitrary . . . or so we thought . . . which one we chose to remove. Little did we know that our hands were being guided to the correct one. . . . Because, Ronnie, once we removed your left kidney, the naked eye was able to see what the ultrasound had failed to show. On the left kidney cortex was a tiny nodule, a nodule of renal cell carcinoma. Had you not elected to donate your kidney to your cousin, you could easily have been dead within a year. And had the kidney not been inspected as thoroughly as it was, Larry would have been dead from *your* cancer. . . . Ronnie, your intentions were indeed very noble. You thought you were saving your cousin's life—but as it turns out, my friend, it was Larry who saved *yours*."

Comment

The universe repays kindness, not measure for measure, as humans do, but with infinite generosity and grace.

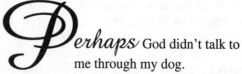**P**_erhaps_ God didn't talk to me through my dog.

Perhaps it just seemed that way—not just to me, but to a friend who witnessed the event. But considering that God—the Judeo-Christian God, at least—has employed burning bushes and ghostly images of the Virgin to communicate with mortals, maybe my lop-eared, Roman-nosed coon hound wasn't such an outlandish choice for a conduit between the mundane and the ethereal.

In any case, the events happened as described. And if what follows wasn't the result of an unseen hand attempting to turn me from my casual agnosticism, it was at least a truly paranormal incident, the only one I've ever experienced.

The time: a few years ago. I was renting a small cabin on the grape ranch my friend David Steiner owned and operated on Sonoma Mountain. One spring day, we decided to go salmon fishing the following morning. And because we're both susceptible to seasickness, we stuck scopolamine skin patches behind our ears before retiring for the night. Scopolamine has some undesirable side-effects—cotton mouth, ringing ears and a sense that roaches are crawling across your skin—but for me, there's no substitute.

The alarm woke me at 3 the next morning. With swollen eyes and parched throat, I dressed and shuffled across the compound to Steiner's house. He was already up, looking as rocky as I felt, dolefully watching his Mr. Coffee fill a pot with viscous, black brew. We drank a couple of cups each and started making sandwiches and collecting our gear: rods, tackle, rubber boots, sweatshirts. It took about a half hour before my truck was loaded and we were ready to go.

My head, sinuses and throat felt like they were packed with wool and cockleburs. The scopolamine was in high gear. I felt like hell, but at least I wouldn't spend the whole day clutching the rail.

Somehow, though, I sensed I had forgotten something. Fishing license? I checked: it was in my wallet. Something still disturbed me, but I didn't have time to dwell on it. We faced an hour drive to Bodega Bay, and the boat left at 5 o'clock—no time to dither. We took off.

From the ranch, Sonoma Mountain Road snakes down a hill for a half mile. Well before we reached the bottom, my vague unease changed to epiphany: the sodas. Or the Pepsi Lights, more accurately—a six-pack of Steiner's favorite nonalcoholic beverage. We had left them in his refrigerator, and it was unthinkable that we could proceed without them.

The prospect of that icy, caffeinated, artificially sweetened nectar trickling down my ravaged throat was too much to resist: I had to have one immediately.

"What's the deal?" grumbled Steiner.

"Pepsis," I rasped. "We forgot 'em."

But as I looked for a driveway to use as a turnaround, my headlights illuminated the eyes of a large animal in the road. It was proceeding toward us with an oddly spavined gait, one I recognized immediately. Megan. The dire hound.

Did I own Megan? No, hounds are the most feline of dogs. She deigned to stay around the place as long as I fed her regularly and granted her access to the compost pile. One of her favorite pastimes was patrolling the road in front of the ranch for road kill. I tied her up or kept her fenced as much as possible, but she found ways to graze the asphalt when my back was turned or I was preoccupied—as I was that morning, with a throbbing skull of scopolamine.

I was irritated to see Megan. She endangered herself by her presence on the road and dealing with her would delay us. We could literally miss the boat.

I downshifted, and she stopped in the middle of the pavement, recognizing the sound of the truck's engine. I could see she had something in her mouth, and I pulled up next to her, opening the door. "Give me that, Megan," I said, grabbing her booty.

It was a six-pack of icy cans. I held them up to the windshield, so we could see what they were. Pepsi Lights, so cold they were rimmed with frost. We knew without checking they weren't the colas from Steiner's fridge. (We looked when we got home; the sodas were still there.)

I could feel the hair stand up on the back of my neck.

I looked down at Megan, who gazed up at me with her blank, vaguely expectant expression.

"Megan," I said. "Bad dog. Go home." She skulked away into the blackness. Steiner popped the top of one of the cans and took a swig. I followed suit. The Pepsi was balm to my throat, exactly what I needed at that moment. We sat for a minute in the dark, spinning through possible scenarios. Had she found an ice chest in the road? Did some friendly passerby give her a six-pack, thinking her a thirsty hound in need of hydration? Had she broken into a neighbor's house, jimmied the refrigerator, padded out with the Pepsi Lights, ignoring sausages, cheese, leftover pot roast?

Or was some higher power involved? How could this happen at the precise moment Steiner and I were discussing not mere beverages, not generic soft drinks—but Pepsi Lights? Was this some kind of a sign??

Such synchronicity of time and events seemed impossible unless a divine intelligence—albeit one with a sense of humor—had chosen to tweak the cosmic clockwork.

"I know this must mean something," Steiner said, "but I'll be damned if I can figure out what it is."

We went fishing and caught nothing all day. The skies were gray, the ambient temperature was low and the seas were high. Despite the scopolamine, Steiner got seasick and spent a considerable portion of his time hanging over the side. I felt queasy, but managed to keep everything down. The colas helped.

I've been importuned by people peddling spiritual nostrums all my life. Neighborhood preachers, evangelical fire-breathers, Hare Krishnites, Jehovah's Witnesses, New Age gurus, crystal hawkers—I've been immune to them all. None offered what I needed most: proof. Only my dog could do that. She's dead now, laid six feet deep at the roots of a gnarled pear tree on the ranch—gone, perhaps, to that great, reeking compost pile in the sky. I could not have entertained the prospect that a heaven existed for either humans or dogs before we saw Megan jackknifed in the middle of the road, a six-pack depending from her maw. Now I'm not so sure. Now I think there may be something—out there. Beyond. After. Something.

Megan: Go Home.

—*Glen Martin*

$\mathcal{O}n$ a sun-splattered June day in 1991, Cantor Michael Weisser and his wife Julie were enjoying a leisurely Sunday brunch in their new home in Lincoln, Nebraska, when the telephone rang. Outside, birds chirped harmoniously and children's sweet voices wafted into the air; from inside the modest, two-bedroom brick ranch came the buoyant sounds of laughter and cheer, as Julie, her close friend Rita Babbitz, and Michael traded quips in an atmosphere of comfort and camaraderie. The telephone had been ringing all morning long; the Weissers were a popular couple in Lincoln, and, as spiritual leader of one of the city's two synagogues, Michael was plied with questions and appeals continuously. There was no reason for him to feel apprehensive as he reached for the phone; no cause for him to suspect that the caller was anyone other than a well-wisher or a congregant. So it was in a spirit of complete ease that Michael crossed the room to answer the phone's insistent ring, unaware that with this simple act the peace and tranquillity of the Weisser household was about to be shattered for a long time to come.

"You will be sorry you ever moved into 5810 Randolph Street, Jew boy," a man's voice—harsh and dripping with menace—rasped. Then the phone went dead.

Michael Weisser had previously served in synagogues in Tennessee, California, Ohio, Florida, and South Carolina—some of these pulpits in towns with minuscule Jewish populations—and although he had encountered subtle forms of bigotry in many of these places, he had never received a hate call before.

From across the room, Julie Weisser observed her husband's pained expression and, more ominously, his silence.

"What's the matter?" she asked.

Michael repeated the warning message and, trembling with anger, said: "I bet it's the Klan."

"I don't think it's the Klan," said his son Dave, who had happened to pick up the extension in his room upstairs and had heard the warning too. "It's probably just some crackpot."

"A crackpot from the Klan," Michael insisted.

He was right.

On the southwest side of Lincoln, a blind bearded man laughed hoarsely as he slammed down the phone. He was wearing a gold swastika on a chain around his neck and a faded red T-shirt with the words "White Power" printed in white next to a black swastika. Blue-gray tattoos—a skull and crossbones with "Hell's Angels" written underneath, a heart pierced by an arrow and an Iron Cross, a German military symbol used as a Nazi emblem—adorned his arms. Nazi rings with swastikas glittered on his fingers.

His name was Larry Trapp and his official title was "Grand Dragon of the White Knights of the Ku Klux Klan for the Realm of Nebraska." His job was spreading hatred throughout the state, and although he was a double amputee confined to a wheelchair, he worked frenetically every day to fulfill his mission. He hated Jews, African Americans, Asians, Mexicans, and Indians. He enjoyed violence, and he particularly liked to scare blacks and Jews. His ugly call to Michael Weisser was just the beginning of a campaign of harassment he planned against the cantor and his wife.

Cantor Weisser was a man fervently dedicated to promulgating the principles of love, tolerance, and nonharmful behavior—three basic ideas he perceived to be at the heart of the Jewish faith. During his first sermon at Lincoln's Bnai Jeshurun Synagogue, Michael had passionately declared: "In Jewish tradition, our role as human beings is to correct the universe. So how do we do that? We look at the things that we have done to place barriers between human beings and the rest of natural creation. Little by little, we need to tear down those barriers and make them disappear so we can experience the fullness of each other and the richness of the creation, which is given to us as a gift and of which we are a part."

Two days after the menacing phone call, Julie Weisser found a thick brown manila envelope in her mailbox, addressed in capital block letters to "RABBI MICHAEL WEISSER." Inside was anti-Semitic literature—flyers, brochures, and horrible, racist cartoons. On top of the stack of material was a card that read: "The KKK is watching you, scum." Other handwritten messages warned: "The 'Holohoax' was nothing compared to what's going to happen to you!"; "Heil Hitler! May his memory refresh your soul and give you inspiration!"; "Your Time is Up"; and "Those responsible for the suffering of our White Race (Jews, Blacks, Race-Mixers, and Whites who support them) will pay the penalty for High Treason with Death by Hanging." The second phase of Larry Trapp's campaign of harassment against the Weissers had been implemented, with a vengeance.

But the Weissers were not the sole focus nor the only target of Larry Trapp's malevolence. He preyed on African Americans and Asians continuously; homes owned by members of these ethnic groups were firebombed, hate literature was strewn across their steps. As part of an ongoing hate campaign that the Grand Dragon labeled "Operation Gooks," a Vietnamese social welfare center was trashed, the furniture inside hacked to pieces, electrical wires ripped from the walls, water pipes broken—the heinous destruction obliterating the center out of existence. Trapp installed a telephone hot line that spewed messages of hate; one particular tape singled out a black woman named Donna Polk whom he had terrorized for months. On this tape, he announced her address with the intimation that she was fair game for hunters seeking good quarry. He convinced the local public access channel to air "Race and Reason," a despicable paean to the White Aryan Resistance Movement.

Michael Weisser was one of those who watched the revolting show, and his horror at the hatred and destruction Trapp had unleashed in Lincoln surged throughout his being like a powerful current. Not only had he and his wife been victimized by the man, but countless others had been swept up by the tide of vitriol coursing through the city. All his life, Michael had challenged, confronted, and acted on his anger. He picked up the phone and called Trapp.

But Trapp didn't answer. Instead, Weisser heard the newest edition of the Grand Dragon's hot line: "Vigilante Voices of Nebraska—where the truth hurts!" The message on this tape was so malignant that Michael could no longer contain his fury. He waited for the beep and said: "Larry, you better think about all this hatred you're spreading, because one day you're going to have to answer to God for all this hatred, and it's not going to be easy."

From that time forward, Michael Weisser began to habitually leave little messages on Larry Trapp's tape. They were impulsive, never prepared or prerehearsed. Michael just said whatever came into his mind. Something in him was compelling him to talk to the Grand Dragon, even though he couldn't know whether he was being heard or understood at all.

Once, after Larry Trapp appeared on a local television program dressed in full Klan regalia standing beneath a Nazi flag, Michael reached for the phone and left another message for Larry.

"I just saw the interview in which you stood so proudly near a Nazi flag," Michael said. "Larry, do you know that the very first laws that Hitler's Nazis passed were against people like yourself who had no legs or who had physical deformities, physical handicaps? Do you realize you would have been among the first to die under Hitler? Why do you love Nazis so much?"

Larry Trapp listened to the message, as he had to all the other messages Michael Weisser had repeatedly left over the last several weeks. The others he had dismissed and scorned, but this one hit home. He knew that Michael's words were true. The Nazis *had* exterminated the physically handicapped, even before they began to gas the Jews.

"What will I do if Trapp ever picks up the phone?" Michael asked Julie one day after he had left a message on Trapp's machine that urged: "How can you feel any real sense of freedom when you're doing all these hateful things? Maybe you should let all that hate go."

Julie had thought about Trapp and his hate-filled existence many times. She had often wondered what terrible circumstances must have wrought such hatred, and had concluded that Trapp must have been sorely deprived of love when he was young.

"If he ever answers the phone, tell him you want to do something nice for him," she said. "Tell him you'll take him to the grocery store or something like that. It'll totally freak him out."

Michael loved Julie's idea and wondered whether he would have the opportunity to implement it. Trapp had never picked up his phone when Michael called. "Had his calls made the slightest dent?" Michael wondered time and time again.

Trapp hated the calls. They were beginning to get under his skin. He had to stop them; he had to stop the man whose warm voice with its undertones of laughter broadcast messages of love into his room. "He's some crackpot," he told another Klansman one day when Michael's voice, coming over the tape machine, exhorted: "Larry, when you give up hating, a whole world of love is waiting for you." "The next time he calls, I'll answer, and put a stop to this harassment once and for all," Larry vowed.

When the call came, Larry was ready.

"What the ——— d'ya want?" he growled.

Michael followed Julie's directive. "Well, I was thinking you might need a hand at something," he said. "And I wondered if I could help. I know you're in a wheelchair and I thought maybe I could take you to the grocery store or something."

For several long seconds, Trapp didn't speak. His shock was palpable, even over the telephone wires. Finally, he coughed and began to speak. Michael fancied that Trapp's voice sounded different than before, less brittle, softer, almost as if the hatred that had laced it before had suddenly, miraculously disappeared.

"That's OK," Larry Trapp said. "That's nice of you, but I've got that covered. Thanks, anyway. But don't call this number anymore. It's my business phone."

"I'll stay in touch," Michael Weisser said quickly before Trapp could hang up the phone.

On Friday night, November 15, 1991, Michael Weisser delivered a Sabbath sermon that electrified his congregation with its warm messages of benevolence, charity, and humanitarianism.

"If we don't communicate our love through the work of our hands, then what kind of love do we have?" he said. "Love means being willing to aid and serve the one who is unloved. And if we keep our tolerance to ourselves, it is not really tolerance at all, but merely silence. In order to express our tolerance, we are called to reach out to those who may seem different—reach out and make them our friends."

Following the sermon, it was traditional for the congregation to engage in a silent prayer for friends and family who were ill. Michael had already stepped down from the dais, when Larry Trapp's image sprang to mind. Impulsively, Michael turned to his congregation and asked them to pray for someone who was sick—not physically sick in the ordinary sense, but "sick from the illness of bigotry and hatred. Please pray that he be healed, too."

That Friday night, as prayers were being said for him, Larry Trapp's sleep was fitful and restive. The swastika ring on his left hand and the swastika ring on his right hand began to feel, for the first time in his life, heavy and uncomfortable. For some odd reason, his ring fingers began to burn, itch, and sting. This had never happened before. He took the rings off because they seemed to hurt his fingers. When his fingers felt better, he put the rings back on. When they started bothering him again, he took them off. He was frightened by what was happening; some thick, impending presence seemed to hang in the air.

All night long, Larry Trapp took the rings off, put them back on, and then took them off again—and couldn't understand why.

The next evening, he called Michael Weisser. "I want to get out," he said, "but I don't know how."

"Would you like some help?"

"I don't know. I don't think so."

"Well, maybe we could talk about this tonight."

"I don't think so. Maybe later sometime."

"Look," Michael said. "Are you hungry? My wife and I'll get some food and come over and bring you dinner."

"Well, I don't know . . ."

"We can have some food and break some bread together."

"Well, OK, I guess that would be all right."

Michael and Julie were inside the car, fastening their seat belts, when Julie had a thought.

"Wait a second, Michael. I think we should bring Larry some kind of gift to show him we're sincere. Let me run into the house and see what I can find."

But once inside the house, Julie was at a loss as to what to bring. "Can't bring a book," she mused out loud, "he's blind. Can't bring sweets—he's a diabetic. Can't bring clothing—don't know what size he wears." She walked into her bedroom, began looking through a little brass jewelry box on the dresser, and saw the perfect gift.

It was a silver ring of intertwined strands she had bought for Michael two years ago. Michael had liked it, but rarely wore it. "It's exactly what I want to give Larry!" she thought with growing excitement.

"Don't you think this ring is perfect?" she asked Michael, returning to the car with her prize. "I like it because it's all twisted up, but it's very beautiful. To me it symbolizes how somebody's life can be all twisted up but still turn out beautifully in the end."

"That's an interesting perspective," Michael responded. "I never looked at the ring quite that way."

"*I've* always thought of it as a brotherhood ring. To me, those strands represent all the different kinds of people on this earth, different, but nonetheless, very much intertwined."

Larry Trapp extended his hand when he opened the door for Michael and Julie. "Hi there," he said.

"It's good to meet you in person," Michael said, warmly clasping Larry's outstretched hand.

At the touch of Michael's hand, Larry winced. He felt as if he had been hit by a jolt of electricity. Then he broke into tears.

Larry didn't know what impulse compelled him, but he suddenly began yanking at the two silver swastika rings on his fingers. "I can't wear these anymore," he cried. "They stand for all the hatred in my life. Will you take them away?"

Michael and Julie stared at each other in shock, stunned by the coincidence. "We will take them away and give you a new one instead," Michael murmured softly.

"Here," said Julie, gently sliding the new ring onto Larry's finger. "We want you to have this. I feel the strands symbolize the beauty of a person's soul, and Michael feels they stand for brotherhood. But one thing is certain. Surely, this ring stands for love."

And then all three clasped hands together and cried.

Epilogue: Larry Trapp resigned his position with the Ku Klux Klan, renounced his membership in all the hate organizations he had joined, and made amends to the people in Lincoln, Nebraska, whom he had harassed over the years. He called each one of them individually and asked for forgiveness. He met with law enforcement officials from various agencies such as the FBI, the Anti-Defamation League, and the local police and gave them inside information on the activities of hate organizations operating underground in the United States. He converted to Judaism on June 5, 1992, and died three months later of diabetic-related illness. During the last several months of his illness, he had moved in with the Weissers, who nursed him tenderly until his death.

Acknowledgments

Our thanks go first and foremost to YOU, our cherished readers, whose enthusiasm for the message of our first book has been boundless and immensely gratifying. Because of *your* warmth and excitement we have been able to proceed with this second book. We have been enormously moved by your kind and sincere letters and are very heartened to know that *Small Miracles* has brought you joy and comfort. *You* our readers are the co-creators of this sequel, and we applaud you for your open hearts and contagious excitement.

Our deep gratitude also goes to everyone at Adams Media, who launched this book with so much trust, belief, and devotion. To the extraordinary Bob Adams, who took such enormous personal interest in the fate of this small book and expended so much creative energy in launching it, who believed in the book even more after he experienced his own first "small miracle" the very night he finished reading the galleys. To Wayne Jackson, innovative and dynamic Director of Marketing, whose zeal for the book was contagious and set booksellers on fire. Thanks also to Melanie Mackinaw for her special efforts and gracious assistance in all spheres of publicity support.

We have been blessed with the most wonderful editor, Pamela Liflander, whose expert advice, gentle wisdom, and intelligent counsel have greatly enriched our writing experience. We have concluded that Pam, whose patience and good humor have proven unflagging over two years of interaction, basically borders near sainthood, and we have been the happy beneficiaries of this paragon's enormous range of estimable virtues. Thanks also to Virginia Ruebens for an extraordinary copyediting job.

During this momentous year in our lives, we have been privileged to meet many wonderful booksellers who believed in our book and hand-sold it magnificently. We are grateful to all of you, too numerous to mention, and we applaud your efforts. There are two small independent stores, however, that deserve special mention. No store has championed *Small Miracles* more fervently than Harnik's Happy House in Brooklyn. Noreen Harnik and Terri Roca and their devoted staff threw such incredible support behind *Small Miracles* that they made it into the number one all-time best-selling book in their store's fifty-year history! We will be forever indebted to them for their tremendous generosity of heart and magnanimity of spirit. Edna Krausz of Inspiration Gallery in New Rochelle, New York, fell in love with *Small Miracles* and sold it in a big way in her neck of the woods. To date, this store—small in size but very large in stature—has sold more than 600 copies of *Small Miracles,* all due to the very devoted hand-selling of the proprietor.

We are both members of an informal women's group, which stresses spirituality and creative living, and we want to thank the very special members of the group for their ongoing support and genuine sharing in our success. Thank you Pessie, Etta, Ruchama, Hadas, Miriam, and Shulamis! We look forward to many years together. Also, a special thanks to Ruth Wolfert for her wisdom and guidance. Anna Ashton deserves tremendous applause for her devotion and help.

Finally, we would like to thank our agents, Gareth Esersky and Carol Mann, for bringing us to Adams Media, and for their guidance and support.

I would like to thank my colleagues at EMUNAH for their gracious support always, and for being willing to overlook many conspicuous absences this past year as a result of both book-tour and book-writing commitments.

Many special people have shared their stories and thoughts about coincidences with me, but I have been most recently touched and moved by the special generosity of Rabbi Hanoch Teller. Rabbi Teller, an outstanding scholar and renowned storyteller, does not jealously guard the gems he has collected, but very generously and graciously shares them with all. Three of the stories in this book are loosely based on Rabbi Teller's wonderful video *Do You Believe in Miracles?*

The greatest moments in life are those shared by friends and family. The enthusiasm and support demonstrated by my dear friends—Raizy Steg, Bella Friedman, Annette Grauman, Babshi Berkowitz, Sarah Laya Landau, and Hindy Rozenberg—are very precious to me. Special thanks also to Ginny Duffy and Marcella Weiner for holding my hand when I most needed it. When the going got tough, I got going to one of the above. My family—my mother, Claire Halberstam; my brother, Moishe Halberstam; and my sister, Miriam Halberstam—have supported my efforts faithfully, as have my in-laws, Leib and Sima Mandelbaum; Suri and Danny Dymshits; Chaim and Bayla Mandelbaum; and Yeruchem and Chaya Winkler. Bayla ran out and bought the first copy of *Small Miracles* sold in Brooklyn the very day it came out, and Chaya threw a little celebration in her home. Both gestures meant so much to me. My sister, Miriam, devotedly scouted for coincidence stories on my behalf. Several of the stories published in this book emanated from her dedicated efforts, and I cannot thank her enough.

My two children—Yossi and Eli—have been joyous participants in the whole wonderful, exciting process and very indulgent of my deficiencies as a mother throughout. They have graciously forgiven me my flaws and absences during this hectic period. Yossi made many expeditions to various bookstores and agents in Israel in an attempt to promote the book there, and his efforts succeeded. Foreign rights to the book have now been sold to that country, and I thank Yossi for his role in making that happen. (Israel now joins Italy, Greece, Latin America, Brazil, China, Japan, Indonesia, Spain, Germany, and Korea in buying foreign rights to *Small Miracles*.)

My husband, Motty, to whom I have dedicated this book, is actually responsible—more than anybody else—for nurturing my creativity during adulthood. (My father of blessed memory was the primary source during childhood.) Throughout the twenty-one years of our marriage, Motty has always insisted, sincerely and with genuine devotion, that I eschew the kitchen in favor of my desk, and he has always reveled in my successes. His wisdom and good counsel have helped me on dozens of occasions, and his feedback and input have proven pivotal. More than anything else, living with him and being exposed to his brilliant insights and original way of thinking has helped me grow.

— *Yitta Halberstam*

I thank Jules, my dear beloved husband who has continuously shown me how to face my perceived limitations, challenge them and move beyond. With an abundance of love, he has stood by me and cheered me on.

I want to acknowledge my little toddler, Arielle who escorted me on the book tour. On the planes and off the planes, she marched like a little trooper, with backpack, stuffed teddy bear, wheeling her little carriage all around town. She made the trips a joy with her ability to delight in it all.

Estee, my sister, friend, and confidant has been a blessing in my life since the moment she was born. My dear mother, Rose, and Hedy and Myer Feiler and children, Isser and Malku Handler, Anne Leventhal, Emery, David and Shulamit Leventhal and children have all provided a loving and supportive family.

Much gratitude is also extended to Pesi Dinnerstein who is my beacon of light. Sara Barris, Deena Edelman, Ruchama and Yisrael Feuerman, and Eta Ansel have been close friends who have been so generous with their enthusiasm. Elli Wohlgelernter is a dear friend and has loved coincidences all his life. And lastly, I want to acknowledge Jonathan and Ruchy Mark who have, through their words, reflected back to us the beauty of our book and together, they have been the catalyst for many miracles.

— *Judith Leventhal*

Permissions

Grateful acknowledgment is made to the following for permission to reprint previously published material:

"Caught in a Firestorm" by Timothy S. Wright, February 1996. Reprinted by permission of *Guideposts Magazine*. Copyright ©1996 by Guideposts, Carmel, NY.

"The Hand of Dog" by Glen Martin, May 19, 1994. Reprinted by permission from *The San Francisco Chronicle*.

"Hands of Fate Reunite Women, Stolen Rolex" by Arnold Markowitz, May 7, 1997. Reprinted by permission from *The Miami Herald*.

"Lessons in Emunah" edited by Naomi Mauer. Reprinted by permission from *The Jewish Press*.

"I Can Do Anything" by Veronica Chater and Arlene Nunes, May 20, 1997. Reprinted with permission by *Woman's World Magazine*, Englewood Cliffs, New Jersey.

Excerpt from *Incredible Coincidence: The Baffling World of Sychronicity*. Copyright ©1979 by Alan Vaughn. Reprinted by permission of Harper Collins Publishers.

"My Life is Yours" by Jeff Smith, July 1996. Reprinted with permission from *Guideposts Magazine*. Copyright ©1996 by Guideposts, Carmel, NY.

Excerpt from *Not by the Sword* by Kathryn Watterson. Reprinted by permission of Ellen Levine Agency, Inc. Copyright ©1995 by Kathryn Watterson.

"Rollaway Plan" by Faye Field, February 1996. Reprinted with permission from *Guideposts Magazine*. Copyright ©1996 by Guideposts, Carmel, NY.

Excerpt from *Shining Lights* by Ruchoma Shain. Reprinted by permission from Feldheim Publishers, Nanuet, BY and Ruchoma Shain.

"Three Sisters Deliver Amazin' Triple Play" by Roger Field, February 1, 1997. Reprinted by permission from *The New York Post*.

Visit Our Website:

http://www.adamsmedia.com/smallmiracles

Meet the authors, read exclusive interviews, catch up with the latest publicity information, correspond with the authors via e-mail, write in your comments, learn more about coincidences, chat with other fans, and much, much more!

You can even submit your own small miracles: Have you ever experienced an unusual, heartwarming, or mysterious coincidence? We would like to hear about these personal events, and possibly use them for an upcoming sequel.

Or mail us your stories to:

Small Miracles
Adams Media Corporation
260 Center Street
Holbrook, MA 02343

Please include your typewritten stories, together with your name, address, and daytime and nighttime phone numbers. All submissions will become the property of Adams Media Corporation.